D1559420

STALLED DEMOCRACY

STALLED DEMOCRACY

Capital, Labor, and the Paradox
of State-Sponsored Development

EVA BELLIN

Cornell University Press

Ithaca and London

The publisher gratefully acknowledges receipt of a grant from
Harvard University, which assisted in the publication of this book.

First published 2002 by Cornell University Press

Printed in the United States of America

Library of Congress Cataloging-in-Publication Data

Bellin, Eva Rana.
    Stalled democracy : capital, labor, and the paradox of state-sponsored
development / Eva Bellin.
        p. cm.
    Includes bibliographical references and index.
    ISBN 0-8014-3942-6 (cloth)
        1. Industrial policy—Developing countries.   2. Labor policy—Developing
countries.   I. Title.
    HD3616.D453 B445 2002
    338.9′09172′4—dc21   2002023727

Cloth printing   10 9 8 7 6 5 4 3 2 1

Contents

Acknowledgments

Scholarly research is ultimately a solitary pursuit, but its successful completion assumes the support of a phalanx of people and institutions. Countless are those who have helped see this project to its end, and so it is a great pleasure to thank them now that it is done.

At Princeton, where this project began, four people proved especially important to me as mentors. John Waterbury was a model of rigor, discipline, and energy, inspiring an entire generation of Middle East scholars to creative effort and steadfast engagement with the region. Atul Kohli was a boundless source of intellectual enthusiasm, insight, and generosity. His intellectual excitement never failed to spark a kindred response from his students. In the Near Eastern Studies Department, L. Carl Brown gave me an essential grounding in the history of the region as well as an important lesson in institution-building. Finally, Nancy Bermeo gave me an early introduction to politics as a discipline and provided me with a broad analytic framework in which to position my own research.

With regard to financing, I was lucky to have the support of many institutions. Graduate studies at Princeton as well as a year of intensive Arabic study in Cairo were largely funded by the U.S. Department of Education (FLAS grants). Preliminary research on Tunisia was conducted in Aix-en-Provence thanks to a grant from Princeton's Council on Regional Studies. Field work in Tunisia was funded by grants from the Fulbright Commission, the Social Science Research Council, and the American Institute for Maghrebi Studies. A Dodd's Honorific Fellowship as well as a grant from the Center for International Studies at Princeton supported the write-up. A follow-up visit to Tunisia was funded by the Johns Hopkins School for Advanced International Studies, with the generous support of my esteemed colleague Fouad Ajami. The Weatherhead Center for International Affairs at Harvard University covered the cost of preparing the book's index. To all these institutions and people, I owe my deepest thanks.

viii   Acknowledgments

Institutional support was also forthcoming abroad. In Aix-en-Provence, the library at the Centre de recherches et d'études sur les sociétés méditerranéennes (CRESM) proved to be a rich resource, profitably mined thanks to the friendly assistance of Vivien Michel. In Tunis, the Center of Maghrebi Studies in Tunis (CEMAT) provided an intellectual home away from home, made especially pleasant by its able director Jean Jeffers Mrad and her gracious assistant, Amal Bel Haj. The Tunisian academic institute Centre d'études et de recherches économiques et sociales (CERES) generously sponsored my visit and also included me in several provocative seminars on state and society in Tunisia. Finally, the libraries of the Central Bank, the Agence de promotion de l'industrie, the École nationale d'administration à Tunis, the Institut du travail, and the Centre de documentation all opened their doors to me and provided documentary resources that proved essential to this project.

Many people in Tunisia—academics, journalists, businessmen, and labor activists—helped me in my quest to understand Tunisian politics and society. Azzam Mahjoub, a model of perseverance and high intellectual purpose, generously guided me to sources and colleagues and helped me find my "sea-legs" in Tunisia. Salah Brik al-Hannachi provided invaluable insights into business thinking in Tunisia as well as an introduction to the world of pure politics. Abdelkadir Zghal provided a wry slant on Tunisian affairs and perspective on how to carry out sociologically informed research. Salah Zghridi showed exceptional generosity in guiding me through the thickets of labor politics and inspired me with his commitment to a life of activism governed by high ideals. Hedi Jelani and Amor Bouchiba spent many hours explaining the workings of the business community and instilled in me a healthy respect for entrepreneurs and the Horatio Alger myth, Tunisia-style. Others who provided invaluable help at different stages include Amor Yumbai, Abdejelil Bedaoui, Mahmoud Ben Romdhane, Mondheur Gargouri, Tawfiq L'Amari, and Michael Lange. Needless to say, none of these people necessarily share my conclusions about politics in Tunisia or elsewhere (a few would heartily disagree!). But without their generous sharing of ideas, my research would not have been possible.

A number of colleagues in the United States proved exceptionally helpful in reading and commenting on my work. My deepest thanks go to Marsha Pripstein Posusney, who painstakingly read every chapter of the manuscript and whose detailed comments made the final version immeasurably stronger. The participants in Harvard University's Sawyer Seminar/Research Workshop on Comparative Politics read different versions of the manuscript's theoretical and comparative chapters, always demanding rigor and extraregional perspective. I am especially grateful to Theda Skocpol, Jorge Dominguez, Susan Pharr, Robert Putnam, Samuel Huntington, and Stanley Hoffmann, who co-taught the seminar with me over the years, as well as the superb graduate students who participated in the venture. Together they gave me a priceless second education in comparative politics. Other colleagues who have read individual chapters along the way and shared their sage advice include Clifford Bob, Joel Migdal, Deborah Yashar, Thomas Ertman, and Lisa Anderson. Clement Henry, I. W. Zartman, and Robert Vitalis also provided critical comments and suggestions at various stages of this project. William Granara generously helped with the transliteration of all Arabic titles and terms (though faults in their reproduction are my own). My thanks to all of these wonderful partners in academe.

Portions of this book first appeared in articles published in *World Development* 22, no. 3 (March 1994), 427–36, entitled "The Politics of Profit in Tunisia: Utility of the Rentier Paradigm," and in *World Politics* 52, no. 2 (January 2000), 175–205, published by Johns Hopkins University Press, entitled "Contingent Democrats: Industrialists, Labor, and Democratization in Late Developing Countries."

Scholars, however, do not live by scholarship alone. In Tunisia, Princeton, Washington, D.C., and Cambridge I was the grateful recipient of much generous hospitality and friendship. Ridha Gharbi and Khedija Annabi, Amal and Edmund Hull, Diane and Terry Hansen, Margaret Koval and Steve Cowley all welcomed me into their homes at different points along the way, making my stays in Tunis, Cairo, and Princeton joyful as well as productive. Others who provided support, companionship, guidance, and goading at different times over the course of this project include Mildred Kalmus, James Ritchey, Jill Frank, Joshua Landis, Deborah Yashar, and Paul Eiss. Most of all I must thank Diane Singerman, who for many years took all the late night calls and gave me the privilege of experiencing what Francis Bacon considers a true friend, who "halveth the grief and doubleth the joy." And deep thanks to my husband, Frank Schwartz, a relative latecomer to the project but whose dry wit, unflappable calm, and keen eye for the extraneous helped see this project to its conclusion.

But when all is said and done I owe the greatest debt of gratitude to my parents, Lowell Bellin and Talah Werbner Bellin. Parents, after all, are our first models of discipline, work, and integrity. They show us the way even before we know we are going. In these models I have been mightily blessed with my father, a man of wit, verve, and stern principle, and my mother, a woman of warmth, wisdom, and very great courage. They have inspired me, guided me, led me, and allowed me to lead. And so it is with great love and respect that I dedicate this work to them.

EVA BELLIN

Cambridge, Massachusetts

STALLED DEMOCRACY

Introduction

On 7 November 1987, the Republic of Tunisia made international headlines. A bloodless coup swept Habib Bourguiba, the country's founding father, from power after thirty years of increasingly autocratic rule. His successor, Zine Abdine Ben Ali, proclaimed a new era for Tunisian democracy. Over the next twelve months Ben Ali embraced a set of sweeping reforms designed to liberalize political life. Presidential decrees of amnesty released hundreds of opposition leaders from prison and exile. Constitutional reform put an end to the institution of "president for life." A new party law paved the way for the doubling of legal opposition parties. And a new press code freed journals and newspapers from many prior constraints. Ben Ali announced: "Our people have attained a sufficient level of responsibility and maturity . . . to contribute . . . to the management of their affairs in conformity to the republican idea. . . . Our people are worthy of a political life . . . truly founded upon multipartyism" (*La presse*, 31 December 1987). This break with autocracy sparked elation throughout Tunisian society and raised high hopes that the country was finally on the threshhold of joining the third wave of democratization.

Five years later, the picture looked very different. Opposition leaders were once again the subject of routine harassment by the regime. The country's most vibrant political movement, the Islamist Renaissance Party, had been declared illegal and its members brutally repressed by state security forces. Newspapers and journals critical of the regime were again the regular victims of government seizure and/or banishment. And human rights abuses by the regime multiplied, carried out in the name of preserving order. By 1992 the door so optimistically opened to democracy had resolutely slammed shut. It was back to authoritarian rule as usual in Tunisia (Gasiorowski 1992).

Retreats from democratic opening, unfortunately, are not all that surprising. What is surprising in the Tunisian case is the muted response it drew from society. News of democratic setbacks elicited little protest from Tunisian citizens. A small coterie of brave-hearted intellectuals and professionals centered in Tunisia's Human Rights League and one or two small opposition parties waged valiant battle against this retreat. And the few Islamist intellectuals not yet swallowed up by the maw of state repression voiced dissent as well. But other groups in society that might have been expected to protest the regime's change of heart proved surprisingly diffident. Most notably, organized labor, long a pole of political activism and opposition in Tunisian affairs, stood stoically by Ben Ali's regime. And the captains of industry, private sector leaders with a presumable interest in the development of predictable, accountable government, also expressed not a hint of dissent at the regime's relapse into authoritarianism.

Capital and labor's response to this relapse is puzzling in two ways. First, it flies in the face of theoretical expectation. A long tradition in political economy leads us to expect the protagonists of capitalist industrialization to be the agents of democratization, not the allies of authoritarianism. Both liberals and Marxists, from Moore 1966, Moraze 1968, Hobsbawm 1969 and Kurth 1979 to Marshall 1950, Thompson 1963, Therborn 1977 and Rueschemeyer, Stevens, and Stevens 1992, argue that capital and labor have played a central role in championing democratization (although there is some disagreement over who the hero of the story is). Some follow Moore's lead, highlighting the contribution that capital makes to democratization ("no bourgeoisie, no democracy"). Others, such as Rueschemeyer, Stephens, and Stephens, are persuaded that labor plays the more redemptive role. But drawing primarily on the historical experience of Western Europe, all agree that capitalist industrialization gives rise to social classes with a material interest in promoting democracy.[1] In fact, it is the development and empowerment of these classes (rather than the more nebulously causal conditions like higher literacy rates and higher standards of living) that best explains the statistically robust linkage found between capitalist development and democracy (Rueschemeyer, Stephens, and Stephens 1992, 13–39). At least this is the pattern suggested by analyses of the early industrializing countries. The Tunisian case stands in stark contrast. Why?

Capital and labor's complicity in authoritarian relapse is puzzling in a second way as well: it runs counter to the historical trajectory of capital and labor's relationship with the Tunisian state since independence. Over the course of Tunisia's first three decades, capital and labor saw their power grow significantly, even if not always unilinearly. This increase in power translated into a growing capacity to make the state responsive to their policy interests. Victories in such policy areas as privatization, trade liberalization, and labor code reform were the result. But if the trajectory of their relationship with the state had been that of promoting ever-greater levels of state responsiveness, this trajectory stopped short of a campaign for the *guarantee* of responsiveness in the form of democratic institutions. Why?

The behavior of capital and labor in Tunisia raises the more general question of the relationship between capitalist industrialization and democracy in the context of late development. Does the socioeconomic change associated with industrialization spell the attenuation of authoritarianism? Will the social classes empowered by industrialization play a central role in authoritarianism's decline? Is there a special pattern to be found among late-developing countries (LDCs) that is distinct from the route followed by first comers? A quick look around suggests that the Tunisian trajectory is far from unique. From Brazil and Mexico to Indonesia and Korea, one finds many cases of social classes developing sufficient power to win substantial policy concessions from the state even as they show remarkable ambivalence about democratization. Under what conditions will they act as agents of democratization? In traversing the path of belated industrialization with all its unanticipated sociopolitical repercussions, Tunisia is illustrative of a larger phenomenon. Investigating it will elucidate a general pattern at work in many late-developing countries.

Stalled Democracy

Why is the relationship between capitalist industrialization and democracy more ambiguous among late-developing countries than among their predecessors? The answer lies in the special character of industrialization in many LDCs and specifically the central role that state sponsorship plays in this process. In Tunisia, as in many other late, but developmentally ambitious countries, the state is committed to encouraging the country's industrial development. To this end the state explicitly nurtures the development of private sector capital and labor, relying on a variety of means—financial, social, political, and infrastructural. The state's project of sponsored industrialization, however, has unintended political consequences. Specifically, it gives rise to two paradoxes that have important implications for both the development of responsive government and its limitation.

First, state-sponsored industrialization gives rise to the "developmental paradox" of the authoritarian state. Once the authoritarian state embraces a developmental logic it is, by its very nature, self-limiting. By sponsoring industrialization, the state nurtures the development of social forces ultimately capable of amassing sufficient power to challenge it and impose a measure of policy responsiveness upon it. In short, the very success of the state's strategy leads to the demise of the state's capacity to dictate policy unilaterally. This is the genesis of state responsiveness and a first important step toward the development of accountable government.

At the same time the central role played by state sponsorship results in a second paradox, the "democratic paradox" of state-sponsored industrialization. The crux of this paradox lies in the fact that the very catalyst that gives rise to social forces capable of eliciting state responsiveness also fatally limits their commitment to democratization. State sponsorship fosters the development of capital and labor but also undermines their enthusiasm for democracy. Classes that have benefited from state sponsorship often exhibit a "pulling up the ladder" syndrome. They are eager to push the state to be responsive to their own interests, but once this has been achieved, they are not eager to generalize such responsiveness to society as a whole through the creation of democratic institutions.

The dual paradoxes of state-sponsored industrialization result in a situation that might be called "stalled democracy." Democracy is stunted halfway between autocracy and fully accountable government. The state is responsive to a few privileged interests but falls far short of being accountable to society as a whole. This situation is found in many late-developing countries that have embraced a strategy of state-sponsored capitalist industrialization, from Mexico to Korea, Indonesia to Egypt. These countries get stuck indefinitely in a messy intermediate category in which the state is neither all powerful nor open to nonprivileged strata. State-sponsored classes are complicitous in this political stasis. To the extent that reform is achieved, it either comes at the initiative of other forces in society (e.g., church activists and students in Korea, a new generation of party activists in Mexico) or else is associated with a retreat in the state's sponsorship policy, leading capital and/or labor to rethink their political disposition.

The above suggests a revised understanding of the relationship between capitalist development and democracy in the context of late development. State-sponsored capitalist industrialization need not lead to democracy (as many apologists for authoritarian models of growth have assumed), although it often leads to a decline in the authoritarian state's autonomy. Capital and labor may push for state responsiveness, but only so far as it guarantees attention to their material interests. In the context of state-sponsored growth, their political project will fall far short of any demand for democracy.

The fact that capital and labor in late-developing countries are driven by their material interests is not unique to LDCs. To the contrary, this stimulus constitutes a thread of continuity with their predecessors who, like them, were contingent democrats, committed to democracy when it served their interests. Rather, what has changed is the context defining those interests. Capital and labor in the early-industrializing countries faced ideological, political, and economic conditions that put them in conflict with the absolutist state and/or in alliance with mass interests. Later classes, enjoying the benefits of state sponsorship, have less interest in challenging the state and allying with the unprivileged masses. There are strong material incentives to stall democracy's progress.

But this analysis also suggests the conditions under which transition to democracy might be "unstalled." By identifying the mechanism driving capital and labor's diffidence toward democracy we can anticipate how their disposition might change. Specifically, factors that change the extent and character of state sponsorship—rapid growth, ideological change, integration into the global economy—may well transform class attitudes about the utility of democracy and increase capital and labor's willingness to throw their weight behind this political project.

The Tunisian Case

The argument outlined above is illustrated clearly in the Tunisian case. Tunisia, like many late-developing countries, embraced a strategy of state-sponsored industrialization. As a corollary to this strategy the state nurtured the development of both private sector industrialists and organized labor. To mobilize financial and human capital for its industrialization project the state conferred countless benefits and incentives on the private sector. To secure economic peace and stability the state subsidized (even as it corporatized) the development of organized labor.

Both private sector industrialists and organized labor grew dramatically during the first three decades of independence. In the interim they amassed power of different stripes, and by the 1970s and 1980s they were able to translate their power into influence over the state's public policy decisions. By its own hand, the state had unwittingly contributed to the reduction of its autonomy.

But despite their enthusiasm for state responsiveness on particular policy issues, both private sector capital and organized labor proved surprisingly ambivalent toward the general project of democratization. Both stood by the regime as it reneged on one promise of democratic reform after another. Tunisia remained stalled between democracy and authoritarianism. The state was neither fully accountable to society nor fully autonomous.

The best explanation for capital and labor's ambivalence toward democracy lies in the character of their origin and growth. That state sponsorship played a central role in their development and, more important, that the state continued to wield its support on a discretionary basis, translated into class ambivalence toward democratization. For while both capital and labor amassed increasing power during Tunisia's first three decades of independence, they fell short on developing autonomy from the state. This spelled diffidence about the democratic project.

Implications of the Argument

This research speaks to three different concerns. Most broadly, it seeks to engage the debate on the relationship between capitalist development and democracy. It seeks to rethink that relationship in the context of late development and suggest modifications that account for the special conditions faced by LDCs. The goal is to recognize capital and labor as perennially contingent democrats while defining the conditions that shape this contingency and suggesting the factors that may change their political disposition over time.

The second goal of this research is to consider how, short of achieving full democratic transition, the peremptory power of authoritarian regimes might be eroded. Does the embrace of capitalist industrialization "pluralize power" in society in a way that will rein in the autonomy of the state and force it to be responsive to nonstate interests? Rooted in this question is the assumption that absolute power is rarely ceded voluntarily by those who enjoy it and that power sharing must be imposed on autocratic elites. To check the state's authoritarian ambition, independent nodes of countervailing power must be created in society. But the "pluralization of power" must be theorized, its sources and trajectory analyzed. To clarify the impact of capitalist industrialization on this process, the concept of power must be disaggregated, the relationship between economic and political power must be parsed, and the effect of non-economic factors (such as institutional endowment and the size of the elite) must be considered.

Focusing on the power implications of capitalist industrialization brings the insights of political economy to bear on the question of authoritarianism's attenuation. It also goes beyond much of the contemporary literature on "civil society," which stresses the democratizing potential of vibrant associational life. This literature highlights the capacity of associational life to imbue citizens with political competence, civility, tolerance, and civic sentiment (Diamond 1993; Norton 1995; Bellin 1995). But by focusing primarily on the positive *cultural* repercussions of a vibrant civil society it ignores the issue of *power* and fails to explain just how associations full of civic-minded citizens might actually wrest control from autocratically minded states. Is the development of public spirit sufficient to cow recalcitrant authoritarianism and force responsiveness on a tyrannical state? The question demands reconsideration of the power dynamics between state and society.

A rich literature on the relations between state and society rejects any depiction of the distribution of power between the two as a zero-sum game (Stepan 1985; Bratton 1989; Evans 1992; Kohli, Migdal, and Shue 1994). Strength on both fronts can go together. A strong society can enhance the state's capacity to formulate and implement policy. And a strong state fosters society's vivacity by delivering political order and a reliable legal system (Schwartz 2003). But even if the power of state and society should not be conceived as zero-sum, this research argues that a zero-sum relationship *does* exist between state and society's respective power and *autonomy*. The more that power is accrued by forces in society, the more the state's autonomy to dictate policy is constrained. This is the crux of the "developmental paradox" of the authoritarian state.[2] Recognizing it suggests one route toward the erosion of authoritarianism.

The third goal is to reflect on the lessons of this research for a subset of late-developing countries, specifically those in the Middle East and

North Africa. While analysis of the Tunisian case may have theoretical value for late-developing countries in general, it has special significance for the Middle East and North Africa (MENA). This region has long been perceived as a site of entrenched authoritarianism. Culture, history, economics, and institutions are all said to conspire to make states "strong" and societies "weak" or, more accurately, to make states unaccountable and societies incapable of imposing responsiveness.[3] For roughly three decades, however, countries in the region (led by Tunisia, Egypt, Turkey, Syria, and Morocco) have embraced a strategy of state-sponsored industrialization, more or less successfully. The question is whether this choice of strategy effectively pluralizes power, diminishes authoritarianism, and enhances the prospects of democratization in these countries. Because Tunisia shares much with its fellow MENA countries in terms of cultural, historical, and institutional endowment, it is well positioned to highlight the transformative potential of state-sponsored industrialization, as well as its limits, for politics in the region.

A Word on Methodology

The argument presented here grows out of extensive fieldwork conducted in Tunisia, beginning with an eighteen-month visit in the late 1980s, and supplemented by four follow-up visits of two weeks to a month's duration during the early and mid-1990s. In the field I consulted both published and unpublished secondary sources on Tunisian politics, economics, and history; collected primary documents from government ministries, agencies, and private associations; and conducted interviews with more than 150 industrialists, labor activists, public officials, opposition leaders, journalists, and academics. The interviews were open-ended yet structured around a consistent set of questions. They generally lasted an hour or so and were conducted in French or Arabic, at the discretion of the interview subject. Interviewees were selected on a non-random basis and were generally chosen for their knowledge of a subject, although an effort was made to select a varied sample. Some subjects met with me several times at length, welcoming return visits over several years; others met with me only once for an hour-long session.

Access to interview subjects (as well as to documents and data) became progressively more difficult after 1991, as the regime clamped down on opposition and people became more circumspect about discussing sensitive matters with foreigners. But I benefited from having forged personal relationships with many key Tunisians during the country's brief moment of political opening and optimism in the late 1980s. These contacts stood me in good stead later on. Even so, the collection of data ran up against all the logistical difficulties that researchers in the MENA region typically encounter (Birks 1980, 3–4). Officially published data are often old, statistics are often of questionable accuracy, and much data can be obtained only through informal personal contacts. Researching the development of private sector industrialists proved especially challenging because there was almost no secondary-source material on the subject (with the notable exception of work by Ridha Gouia). As for organized labor, secondary sources on the history of the trade union movement were abundant, but primary material was scarce. Throughout the period of my research, the archive of the Union générale de travailleurs tunisiens (UGTT) was in absolute shambles. Trade union activists were often wary of sharing sensitive information with an outsider, and even a simple question such as the number of members in a particular syndicate might be deemed sensitive. Written documents are often unavailable. Either the documents had never been generated (union leaders in Tunisia are often uninterested in, or actively opposed to, leaving a paper trail), or else they had been destroyed in the course of an incident of government repression. Documents from one trade union, for example, turned up as paper cones for peanut sellers in the central market. Apparently, an enterprising official had sold them en bloc to a paper wholesaler after storming the union local.

As a consequence, certain information that would be taken for granted by researchers in other parts of the world was very hard to come by in Tunisia. Figures for things like strikes and union membership should be taken as estimates, valid to an order of magnitude only. Although this makes for some imprecision in the description of the Tunisian case, it does not do violence to the credibility of the overall argument presented here.

Single case studies have fallen out of favor in political science in recent years, primarily for their inadequacy for *hypothesis testing*. But in-depth, culturally sensitive, and historically informed understanding of a single case is still ideal for *hypothesis generation*. That is the goal here. The Tunisian case suggested some generalizable hypotheses about the relationship between state-sponsored capitalist industrialization and the retreat of authoritarianism. Comparison with several other late-developing countries confirms the plausibility of these hypotheses. Systematic testing across many cases would be necessary to establish the validity of these hypotheses further.

Plan of Book

The book begins with an exploration of the logic that compelled the state to sponsor the development of private sector industrialists in Tunisia. Chapter 1 documents the measures taken to foster the development of these industrialists and profiles the growing role they have come to play in the economy over the past three decades. Chapter 2 analyzes the emergent power enjoyed by private sector industrialists and their growing capacity to make the state responsive to their interests. This is contrasted with the limits that state sponsorship spells for the industrialists' autonomy and the constraint thus posed for their erosion of authoritarianism. Chapter 3 studies the development of organized labor and the logic driving the state both to sponsor and to disorganize this social force over time. Chapter 4 explores the power and autonomy of organized labor and the vector of its influence over the state. Chapter 5 explores the possibility that private sector industrialists and organized labor will serve as the agents of democracy. It reflects on the peculiar characteristics of late, state-sponsored industrialization that prevent the protagonists of industrialization from replicating the experience of the early industrializers in championing democratization. Finally, Chapter 6 puts the lessons of the Tunisian case in comparative perspective. The chapter highlights the generalizability of "stalled democracy" in the context of late development by drawing on the experience of Mexico, Korea, Indonesia, and other LDCs. The chapter also explores the specific implications of this argument for countries in the Middle East and North Africa by drawing comparisons with Egypt, Turkey, and Syria. These compansons permit reflection on the transformative capacity of state-sponsored industrialization and its prospects for reconfiguring state-society relations in this region of long-entrenched authoritarianism.

CHAPTER I

Genesis of the Private Sector in Tunisia: The Logic of State Sponsorship

Why would an authoritarian state nurture the development of private sector industrialists? To read the social science literature, one would think that few social forces are better positioned to compromise the state's autonomy in the policy-making process. Whether portrayed as a hidden "executive committee," secretly controlling the state's agenda, or merely an especially privileged player operating in a stacked pluralist game, private sector industrialists have long been perceived by social scientists, from Marxists to liberals, as uniquely positioned to control the state's policy direction. It is thus somewhat surprising to find that many states jealous of their power have expressly chosen to nurture the development of this stratum. What drives this apparently paradoxical behavior?

Typically, the pairing of developmental ambition with financial constraint forces the state to sponsor the development of private sector industrialists. In general, states pursue this path because they are committed to fostering their country's rapid economic development but lack the resources to finance such development unilaterally. Strapped for capital, the state turns to the private sector (both domestic and foreign) to coax investment in the economy. To sweeten the prospects of such investment the state may enact a battery of supports and incentives aimed at encouraging private sector investors. If successful, the state fosters the development of a robust private sector, which is then expected to fuel the country's advance into greater prosperity.

This is the route that Tunisia has followed over the past few decades. As is documented in this chapter, the Tunisian state has long embraced a

strategy of state-sponsored capitalist industrialization, consciously nurturing the development of private sector industrialists in the process. The
logic driving this choice of strategy stems from the state's consistent
commitment to a developmentalist ethos even as it faced the persistent
constraint of limited resources. Pragmatism, not ideological dogmatism,
has governed the state's embrace of the private sector. As a consequence,
for decades both the character and extent of state sponsorship has been
characterized by a certain eclecticism, ruled by the vagaries of fiscal crisis
and international trends, not to mention domestic political intrigue.

In Tunisia, this phenomenon has resulted in a four-part periodization
of state support. In the early years of statehood, political weakness, international pressures, and economic constraint led the state to endorse the
development of private sector industry but also limited state support
to infrastructural assistance. By the sixties, economic windfalls as well as
international currents pushed the state to embrace an etatist development
strategy, although it continued to encourage the private sector through
the mounting of joint ventures and through the provision of infrastructural support. By the seventies, economic difficulties undermined etatism
and breathed new enthusiasm into a so-called liberal development strategy. That strategy entailed legislative reforms, institutional innovations,
and clearly illiberal market controls that favored the development of
private sector industry. These were soon supplemented by a wide range
of subsidies financed by the sudden influx of petroleum and phosphate windfalls. Finally, by the mid-eighties, renewed fiscal and foreign
exchange crisis forced the state to embrace a more market-disciplined
development strategy. Sponsorship of the private sector moved away from
subsidies and market controls and toward measures that did not violate
market logic.

What follows is an account of the development of private sector
industry in Tunisia and the central role played by state sponsorship in
this process. The chapter starts with a brief survey of Tunisia's industrial
development prior to independence in order to establish the country's
poor initial endowment in both industrial entrepreneurs and enterprises.
The chapter proceeds with an account of each of the four stages in the
state's sponsorship of the private sector, documenting the growth of
this sector over time. By the 1980s, a significant group of private sector
industrialists had emerged in Tunisia. State sponsorship had given rise to
a class of industrialists whose contribution to the Tunisian economy was
undeniable.

Tunisian Industry and Industrialists prior to Independence

Tunisia is a latecomer to industrialization. Although the country had long produced sophisticated consumer goods, exporting ceramics, textiles, and leather goods far and wide since medieval times, production processes remained largely artisanal well into the twentieth century (Mahjoub 1978, 28). Nor did the arrival of European capital in the early 1800s speed the course of industrialization. French and British capitalists were drawn to Tunisia to exploit the country's agricultural and commercial potential, not to implant indigenous manufacturing rivals.[1] Surprisingly, the traditional Tunisian state started the country on a path toward industrialization (Brown 1974). Challenged and enthralled by the example of European power, the local ruler, Ahmed Bey, began an experiment in "defensive modernization," ordering the creation of several mechanized oil presses, flour mills, cannon and gunpowder factories in the mid-nineteenth century (Mahjoub 1978, 84). But financial difficulties soon forced Ahmed Bey to abandon this experiment in state-led industrialization. Thus, save for the mechanization of the odd flour mill or oil press by a local notable or foreign trader, Tunisia remained largely devoid of industrial enterprises well up to French colonial occupation in 1881.

French rule did not much speed the industrialization process in Tunisia. Like their fortune-seeking predecessors, French colons focused primarily on developing the country's agricultural potential, investing in olive, vine, and cereal culture. Only the discovery of mineral deposits in the late nineteenth century spurred a minor interest in industrial ventures.[2] A handful of major European trusts undertook the development of Tunisia's mining sector; they simultaneously developed a few collateral "industries" (railways and ports) that were necessary to make the mines profitable (Sebag 1951, 52–65). This investment gave the Tunisian economy the character of a classically peripheralized economy, with industry limited to an enclave sector dominated by foreign monopolies and oriented toward the demands of the colonial center (Romdhane 1981, 6).

As for industry that might have been more oriented to the needs of the domestic market (e.g., manufactures), the colonial regime provided little encouragement. The creation of a customs union with France in 1904, redefined in 1928, contributed to the "deindustrialization" of Tunisia by opening the Tunisian market to French manufactured goods. The latter undermined the health of Tunisian artisanry and hampered the growth of infant industries in the colony (Pennec 1964).

Official statistics make clear the sorry state of Tunisian industry during the first half century of colonial rule. For the year 1896, Mahjoub counts only 103 industrial enterprises in Tunisia. By 1928, the number had risen to only 428. At both points, moreover, the lion's share of industrial ventures were in the agro-alimentary sector; many consisted of little more than mechanized olive-oil presses (Mahjoub 1978, 234).

Tunisia's industrial sector began to expand during the mid-1930s. And like many other late-developing countries (notably those in Latin America), Tunisia enjoyed its biggest spurt of industrial growth during World War II and the years immediately following the war (1938–51). Warfare cut off North Africa's supply of European manufactured goods, and under these artificial conditions an indigenous industry grew up to answer local demand for manufactured products (Mahjoub 1978, 311–12; Amin 1970; Leduc 1952, 234–35). Moreover, for the first time in its history the colonial state expressly encouraged the development of local manufacturing capabilities. It now perceived the "under-industrialization" of Tunisia as a strategic risk since France could not guarantee the provision of essential goods to its citizens living in Tunisia during wartime (Signoles 1984, 556). To encourage investment in industry the state went so far as to issue a series of decrees between 1942 and 1956 that offered tax breaks, customs exemptions, and guaranteed credit to all potential investors in new industrial ventures in the colony (Gouia 1987, 201–2; Lepidi 1955, 52–53; Signoles 1984, 735; Romdhane 1981, 180).

Given state encouragement and the absence of foreign competition, local industry flourished for a time in Tunisia. Existing industries dramatically expanded their production capacity (the metalworks sector was notable for its growth), and entirely new industrial ventures sprang up, primarily in consumer goods industries (e.g., canned foods and textiles) (Mahjoub 1978, 315–17). Unfortunately, a good many of these firms, launched under the artificial conditions of war-imposed autarky, were not sufficiently competitive to survive the resumption of foreign trade with Europe at the war's end (Mahjoub 1978, 556). Tunisian industry remained lopsided, heavily weighted toward the mining and agro-alimentary sector. European trusts continued to dominate the largest firms in most industrial sectors (Sebag 1951, 89–100; Romdhane 1981, 8–23). Moreover, as independence approached, industrial development slowed. During the late 1940s and early 1950s, the economic and political uncertainty associated with separation from France led to stagnation in industrial investment and production (Mahjoub 1978, 324–25). Thus, Tunisia faced the prospect of independence equipped with an industrial sector that was still far from strong.

But if the industrial sector as a whole was weak, even more wanting was the development of Tunisia's indigenous industrialists. Tunisians had always been slow to engage in industrial ventures. In a survey of the country's earliest industrial enterprises, few Tunisians were counted among the proprietors of industrial firms. The steam-powered flour mills and mechanized olive oil presses that composed the core of Tunisia's industry in the late nineteenth century were largely the work of transplanted French and Italian entrepreneurs and merchants (Mahjoub 1978, 106). In the mining sector, European trusts monopolized production, thanks to exclusive concessions granted them by the state. And even during the country's industrial spurt during the 1930s and 1940s, the participation of Tunisian entrepreneurs was disappointing. Although Tunisians began to invest in increasing numbers in food-processing factories, brickworks, and metal shops, they continued to be overshadowed by their European counterparts even in these sectors. A survey of Tunisia's manufacturing industries from this period finds nearly every sector dominated by European-owned firms (Sebag 1951, 89–98). Even following World War II, Tunisian entrepreneurs had not established predominance. A 1953 census of 141 of the largest industrial firms in Tunisia found that only 8% (i.e., 11) were owned by native Tunisians (Mahjoub 1978, 338).

Why this relatively poor showing for Tunisians in the country's industry? The question recalls the rich debate over the best explanation for the belated development of industrial capitalism in many parts of the world. "Culturalists" (often inspired by Weber's work on the Protestant ethic) tend to blame the late emergence of capitalist industry on the absence of a cluster of values that inspire entrepreneurs to rational, self-sacrificing, long-term capital accumulation (Turner 1978).[3] "Structuralists" (also inspired by Weber) attribute this delay to the presence of structural impediments to capital accumulation, especially the presence of a predatory, patrimonial state (Callaghy 1988). Such a state, they argue, undermines the security of private property and makes the long-term investment horizons that are essential for industrial development inadvisable for the propertied classes (Ashraf 1969; Anderson 1979).

In the Tunisian case, neither of these arguments proves terribly useful in explaining the reluctance of Tunisian entrepreneurs to embrace industrial ventures in the nineteenth and twentieth centuries. Sweeping assertions that portray the cultural predispositions of Tunisian entrepreneurs as incompatible with rational, long-term, self-sacrificing accumulation do not square with empirical evidence from the time. Capitalist rationality had long been the rule in much of the artisanal production in Tunisia, especially in the country's complex "putting out" system for the production of chechias, the woolen caps once worn throughout the Muslim world (Valensi 1969).[4] The chechia industry embraced the deliberate and systematic pursuit of profit through the use of formally free labor, rational accounting procedures, and impersonal exchange on the market.[5] The production process was long and complex, requiring considerable delay between capital investment and return. Cultural predispositions in Tunisia did not stand in the way of this long-term, rationally organized capitalist accumulation when production processes were artisanal. Why should they suddenly obstruct such accumulation when steam power and machinery were introduced?

With regard to structural impediments, it is true that a long history of a predatory patrimonial state may have inculcated a wariness of long-term investments among Tunisian entrepreneurs. However, the state ceased to be patrimonially organized shortly after European intervention in 1881. After that, the state became significantly more rule-bound. In general, it respected private property in industry, although not necessarily in land. For this reason many European settlers, and some Tunisian Jews, felt sufficiently secure to invest in industry in Tunisia at this time.[6]

Instead, Tunisians' general reluctance to invest in industry might best be explained by their level of technical know-how and their access to capital. In the late nineteenth and twentieth centuries most Tunisians were simply unfamiliar with industrial processes and were thus reasonably hesitant to invest in terra incognita. That European industrialists, often backed by foreign capital, quickly established themselves in many industrial sectors made this realm appear all the more foreign to Tunisian newcomers. In addition, credit does not seem to have been easily available to most Tunisian investors. Prior to World War II, banks in Tunisia without exception were owned and managed by Europeans, and credit was apparently granted on a preferential basis to investors of European origin (Sebag 1951, 52, 156; Romdhane 1981, 54). Lacking access to capital and experience in industrial ventures, the propertied natives of Tunisia avoided investment in industry and instead sought financial security in land, quick profits in commerce, and status mobility through education and entry into the free professions and the civil service. For these reasons, Tunisia arrived at independence endowed with neither an impressive industrial infrastructure nor a robust class of indigenous industrial entrepreneurs.

Independence and the First "Liberal" Experiment, 1956–1961

With the achievement of independence in 1956, Tunisia was at least positioned to steward its own economic destiny. The new president, Habib Bourguiba, came to power committed to the economic development of his country. Tunisia's industrialization was clearly part of his agenda. The question was how to proceed. Should the state take the lead in the industrialization effort, or should the private sector be designated the engine of growth?

After some debate, Bourguiba opted for a self-described "liberal," as opposed to "etatist," approach to the country's development. Both political and economic weakness obliged this approach. Politically, Bourguiba's hold on society and party during the first years of independence was still somewhat tenuous, and so the new president was eager to preserve national unity. A statist development strategy threatened to divide the national consensus by provoking the ire of Tunisia's wealthy merchant and landed classes. This was a risk Bourguiba apparently did not yet feel strong enough to take. In addition, the etatist strategy was identified with Tunisia's trade union federation, the UGTT, and its dynamic leader, Ahmed Ben Salah. Bourguiba likely feared being politically upstaged by the young, charismatic trade union leader just as he likely feared that an ascendant UGTT, encouraged by this policy victory, might overshadow his own still rather weak party. From a more economic perspective, the Tunisian state was capital poor. Bourguiba was anxious not to alienate Western aid donors nor to encourage further (French) capital flight from the country. It is likely he feared that a development strategy with the slightest taint of "socialism" might do just that (Dimassi 1983). In this way, Bourguiba's commitment to development, paired with the evident political and economic constraints of the time, nudged the state toward a liberal approach to the country's industrialization.

The choice of a liberal strategy, however, did not mean that the state took a completely hands-off approach to the development of Tunisian industry. To the contrary, even at this stage the state took explicit measures to encourage private sector investment in industrial ventures. The state preserved (and improved on) pre-existing colonial decrees that guaranteed loans and extended tax holidays to investors in industry. It set in place prohibitive customs tariffs to protect infant industries and, in some sectors, expanded this protection to include comprehensive import bans (Dimassi 1983, 126–28). Finally, the state created several financial institutions, including the Fond d'investissement et développement (FID), the Société tunisienne de banque (STB), and the Société nationale d'investissement (SNI), with the express mandate to make credit easily available to private sector investors in Tunisia (Dimassi 1983, 133).

Aside from these measures, the state refrained from any direct management of the industrialization process. During its first years of independence, the Tunisian state was primarily preoccupied with setting in place the accoutrements of independent sovereignty (flag, army, "tunisified" bureaucracy). In the economy this meant creating a national bank, establishing an independent currency, and progressively buying up (though not unilaterally nationalizing!) the country's "national patrimony" from European companies. Within six years the state had bought majority shares in nearly all the country's major mines, utilities, and transport facilities previously controlled by Europeans. But save for these exceptional ventures, the state by and large refrained from an active entrepreneurial role in the economy. According to official rhetoric, the driving force behind industrialization and economic development was to come from the private sector, not from the state.

But in their hopes that the private sector would be the motor of Tunisian industrialization, Bourguiba and other exponents of the liberal development strategy were sorely disappointed. Private initiative lagged. Investment funds made available for industrial projects went begging; Tunisian entrepreneurs apparently preferred to buy up abandoned French businesses rather than risk inaugurating new industrial ventures (Romdhane 1981, 200). Investment levels stagnated in the mid- to late 1950s, as did industrial activity (Table 1.1).

In addition, capital flight proved epidemic, despite Tunisia's cautious handling of foreign interests.[7] In 1957–58 alone, this loss of capital was estimated at 100 million dinars (Bedaoui and Manoubi 1987, 50–51; Romdhane 1981, 131–37; Signoles 1984, 742). Nor did new foreign investors take much interest in Tunisia. Thus, the performance of private capital, both domestic and foreign, proved disappointing. During the first five years of independence, per capita GNP remained constant, and by 1961 it was at risk of declining. The imminent threat of negative growth disenchanted many political elites with the liberal approach to development. Poor growth and low levels of investment clashed with the state's

Table 1.1. Census of Industrial Activity, 1957–1960

Industrial Sector	Number of Enterprises				Value of Production (in thousand dinars)*			
	1957	1958	1959	1960	1957	1958	1959	1960
Extractive	19	17	19	18	10,752	12,380	10,046	11,152
Wood, paper	3	3	3	3	49	53	49	39
Cork	4	5	4	4	448	449	421	363
Paint	3	4	4	4	204	238	240	280
Fertilizer	10	10	10	11	4,538	5,311	5,390	5,134
Soap	30	31	31	29	1,992	1,710	2,211	2,199
Construction materials	92	91	92	54	4,287	3,797	3,821	4,461
Metalworks	4	4	5	5	3,203	2,726	1,961	1,790
Alimentary	159	163	167	(152)**	10,334	21,988	35,239	35,239

Source: Gouia 1976, 209.

*Original table does not specify unit of measurement for value of production. My presumption is that unit of measurement is in thousand dinars (current). No matter the unit of measurement, one sees stagnation in the production value in nearly all sectors.

**Original table seems to contain a typographical error here, listing the number of alimentary enterprises in 1960 as 552 (a dramatic increase that is not matched by the stagnation in alimentary sector production observed between 1959 and 1960). My best guess is that the number should read 152 alimentary enterprises for 1960.

developmentalist ethos and forced state elites to reconsider a state-led, planned strategy after all.

The State Takes the Lead: Tunisia's "Socialist" Period, 1962–1969

Reconsideration became official policy in 1962, the year Tunisia published its first economic plan. Under the leadership of Ahmed Ben Salah, Tunisia embarked on nearly a decade of planned, state-led development.[8] Failures of the private sector, regional and international ideological trends, not to mention the state's endowment with various economic windfalls, help explain the triumph of a dirigiste vision of development in Tunisia.

First, stagnant investment levels and GNP persuaded Tunisia's political leaders that the country suffered from a problem of "class vacuum." Despite numerous financial and legal inducements the state provided, an entrepreneurial industrial bourgeoisie failed to emerge and play the dynamic development role expected of it. State elites thus felt obliged to fill the entrepreneurial gap.

Second, a state-centered development strategy was encouraged by windfalls enjoyed by the state in the early postcolonial period. Within eight years of independence, the state found itself in possession of more than 500,000 acres of Tunisia's most productive land. More than half of this land (300,000 acres) had either been abandoned by departing French colons at independence or had long been in the possession of the state (e.g., beylical properties). The remainder of this land was still held by foreigners at independence; however, in the wake of political conflicts with France in 1964, the Tunisian state unilaterally nationalized it.[9] When partial sale of this land to the private sector rendered poor economic results—many of the buyers, who had ambitions to be absentee landlords, were more interested in prestige and security than increased agricultural production (Dimassi 1983, 113)—the state decided to step in as a direct agricultural producer. Thus, a windfall of land, combined with the state's commitment to rapid economic growth, also pushed state elites to embrace a state-led development strategy (Gouia 1976, 233; Poncet 1969, 100–103; Bedaoui and Manoubi 1987, 59–60).

Third, the conventional development wisdom of the period, along with the hard currency that foreign powers used to back this wisdom up, also encouraged Tunisia along a path of state-led development. In the early 1960s, "planning" was the new gospel of development policy circles, and the United States was one of its most outspoken advocates. In May 1961, President Kennedy announced the willingness of the United States to provide financial aid to those developing countries that met certain conditions; chief among these was a commitment to rational planning. Six months later, a mission of American experts visited Tunisia and recommended that the U.S. government grant $180 million to Tunisia to help realize the country's first economic plan (Dimassi 1983, 143–45). Thus, Tunisia's first venture into planning was both encouraged and subsidized by Western governments and financial institutions.

Finally, regional trends also encouraged Tunisia's swing toward etatism. The early 1960s were the heyday of Arab socialism, when firebrands like Gamal Abdul Nasser of Egypt captured the imagination of the Arab world, preaching a combination of socialism and Arab nationalism. Bourguiba, who personally preferred to situate Tunisia in a Euro-Mediterranean context rather than an Arab one, was largely hostile to these trends. Nevertheless, the Tunisian leader was not about to pass up an effective mobilizing slogan that could be used for his own ends. "Socialism" and "planning" were two potentially powerful mottos that might galvanize

Tunisian citizens to support the development process, as well as win the hearts of the intellectuals and stave off the development of a real left alternative.

Bourguiba thus threw his weight behind etatism and planning. The publication of the government's official overview of the economy (the *Perspectives décennales*) in 1960 and Tunisia's first Three-Year Plan in 1962 assigned the state a larger and more direct role in the development process. This shift in policy was given further official seal in 1964, when Bourguiba changed the ruling party's name from the Neo-Destour to the *Socialist* Destour Party (PSD).

What followed was a decade of ambitious state intervention in every sector of the economy. In agriculture, the state began a program of forced cooperativisation, using the windfall of state lands as the core of its cooperative program (Romdhane 1981, 313; Dimassi 1983, 329). In commerce, the state sought to "rationalize" foreign and domestic trade by establishing a string of state offices to monopolize much of the import/export trade and force wholesalers (and, ultimately, retailers as well) to regroup under state supervision (Dimassi 1984, 297–306; Ayadi 1969, 85–89; Romdhane 1981, 243–50).

But the state was ultimately most ambitious in industry.[10] The very first plan contained a declaration that the state intended to play the role of industrial entrepreneur, with the aim of creating a more autonomous, better integrated, and more regionally balanced economy. To achieve this goal, the state planned to set in place "industrializing industries" that would foster backward and forward linkages with other industries and promote the economic integration of Tunisia.[11] In addition, the state committed itself to the creation of import-substituting industries that would supposedly reduce Tunisia's dependence on imports and scattered these industrial projects throughout the country to encourage a more even geographical development of the national economy.

The result was massive state investment in a wide range of industrial projects, from heavy industry to light. By 1969 the state counted more than eighty public sector industrial enterprises, producing everything from paper, steel, cement, and chemicals to dairy foods, cigarettes, ovens, and clothing (Ayadi 1969). The extent of state engagement in the industrialization effort is evident from statistics on capital formation in industry during this decade. In nonmanufacturing industries (such as mining and utilities), the state contributed nearly 100% of gross capital formation (Gouia 1976).[12] In the manufacturing industries, the state played an impressive role as well (Table 1.2).

Table 1.2. Public and Private Participation in Gross Fixed Capital Formation, 1961–1969 (in %)

Industrial Sector	Public Enterprise	Private Enterprise
Agro-alimentary	72	28
Metal, glass, construction materials	93	7
Electrical appliances, machinery	92	8
Chemicals	62	38
Textiles	83	17
Diverse	79	21
Total	84	16

Source: Romdhane and Signoles 1982, 73.

Thus, the state clearly took the lead in the industrialization of Tunisia during the 1960s. But none of this is to say that the regime was hostile to private sector participation in the economy. In contrast to other governments in the region (rhetorically) committed to "socialism" (e.g., the Nasserist regime in Egypt), the government led by Ben Salah never wholly discredited the private sector, neither in rhetoric nor in practice. In terms of rhetoric, from the first days of "planned development," political elites from Bourguiba to Ben Salah proclaimed their commitment to the private sector, arguing that the Tunisian economy would be the work of three sectors: state, cooperative, and private.[13] In terms of practice: the regime encouraged private participation in many of its industrial ventures. Joint ventures between the state and private capital were quite common in consumer goods industries (glass, razors, ice cream, and ovens were all produced in mixed enterprises) (Ayadi 1969, 128–38; Bedaoui and Manoubi 1987, 205–6), and public-private cooperation was embraced even in the state's most ambitious industrial ventures. For example, private capital owned 50% of El Fouledh, the steel processing complex that was the centerpiece of Tunisia's "industrializing industries." Similarly, the private sector owned 40% of the state's paper processing plant in Kasserine and 20% of its sugar factory in Beja—two other key "poles" of the state's industrialization program (Ayadi 1969). In addition, the regime upheld and augmented earlier decrees designed to subsidize the development of the private sector through tax holidays, protected local markets, guaranteed loans, and subsidized credit, inputs, and infrastructure.[14] The private sector, then, was not squelched, although the state remained the primary force behind Tunisian industrialization throughout the decade.

Tunisia's Return to "Liberalism": Phase I, 1970–1986

Ben Salah's program of state-led development counted some important successes during the 1960s. Most important, the industrial sector expanded dramatically during his tenure.[15] Despite this success, however, Ben Salah's strategy ran up against structural barriers that are by now familiar to any student of the state-led import substituting strategy of industrialization so popular in the 1960s.

First, a limited local market meant limited room for industrial growth in Tunisia.[16] It also led to inefficient industrial production.[17] Second, import-substituting industries did not reduce Tunisia's level of imports; they merely changed the composition of the country's imports. (Industrial inputs and machinery increasingly replaced finished consumer goods as the leading imports to Tunisia.) As a result, Tunisia's balance of trade remained in serious deficit throughout the course of the decade, averaging a 42% gap between 1962 and 1969 (Tunisian Central Bank, *Statistiques financières*, September 1972, December 1974). Third, the state's ambitious development plans but relatively small tax base meant the Tunisian government was increasingly plagued by fiscal crisis. New sources of investment capital had to be found if the state wished to keep growth rates high (Dimassi 1983, 166–68; Ghabi 1978; Bennour, 1977; Romdhane 1981, 368).[18] These difficulties, together with the colossal failure of the regime's cooperative venture in agriculture, increasingly discredited Ben Salah and the etatist strategy identified with him.[19] The state's commitment to rapid economic development demanded a change in policy. In 1969 a serious harvest failure signaled the end for Ben Salah. Bourguiba removed the ambitious prime minister from power, and Tunisia's experiment in etatist "socialism" came to an abrupt end.[20]

The dismissal of Ben Salah gave rise to a new elite more liberal in outlook that favored a smaller role for the state in the industrialization process and advocated further integration of Tunisian industry into the world economy. Hedi Nouira, the new minister of economy, denounced Ben Salah's socialism as little more than "a dictatorship of the bureaucracy," responsible for fostering inefficiency and corruption in Tunisia. He also assailed the regime's primarily import-substituting approach to industrialization, arguing that it condemned Tunisia to blocked development (Dimassi 1983, 648).[21] Instead, Nouira sought to expand Tunisia's horizons outward by developing the country's export-oriented industries and courting foreign investment to fund such ventures. Nouira also advocated a retreat of the state from its "omni-interventionist" mode (Nouira, cited in Signoles 1984, 787), calling for the state's progressive replacement in the economy by a consciously sponsored private sector.

Commitment to the development of the private sector was first given policy expression in the dismantlement of the cooperative sector in agriculture and commerce. In September 1969 the prime minister called on Tunisia's governors to dissolve all agricultural coops "not viable from either a psychological, technical, or financial point of view" (Bahi Ladgham, cited in Signoles 1984, 785). Within a year, nearly all the land that, prior to the cooperative experiment, had been privately owned was withdrawn from collectivization.[22] With regard to commerce, the regime once again authorized the free practice of retail and wholesale trade in the domestic market, although the state sustained price controls on most consumer staples and monopolistic control over the distribution of sugar, tea, coffee, pepper, matches, and cigarettes. The regime also liberalized export trade.[23] Finally, it eased import trade in those goods essential to the development of domestic industry.[24]

But it was in the industrial sector that the regime undertook the most ambitious measures to encourage private sector development. The minister of national economy, C. Ayari, made clear the new regime's vision: "the state wishes to create a generation of industrialists who tomorrow will be the masters of the country" (*La presse*, 6 February 1974, cited in Signoles 1984, 790). To accomplish this, the state undertook a wide variety of measures favorable to industrial investment, ensuring extensive institutional support to the private sector, generous subsidies for credit and inputs, highly protected markets, and professional training for private sector entrepreneurs.

Measures of Support Offered to Private Sector Industry

In terms of legislative rubrics, the state introduced two new investment codes in 1972 and 1974 designed to encourage private sector development in industry. The 1972 code aimed primarily at stimulating investment (both foreign and domestic) in *export-oriented* activities. Its chief incentives were fiscal, with generous tax exemptions granted to firms in proportion to the share of production they exported. Additional incentives included the right to repatriate profits (for foreign investors) and wide liberty to import industrial inputs. By contrast, the 1974 code aimed at stimulating *domestically oriented* industry. Again, generous tax exemptions were offered as incentives, with concessions granted in proportion to the firm's fulfillment of stipulated state objectives (e.g., employment creation, economic integration, location in disinherited regions, and energy conservation).

Besides favorable legislative rubrics and tax regimes, the state also created new institutions designed to help nurture the development of private sector industry. These institutions included API (Agence de promotion industrielle), created in 1973 and mandated to help entrepreneurs identify potentially profitable industrial projects and facilitate their realization;[25] AFI (Agence foncière industrielle), also created in the early 1970s and designed to make land available to industrial investors, often at subsidized prices; and CEPEX (Centre de promotion des exportations), created in 1973 and designed to help exporters identify market opportunities and improve their marketing techniques as well as their packaging and transport facilities (*Conjoncture,* no. 46, [May 1980]).[26]

Financial support and input subsides were also part of the state's arsenal in its campaign to nurture private sector development. To foster the financing of new industrial projects, the state (as of 1973) essentially guaranteed credit to all industrial projects that had received API approval (Signoles 1984). Special funds and institutions were created to back these guarantees;[27] they were also used to finance investment directly.[28] In addition, the state continued to subsidize interest rates, consistently underpricing this commodity so that interest rates barely kept pace with inflation (Dimassi 1983, 519–20; Sellami 1975, 7–14). In the same spirit, the state underwrote infrastructural support to industry, providing water, power, and transport at subsidized prices (Dimassi 1983, 516).

To stimulate further private sector interest in industry, the state boosted the profitability of industrial ventures through three forms of state regulation. The state guaranteed protection from foreign competition by erecting high tariff barriers and import quotas. It retained dozens of laws from the late colonial era and the Ben Salah period that protected more than eighty-four categories of goods produced in Tunisia (Dimassi 1983, 128; 502–6). Such extensive protection of the local market created extremely comfortable conditions for local industrialists. In the words of one textile manufacturer, "Profits were there for the asking" (interview, 15 March 1988).

Besides protection from foreign competition, the state also guaranteed local industrialists protection from domestic competition. Until 1987, all industrial ventures had to be licensed by API.[29] These licenses were typically denied in sectors that API ruled "saturated." Given the small size of Tunisia's domestic market, "saturation" was often achieved with the creation of one or two firms per sector. Consequently, the licensing system guaranteed monopolies (or at best oligopolies) to investors in many sectors of the domestic market, providing them with opportunities to reap "super-profits" (*Conjoncture*, no. 125 [June 1988]: 19).

In 1970 the state also imposed a comprehensive system of price controls that set the prices of the lion's share of the goods bought and sold in Tunisia. For goods manufactured in Tunisia, prices were largely set on a cost-plus basis, guaranteeing generous profit margins to local manufacturers (no matter their inefficiency). Legislated profit margins varied from 12% for the production of TV aerials to 23% for the production of chemical goods such as glue and paint, an attractive prospect to potential investors (*Annuaire de UTICA*, 1987–88, 77).

In addition to favorable regulation of the market, the state also fostered the development of private sector industry through the professional training of industrial entrepreneurs. In a survey of 140 large private sector industrial enterprises, Gouia found that nearly a third of the entrepreneurs owning or managing these firms had previously served in the public sector (Gouia 1987, 431). Prior to their jump to the private sector, these entrepreneurs (for the most part engineers, technicians, and highly skilled cadres) had served primarily as administrators in the government ministries or as managers in large public enterprises. Many were encouraged to make the jump by the state's generous furlough policy. Under this system, the state permitted employees to take a two-year leave of absence from their jobs to try their hand in the private sector. Their position, salary, and seniority in the public sector were guaranteed for this period. The furlough system essentially made the transition to the private sector risk-free, encouraging many state employees to take the chance (interview, 8 July 1988). In this way, the public sector served as a crucial training ground for many of Tunisia's most successful entrepreneurs.[30] Simply put, the state acted as a "school for entrepreneurs" in Tunisia.

Growth of Private Sector Industry

As we have seen, the Tunisian state spared no effort to nurture the development of private sector industry. The results were not disappointing. The 1970s saw spectacular industrial growth (Table 1.3). Signoles, for example, counts more than eight hundred new industrial enterprises created during this period, doubling Tunisia's industrial capacity (Signoles 1984, 568). The value added of manufacturing industry nearly tripled

Table 1.3. Industrial Firms with Ten or More Employees

1967	1970	1975	1978
553	640	927	1,205

Source: Romdhane and Signoles 1982, 60–63.

during the decade and, by 1979, represented 12.2% of GNP (up from 9.2% in 1970) (Romdhane and Signoles 1982, 62).

The private sector's share in this growth was impressive. Private sector investment in industry multiplied more than sixfold, surpassing public sector investment for the first time in the mid-1970s (see Fig. 1.1). Private sector involvement was especially strong in four subsectors of manufacturing industry: textiles, agro-alimentary, electrical appliances and machinery, and "diverse" industries (a catch-all category that embraces plastics, wood products, publishing, and paper goods), equaling or outpacing the public sector's role (see Table 1.4).

In terms of contribution to value added, the private sector also made a strong showing in these subsectors, as determined by a 1983 enterprise survey conducted by the Tunisian National Institute of Statistics (Institut national de statistiques [INS]) (Table 1.5). But the private sector's

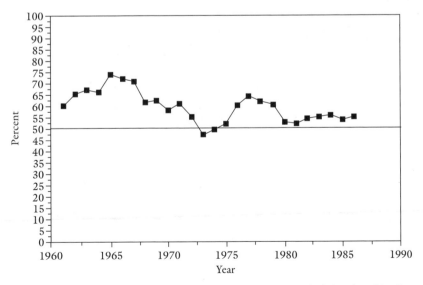

Figure 1.1 Public sector investment as share of total investment. Calculations based on *Retrospectives décennales*, National Institute of Statistics, Tunisia.

Table 1.4. Average Annual Share of Investment of Private
Enterprises in Manufacturing Industry (in %)

Industrial Sector	1961–69	1970–81
Agro-alimentary	22.9	62.2
Textiles, leather	23.4	78.5
Diverse	26.9	78.9
Electrical appliances, machinery	26.8	48.4
Construction materials	27.2	24.0
Chemicals	22.5	18.5

Source: Calculations based on Retrospectives décennales, National
Institute of Statistics, Tunisia.

Table 1.5. Contribution of Value Added by Private Enterprises, Manufacturing Industry,
1983

Industrial Sector	% Private	Amount of Contribution (in million dinars)
Construction materials	32.9	38.4
Chemicals	47.1	29.5
Electrical appliances, machinery	53.4	77.1
Agro-alimentary	46.4	59.8
Textiles, leather	82.9	126.0
Diverse	85.1	54.8

Source: Tunisia, National Institute of Statistics, 1983 Enterprise Survey.
Note: The value added does not include that of enterprises employing fewer than ten workers.

new-found enthusiasm for investment in industry was most evident in the
sheer number of new industrial ventures mounted. Over thirteen years,
Tunisia saw a veritable explosion in the number of private manufacturing
enterprises (Table 1.6).[31] As one civil servant-turned-industrialist
explained, "There was a great feeling of optimism in the air. Everyone was
saying, 'I'm going to start an enterprise!'" (interview, 3 August 1988).

Persistent Weaknesses of the Private Sector

The rapid expansion of private sector industry should not lead us to
overestimate its robustness or strength. A profile of private industrial
enterprises at this time reveals weaknesses relating to sectoral concentration, firm size, management structure, and managerial experience.

Table 1.6. Number of Private Manufacturing Enterprises, 1970–1983

Industrial Sector	1970	1980	1983
Agro-alimentary	203	300	692
Construction materials	84	181	357
Metalwork, electrical appliances, machinery	157	204	396
Chemicals	91	76	156
Textiles, leather	172	390	763
Diverse	158	244	502
Total	865	1,395	2,866

Sources: Tunisia, National Institute of Statistics (INS), Industrial sector for 1970, 1980; INS internal document for 1983; Ministry of Plan, *Sixième plan de développement (1982–86)*; Ministry of Plan, Preparation for Seventh Plan (internal document).

First, with regard to sectoral concentration, we have seen that private entrepreneurs interested in industrial ventures tended to gravitate toward a few industry subsectors, namely textiles, agro-alimentary, diverse, and electromechanical projects. Even within subsectors, private sector entrepreneurs tended to undertake technologically simple endeavors that answered local demand for basic consumer goods. These included furniture making (51% of diverse private sector industrial firms), grain processing, olive oil processing, and canning (91% of agro-alimentary private sector firms), and the production of hats and ready-to-wear clothes (70% of textile firms) (National Institute of Statistics 1983, internal document). This clustering of private sector enterprises in what API called "classic, repetitive projects" (*Conjoncture,* no. 59 [July 1981], supplement) made for limited growth opportunities at home and abroad, especially given the small size of Tunisia's domestic market and the relatively high price of Tunisian labor compared to other less-developed countries specializing in such labor-intensive industries.

As for size, most of these enterprises were rather small. API calculated that 94% of all industrial projects entailed less than 500,000 dinars' worth of investment, while the average investment per enterprise fell below 100,000 dinars (API, "Al-Mu'assasāt al-ṣaghīra," internal document, n.d., 1). Measured in terms of employees, the vast majority of firms employed fewer than fifty workers (Table 1.7). In fact, if "informal" industrial enterprises are included in the count (informal here meaning the tiny firms employing two or three workers that generally escape the INS censuses of industry), one finds private industrial enterprises even more heavily weighted toward small-scale ventures. When the INS included these firms, as was the case in an in-depth census carried out in 1976–78, the census

Table 1.7. Distribution of Private Manufacturing Enterprises by Number of Employees, 1983

	Number of Employees		
Industrial Sector	10–49	50–99	100+
Agro-alimentary	529	52	32
Construction materials	248	40	26
Metalwork, electrical appliances, machinery	204	54	42
Chemicals*	(128)	(39)	—
Textiles, leather	541	99	201
Diverse	361	36	33

Source: Interview with M. Sellami of IACE, who provided figures based on National Institute of Statistics data.
 * Statistics for the chemicals sector roughly calculated from INS figures.

revealed that 62% of all establishments in the industrial sector employed fewer than ten workers. Moreover, in some sectors like textiles, leather, woodworking, and electromechanics, the number of such small firms jumped to 95% (Table 1.8). Small size was thus generally the rule, rather than the exception, for private sector industry in Tunisia.[32]

Besides being small, most of these firms were run as family concerns, a factor that compromised the professionalism of their management. This was true even for firms that had adopted "modern" juridical status (e.g., incorporation), as Fakhfakh found in his 1975 study of industry in the region of Sfax:

> The family aspect of management . . . is transmitted to modern industry as well. In effect the cadres and even the workers of industrial establishments . . . are chosen from among the family of the patron or are neighbors or friends. . . . Even if the organization of work in the factory is of a modern type, the social relations between patron and worker . . . retain a family character." (Fakhfakh 1975, 66)

By the mid-1980s, the familial nature of enterprise management had not changed much in Tunisian industry. Gouia found in a survey of two hundred private industrial enterprises that only 13% of the respondents were governed by a formal board of directors (1987, 422). Management and control of the industrial firm remained highly personal, and like entrepreneurs in many developing countries, Tunisian businessmen generally did not resort to the stock market to expand capital. (The issuing of public

Table 1.8. Distribution of Manufacturing Enterprises by Number of Employees, 1976–1978

Industrial Sector	Number of Workers		Average Number of Workers per Enterprise
	<10 (%)	≥ 10 (%)	
Agro-alimentary	83.8	16.2	8.5
Textiles	94.6	5.4	5.5
Leather	95.2	4.8	5.0
Wood	94.6	5.4	5.5
Paper	69.3	30.7	13.3
Chemicals	82.8	17.2	10.2
Construction materials	80.5	19.5	11.9
Metalwork, electrical appliances, machinery	94.5	5.5	4.8

Source: Tunisia, National Institute of Statistics, *Recensement des établissements, Tunisie entière,* 1976–78.

stock might involve outsiders in the management of the firm, which was anathema to the average Tunisian entrepreneur [Huppert 1971].) This insistence on highly personal control of the firm as well as resistance to issuing public stock undermined the professionalism of industrial management in Tunisia and limited the possibilities of rapid growth, for example, through the public expansion of capital.

Finally, the industrial experience of many Tunisian industrialists was often quite limited. Industrialists as a group are a young class in Tunisia; most industrial ventures date from the early 1970s, if not later. Moreover, most industrial entrepreneurs have relatively shallow roots in industry, having come to the sector from a wide variety of professional backgrounds. A study conducted by API in the late 1970s found that 64% of all industrial entrepreneurs licensed between 1974 and 1977 had no prior industrial experience (Table 1.9). A later survey conducted by Gouia (1987) found that fewer than 20% of industrial entrepreneurs had begun their professional careers in industry (Table 1.10).

The professional background of these industrialists had a direct impact on the character of the industrial projects they undertook. Those who began as merchants, for example, typically ended up producing goods they once sold. This explains the clustering of many industrialists in ready-to-wear clothes, shoes, furniture, and small metal shops (Signoles 1984, 613). In general, then, the lack of deep industrial roots among private sector entrepreneurs further handicapped the sophistication of Tunisian industrial development.

Table 1.9. Professional Background of Industrial
Entrepreneurs Licensed by Agency for the Promotion of
Industry, 1974–1977 (in %)

Industrialists, employees of industrial firms	36
Merchants	35
Civil servants, engineers, technicians, liberal professions	24
Artisans, workers, farmers	5
Total	100

Source: Romdhane and Mahjoub, n.d., 72.

Table 1.10. First Occupation of Selected Industrialists

Occupation	Number	Percentage*
Commerce	66	36
Industry	35	19
Engineering	28	15
Civil service	25	14
Liberal profession	18	10
Artisanry	9	5
Agriculture	3	2
Total	184	

Source: Gouia 1987, 438.
* Percentages do not add up to 100 because of rounding.

Contribution of Private Sector Industry

Despite these weaknesses, however, private sector industry was exercising significant weight in the Tunisian economy by the early 1980s. Its contribution proved especially important in the areas of industrial investment, production, exports, and employment creation. First, with regard to investment, the private sector's contribution to the financing of industrial development in Tunisia rose steadily during the first thirty-five years of independence, increasing from 21.8% during the 1960s, to 41% during the 1970s, to 43% by the close of the Sixth Plan (in 1986). Private investment proved especially important in specific subsectors such as textiles, agro-alimentary industries, and diverse industries (Table 1.4). By the early 1980s, the private sector had overtaken public sector investment in each of these branches.

Second, with regard to production, the private sector's contribution to value added rose steadily during the 1970s. By 1983 it had surpassed the public sector in at least three branches of industry (textiles and leather,

Table 1.11. Contribution of Major Export Earners to Total Exports, 1970–1986 (in %)

	1970	1975	1980	1985	1986
Petrol and derivates	27	44	52	41	24
Phosphates, minerals	12	14	3	2	3
Olive oil	9	9	3	3	4
Fertilizer	9	5	7	10	12
Textiles	2	8	17	20	28
Electrical appliances, machinery	0.1	0.5	2	2	3
Chemicals	0.01	4	6	6	7
% of total export earnings	59	84	90	84	81

Source: Calculations based on Central Bank of Tunisia, *Statistiques financières*, March 1988, 64.

electrical appliances and machinery, diverse) while reaching near parity in two others (chemicals and agro-alimentary industries) (see Table 1.5).

Third, with regard to exports, by the early 1980s manufactured goods were fast replacing Tunisia's traditional export earners (petroleum, phosphates, olive oil) as the country's major hard currency earners. The Sixth Plan predicted that manufactured goods would constitute more than half of all exported goods and services by 1986. Table 1.11 documents the growing role of manufactured goods in exports during the 1970s to the mid-1980s. Within manufactured goods, moreover, textiles (an industry where the private sector predominates) contributed the largest share of exports. Textiles surpassed petroleum as the *leading* export earner in 1986, providing 28% of export earnings (compared to 24% for petroleum). If the performance of textiles is combined with that of shoes/leather and electrical appliances/machinery (two other areas where the private sector predominates), the contribution of the private sector industry to export earnings (roughly calculated) jumps to 34%.[33]

But perhaps even more impressive than its contribution to investment, production, or export earnings was the private sector's role in the creation of employment. In a country where unemployment levels routinely hovered around 14% (*Réalités*, 1 December 1990, 19), job creation was an extremely important political goal. Industry played a key role in creating new jobs: 37% of all new jobs created between 1972 and 1976 were in industry. That percentage jumped to 48% between 1976 and 1980 (*Conjoncture*, no. 59 [July 1981], supplement). Within industry, private sector manufacturing industry was the fastest-growing employment creator. For the period 1971–75, an API report showed that 91% of all new jobs in industry were created by the private sector (API report, cited in Gouia 1987). A more recent report by the same agency showed that

72% of all industrial workers in Tunisia were employed in predominantly private sector, small-scale enterprises (API, "Al-Mu'assasāt al-ṣaghīra," internal document, n.d., 1).

Persistence of the Public Sector

By the mid-1980s, then, private sector industry represented an important force in the Tunisian economy. Still, the private sector did not prevail in all parts of the economy. In industry, the public, not the private, sector continued to dominate investment and production in sectors like chemicals, construction materials, mining, and utilities. In other sectors where the private sector proved stronger (e.g., agro-alimentary, textiles, diverse, and electromechanical) the state continued to play an important role, thanks to its commitment to investing in capital-intensive and technology-intensive projects such as naval construction or sugar processing. Throughout this "liberal" period, the regime continued to abide by the logic defined by Tunisia's very first economic plan (1962–64), namely, that the state would assume responsibility for those projects that "exceed the capabilities of private initiative" (Ministry of Plan, *Troisième plan de développement*, 141–42). In other words, the state embraced a clear division of labor between the public and private sector, with the state taking responsibility for the development of those industrial sectors that were most capital intensive, most costly in terms of technology, and least immediately profitable; left to the private sector were the industrial ventures that were less costly, less technologically sophisticated, and more immediately profitable (Romdhane and Mahjoub, n.d., 77; Romdhane and Signoles 1982, 76).

As a consequence, the public sector continued to grow throughout Tunisia's first "liberal" phase (1970–86). The public sector's contribution to overall investment levels in Tunisia remained high, staying well above 50% for the entire period, save for the years 1973 and 1974. The dinar value of its contribution to value added grew fourfold during the first decade of the "new era," with the state's contribution to GNP always hovering around 20–25% (Ministry of Plan, *Réforme des entreprises publiques*, Commission de synthèse du VIème plan, February 1982, 9). Employment in the public sector tripled, rising from 51,500 employees in 1971 to 173,000 employees in 1981 (Ministry of Plan, internal document, n.d., 8). Even the sheer number of public enterprises mushroomed, rising from 180 in 1970 to 297 in 1981 (*Réforme des entreprises publiques*, 7).

In short, the state did not wither away during this first "liberal" phase in Tunisia. The private sector certainly grew, but then so did the public. In this way, Tunisia resembled many other countries (e.g., Greece, Spain, Portugal) in that the regime's official rhetoric and professed ideological convictions often sustained a paradoxical relation to policy (Bermeo 1990). In Tunisia the public sector expanded much more rapidly during the reign of Hedi Nouira, who came to power committed to paring down the omni-interventionist role of the state, than it did during the reign of Ben Salah, who was frankly committed to etatism.

How, then, might public sector expansion and contraction be explained? Certainly, ideology was not irrelevant, but more important was the condition of the state's coffers. One finds that during the first years of Nouira's rule public sector investment *did* contract, in line with Nouira's professed liberal convictions (see Fig. 1.1). However, in 1974–75 public sector investment began to rise again, and this increase directly coincides with the period when Tunisia's revenues from petroleum sales began to rise dramatically. In the wake of the 1973 oil crisis, Tunisia's oil revenues nearly tripled overnight (see Fig. 1.2). Awash in

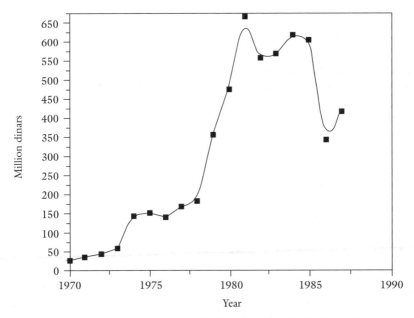

Figure 1.2 Earnings from petroleum and derivatives. Data from Tunisia Central Bank annual reports, various years.

petroleum rents, the Tunisian elites found the allure of expanding the public sector irresistible.

Expansion of the public sector did not spring from elite conviction that the state would make the most efficient use of Tunisia's surplus. Although some public sector expansion could indeed be justified on purely economic grounds (e.g., to remedy choke points in the country's transport, energy, and hydraulic infrastructure) (Signoles 1984, 807–8), the elite's embrace of public sector expansion stemmed more from calculations of political than of economic interest. Public sector expansion promised to alleviate three crucial political problems faced by the regime: (a) unemployment, (b) regional economic imbalance, and (c) overly rapid rural-to-urban migration. The expansion of the public sector would generate jobs and permit the creation of more enterprises in economically disinherited rural areas, thereby redressing each of these problems. This political logic proved irresistible to the state elite and explains their embrace of public sector expansion despite their much-professed liberal rhetoric.

Liberal Era: Phase II, 1986–Present

But the very same factors that fostered the state's expansive role in the economy in the 1970s contributed to its contraction in the 1980s. Specifically, during the first half of the decade the state saw significant reduction in its petroleum rents as well as reduction and/or stagnation in many other principal foreign exchange earners. Petroleum revenues, which typically accounted for nearly half of the country's foreign currency earnings in the mid- and late 1970s, dropped for the first time in 1982 (at a rate of nearly 20%, owing to a decrease in the quantity of petroleum produced and exported). This decline led the authors of the Sixth Plan (1982–86) to predict the imminent exhaustion of Tunisia's petroleum resources. The planners' dire predictions ultimately proved unfounded: quantities produced and exported remained relatively constant at 1982 levels for the duration of the decade (Central Bank, *Statistiques financières*, September 1996, 74). Nevertheless, petroleum revenues took a second major plunge when oil prices collapsed to nearly half their prior value in 1986.[34]

Besides the decline in petroleum revenues, Tunisia also experienced significant contraction and/or stagnation in several other sectors that were strategic foreign currency earners for the country. Phosphates, which in the 1970s had accounted for as much as 10% of hard currency earnings, saw an overall stagnation in production and, in some years, experienced a significant decrease in world price as well (Central Bank, *Annual Report*, 1982, 1984, 1985). Worker remittances, which accounted for 6–8% of foreign currency receipts in the 1970s, stagnated between 1980 and 1986, and even registered an absolute decline in 1985, due to economic recession in Western Europe (where most Tunisian migrant workers were employed). Finally, tourism, which accounted for an average of 13% of the country's foreign currency receipts in the 1970s also experienced stagnation and even regression, thanks to the recession in Western Europe, and international disturbances in the region, such as the American bombing of Libya in 1986, which reduced the number of European holiday makers in Tunisia. In short, the period 1980–86 was one of economic difficulty for Tunisia, with foreign exchange in ever-shorter supply (Elmanoubi 1993, 94–95).[35] These economic difficulties culminated in crisis in 1986. That year, the conjuncture of severe drought and very poor harvests compounded with collapsed oil prices, decreased worker remittances, and a decline in tourism to result in a negative growth rate for the country (−1.6 in real terms) as well as the exhaustion of foreign reserves. To forestall economic disaster, the Tunisian government was forced to appeal to the IMF. Ultimately, the prescriptions proposed by this agency nudged Tunisia into phase two of "liberal" development.

This second phase of liberal development is noteworthy for putting the market back into "liberal." Whereas during the earlier phase of "liberalism" the state had focused primarily on encouraging growth of the private sector (even as it expanded the size of the public sector and retained control of prices, interest rates, and the terms of international trade), during this second phase the state embraced widespread market reform as well as contraction of its role in the Tunisian economy. The specific measures adopted by the regime are by now the familiar stuff of International Monetary Fund (IMF)/World Bank-inspired programs of economic stabilization and structural adjustment implemented in many countries around the world. In Tunisia these measures included liberalization of prices, interest rates, and imports, reductions in public spending, devaluation of the dinar, legal innovations to improve the functioning of the market (including tax reform, financial sector reform, and investment reform (no more API licensing!), privatization of public enterprises, and ever-stronger emphasis on export orientation and the integration of the Tunisian economy into the international system.

In the decade following Tunisia's first embrace of structural adjustment, the country showed differential success at reform, performing better in some areas than others. The regime was most successful at reducing the budget deficit, liberalizing prices, reforming the tax system, simplifying the investment code, and devaluing the dinar. By 1994 the regime had reduced the budget deficit to less than 2.6% of GNP, down from 5.5% in 1986 (*Conjoncture*, no. 192 [July–August 1995]). By 1995, prices had been liberalized for nearly 90% of goods in Tunisia, leaving only a small group of basic consumer goods (e.g., bread, sugar, oil) still subject to price control and subsidization by the government (Central Bank, *Annual Report*, 1995, 73). With regard to reform of the tax and investment codes, the regime undertook extensive measures to rationalize the income tax system and create a standard value-added tax in the late 1980s and in 1993 introduced a unified investment code designed to streamline the investment process across sectors (API, *Investment Incentives Code*, n.d.). Finally, the regime began devaluing the dinar as early as 1986 and, by December 1992, had made the dinar largely convertible for current account purposes (Central Bank, *Annual Report*, 1992, 147–48).

But the regime was less successful in other areas of reform. Least impressive was its performance in the area of trade liberalization. Although by 1995 the regime was boasting that 91.5% of imports had been liberalized, in fact this liberalization referred only to exemption from quantitative restrictions (EIU [Economist Intelligence Unit], *Country Report: Tunisia*, January–March 1995, 17). The vast majority of imported manufactured goods (for which an equivalent was manufactured locally) remained subject to sizeable tariff barriers.[36] The maximum tariff barrier was officially set at 43%, although "temporary tariff surcharges" were added to "tide enterprises over the adjustment to the removal of import restrictions" (World Bank 1994, ii). In a 13 December 1996 speech given at an IACE conference in Sousse, the minister of international cooperation and foreign investment, Mohamed Ghannouchi, admitted that the effective rate of protection in Tunisia was closer to 52% overall, while a brief glance through the official *Nomenclature de dédouanement des produits*, published by the director general of customs in 1995, turned up many locally manufactured goods, with customs protection edging well past the 73% mark.

Similarly, the regime lagged in its embrace of privatization. Out of more than four hundred public enterprises slated for privatization, only sixty had been privatized by 1996. The slow pace of privatization was attributed to a variety of state concerns, such as the fear of generating unemployment and concern that public enterprises would be sold too cheaply (EIU, *Country Report: Tunisia*, October–December 1996, 15). But aside from this less-than-stellar showing in the areas of privatization and trade liberalization, Tunisia performed relatively well in its embrace of structural adjustment. By the early 1990s the government's reform efforts were sufficiently praiseworthy that the IMF was touting Tunisia as the "model" of reform for other countries (*IMF Survey*, 18 June 1990, 9 November 1992).[37] Similarly, in 1996 the Heritage Foundation ranked Tunisia thirtieth-seventh out of 140 countries evaluated in its Index of Economic Freedom; this ranking placed Tunisia among countries described as "essentially free." The foundation found Tunisia to have low levels of inflation, government consumption, wage and price control, restrictions on banking, and barriers to foreign investment; it judged Tunisia's levels of taxation and black market activity to be moderate. Only Tunisia's trade policy was branded as highly protectionist. As such, the foundation ranked Tunisia above Italy, Spain, and Greece and placed it fourth-highest among Arab countries, following Bahrain, the UAE, and Kuwait (EIU, *Country Report: Tunisia*, April–June 1996, 16).

Impact of Reform on Private Sector Industry

What has economic reform meant for private sector industrialists in Tunisia? Clearly, these reform measures have posed a hardship for some private sector industrialists, especially those whose operations were marginal to begin with and whose production was oriented solely toward the domestic market. Many Tunisian industrialists prospered during the 1970s and 1980s, thanks to years of state-subsidized credit and inputs, protected markets, and inflated (but state-mandated) prices. The introduction of economic reform exposed their inefficiency to the rigor of market discipline and threatened the long-term survival of some. Already by April 1987, 389 firms had gone bankrupt and 630 more were in trouble (*Réalités*, no. 148 [10 June 1988]: 6–11). Between 1987 and 1994 the Ministry of Social Affairs registered an annual average of 117 manufacturing enterprises "in economic difficulty" (Ministry of Social Affairs, Service des statistiques, internal document).[38] And in the wake of the free trade accord reached between the European Community and Tunisia in 1995, official sources estimated that somewhere between 15 and 30% of Tunisia's industrial enterprises might not survive if tariffs on European industrial imports were removed immediately. Consequently, the regime negotiated a gradual lifting of tariffs over a twelve-year period to allow Tunisian industry time to adapt to European competition (EIU, *Country Report: Tunisia*, July–September 1995, 16).

Persistent Importance of the Private Sector

Despite these challenges, however, private sector industry did not collapse in Tunisia. To the contrary, in the decade since the country first began its program of structural adjustment, private sector industry flourished and expanded its role in the economy. A number of key indicators make this clear.

In terms of the sheer number of private sector industrial firms, Tunisia saw dramatic expansion. In 1996, API counted 10,304 manufacturing enterprises in the country, nearly all of which were privately owned (interview, 17 December 1996). This represented more than a threefold increase over the 2,866 private manufacturing firms counted by the INS in 1983 (compare Table 1.12 to Table 1.6).

In terms of exports, the role of private sector industry mushroomed, growing at a rate of 10% per year between 1986 and 1993 (World Bank 1994, 5), and representing more than 70% of all export earnings by 1995 (Table 1.13).[39]

In terms of employment, the manufacturing sector (which was primarily dominated by the private sector) accounted for 25% of all the country's nonagricultural employment by 1994 (National Institute of Statistics, *Recensement général de la population et de l'habitat*, February 1994).[40] This sector proved to be a leading creator of jobs, generating 27–33% of all new nonagricultural jobs in the economy between 1986 and 1995 (Table 1.14).

In terms of contribution to value added, manufacturing industry (again, private-sector dominated) saw strong growth averaging 6% per

Table 1.12. Number of Private Manufacturing Enterprises, 1996

Industrial Sector	Number of Enterprises
Agro-alimentary	2,213
Construction materials	737
Metalwork, electrical appliances, machinery	1,343
Chemicals	437
Textiles, leather	3,955
Diverse	1,619
Total	10,304

Source: Agency for the Promotion of Industry, internal document.

Table 1.13. Sectoral Contribution to Export Earnings, 1995

Sectoral Type	Percentage Contribution
Textiles, leather	49.9
Metalwork, electrical appliances, machinery, construction materials, ceramics, glass	13.8
Chemicals, misc. industries	7.6
Phosphates and derivatives	10.3
Agro-alimentary	10
Energy products	8.4
Total	100

Source: Centre de Promotion des Exportations, "Commerce extérieur de la Tunisie," 1995.

Table 1.14. Creation of Nonagricultural Employment, 1986–1995

Year	Total New Jobs Created	Manufacturing Jobs
1986	29,320	12,000
1987	35,000	11,000
1988	42,000	14,000
1989	44,000	14,000
1990	46,000	15,000
1991	37,000	11,000
1992	51,000	14,000
1993	54,500	15,800
1994	58,000	16,000
1995	61,000	17,000

Source: Central Bank, Annual Report, 1990, 86; 1995, 79–81.

year between 1987 and 1995.[41] This increase made up for the decline in the nonmanufacturing industrial sector, specifically in the hydrocarbon sector, which saw an average drop of 2.4% per year during this period (Central Bank, Annual Report, 1995, 44; 1991, 51). Overall, manufacturing industry accounted for the growing share of GNP in Tunisia (Table 1.15).

Finally, in terms of contribution to investment, the private sector accounted for 78% of total investment in manufacturing industry in 1995, up from 76.4% in 1994 (Central Bank, Annual Report, 1995, 86) and 70% for the period of the Seventh Plan (1988–92) (Ministry of Plan,

Table 1.15. Manufacturing Industry: Contribution to GNP, 1986–1996

Year	Percentage Contribution
1986	13.1
1987	13.1
1988	13.9
1989	17.4
1990	16.9
1991	17.1
1992	16.5
1993	17.1
1994	18.3
1995	18.8
1996	18.4

Source: Central Bank, *Statistiques financières*, September 1989, September 1991, September 1993, September 1996.

Huitième plan de développement, vol. 2, 50). Overall, the private sector accounted for 50% of all investment in the Tunisian economy between 1991 and 1994, consistent with its 49.5% share of total investment under the Seventh Plan (*Huitième plan*, vol. 1, 80).

Persistent Weaknesses

Of course, despite this impressive showing, private sector industry continued to exhibit certain important weaknesses in Tunisia. Individually, most private sector firms remain quite small, employing on average only thirty-five workers (World Bank 1994, 14). Recent API statistics confirm this (Table 1.16).

In addition, most private sector industrial firms continued to be family-run operations or, at best, run by small groups, with the attendant negative consequences in terms of undercapitalization and less than professional management.[42] Private sector industry in Tunisia also continued to be characterized by a low level of value added. The leading manufacturing sectors, textiles and machinery/electrical appliances, tended to import semifinished goods (fabric, appliance parts) and focus primarily on the assembly of these inputs. Finally, private sector investment confidence tended to flag a bit in the mid-1990s, evidenced by a slight slowdown in investment levels at this time (Central Bank, *Annual Report*, 1995, 83).

Table 1.16. Size of Industrial Enterprises by Number of
Employees, 1996

Number of Employees	Number of Enterprises	Percentage
Fewer than 10	3,822	37.2
10 to 100	4,543	44.2
100 to 500	643	6.3
500 to 1,000	39	0.4
1,000 to 5,000	9	0.1
No response	1,221	11.9
Total	10,277	100

Source: Agency for the Promotion of Industry, internal
document.

No doubt, this was a consequence of business fears, spurred by the
EU–Tunisian free trade accord of 1995, concerning further liberalization
of imports and further integration of the Tunisian economy into the international system.

Nevertheless, after more than two decades of growth, the private sector
industry constituted an important force in the Tunisian economy, providing a crucial source of investment, employment, exports, and value
added. And, as before, its expansion had been actively embraced and
encouraged by the state.[43] In fact, the adoption of a more liberal strategy
of economic development only reinforced the centrality of private sector
entrepreneurs to the regime's strategy for economic growth and re-
doubled the state's commitment to "pass the baton" to the private sector.

State Sponsorship in the Context of Economic Reform

To encourage this process the state continued its tradition of providing a wide variety of supports and concessions to private sector industrialists. This time around, however, many of the sweeteners were designed
not to contradict the logic of the market. Thus, for example, instead of
providing investors with subsidized inputs or underpriced interest rates
(as it had in the 1970s and early 1980s), as of 1987 the state decreed the
simplification of start-up procedures for new industrial ventures, abolish-
ing the old requirement that obliged entrepreneurs to obtain government
approval before launching new projects. The new projects, however, still
had to be registered with API (Law 87-5 of August 1987). In addition,

the state streamlined the country's investment code in 1993 to further simplify the start-up process. In the late 1980s the state simplified the tax code to encourage compliance and, by 1993, made the dinar convertible for current account purposes, thereby making business travel easier and industrial imports easier to obtain. Finally, the state remained true to its role as "school for entrepreneurs," offering API-sponsored seminars to recent university graduates on "how to be an entrepreneur" (*La presse*, 16 June 1988) and even expanding this program to target promising women candidates (*Réalités*, 5 January 1990).

But not all the state's measures to support private sector industry during this period conformed to the logic of the market. For example, while the regime theoretically embraced the principle of trade liberalization, it was slow to implement this ideal in practice. Although raw materials, equipment, and spare parts could be imported largely without restriction in Tunisia, high tariff barriers remained in force to protect locally produced finished consumer goods. These tariffs generally ranged from 43% to 75%, permitting local industrialists a comfortable margin of inefficiency (by world standards) without loss of profitability. Tunisian officials defended the slow pace of trade liberalization, arguing that "to preserve [Tunisia's] industrial tissue, we must be careful that [liberalization] is not carried out brutally or in a disloyal fashion" (Mouldi Zouaoui, secretary of state of industry and commerce, *Réalités*, 5 January 1990). The persistence of such protection was anticipated for a relatively long period. For example, the 1995 free trade accord with the European Community envisioned a gradual lifting of such tariff protection, to be spread out over a twelve-year period for Tunisian goods not yet competitive with European products. Tariffs on imports of non-European provenance would doubtless remain in force even longer.

Besides retaining such trade protection, the state also took steps to protect local industry from the full impact of market discipline. When rising bankruptcy rates threatened recession and the loss of thousands of jobs in the late 1980s, the state stepped in with a program designed to save those firms it considered viable (i.e., capable of future growth and profitability). The program included the provision of subsidized credit for debt consolidation, generous fiscal concessions, and a reduction of social security obligations (Central Bank, "Measures to Help Enterprises and Sectors in Difficulty," internal document, 7 March 1988). In addition, the state created a variety of new funds, such as FODEC (Fond de développement de compétitivité de l'industrie) and FOPROMAT (Fond de promotion et de maîtrise de la technologie industrielle), even as it has financially reinforced old ones (e.g., the Agence foncière industrielle) to help in its ambitious program of "Mise à niveau de l'industrie," a program devoted to renovating Tunisian industries and making them competitive with foreign firms.[44] And, of course, the state continued to grant generous fiscal concessions to firms that were export-oriented or located in disadvantaged regions. In short, the state continued to act as caretaker/handmaiden for private sector industry in Tunisia, even during this second stage of "liberal" development.

Conclusion

As we have seen, the Tunisian state has long embraced a strategy of state-sponsored capitalist industrialization, consciously nurturing the development of private sector industry. Committed to a developmentalist ethos but constrained by limited resources, the state has long sought to coax investment from the private sector to foster Tunisia's economic growth. Successive experiences of fiscal constraint, especially in the late 1960s and again in the mid-1980s, drove the state to champion the private sector—first, through measures that violated market logic, among them subsidies, protection, and controls, but later through measures that embraced it as well, for example, termination of the licensing system, simplification of start-up procedures, and more efficient institutional support. Thanks to such sponsorship, a significant class of private sector industrialists has emerged in Tunisia over the past twenty years, one that plays an ever more redoubtable role in the national economy. Whether this economic position translates into political power and autonomy sufficient to shape the state's policy agenda and constrain the state's autonomy in the policy-making process is the subject of chapter 2.

CHAPTER 2

The Developmental Paradox: Capital's Emergent Power and Autonomy

What does state sponsorship mean politically? Does a debt of origin condemn private sector industrialists to persistent submissiveness vis-à-vis the state? Or does state sponsorship contain the seeds of a paradox, giving rise to a social force capable of challenging the state and eroding its capacity to dictate policy unilaterally?

The answer turns in large part on the power and autonomy that private sector industrialists manage to carve out in the context of state sponsorship. As the Tunisian case shows, the state's decision to sponsor the development of private sector industrialists can significantly boost the structural power of this class. But access to other classic sources of private sector power (instrumental power, cultural power) may still be constrained by factors such as the size of the elite and the country's institutional legacy. The private sector's policy influence may thus increase thanks to its enhanced structural position but still fall short of what would be predicted by its structural position alone.

As for autonomy, common sense suggests that state sponsorship will compromise private sector autonomy, especially when the state distributes its favors on a discretionary basis. Discretion opens the door to sycophancy and cronyism, where currying favor with the state, not political assertiveness, is the key to business survival. While this has proven true in Tunisia, the case is especially interesting because it shows that cronyism need not spell complete political self-effacement so long as the state is driven by developmental logic. Further, the Tunisian case shows that the discretionary character of state sponsorship is likely to decline as states embrace increasingly market-driven development strategies.

Chapter 2 elaborates this argument. The chapter starts by disaggregating the concepts of power and autonomy and clarifying the need for analytic distinction between the two. It then turns to the Tunisian case, evaluating the parameters of power and autonomy enjoyed by private sector industrialists in the context of state sponsorship. Finally, it reflects on the policy influence exercised by industrialists in Tunisia. The goal is to determine whether state-sponsored industrialization has indeed given rise to a developmental paradox such that the state, by its own logic, has inadvertently given rise to a class that can erode state power to make policy unilaterally.

Power and Autonomy: Definitions

To evaluate the position of private sector industrialists and their capacity to influence state policy we must assess their evolving power and autonomy. Given the ambiguity of these terms the chapter begins by defining them, disaggregating their component parts, and highlighting their analytic distinctiveness.

Power

When used with reference to private sector industrialists, power refers to the capacity of these private sector actors to work their will upon the state, that is, to impose their preferences on the state and state policy. The vast literature devoted to this subject typically identifies three sources of private sector power: structural, ideological, and instrumental (Gold, Lo, and Wright 1975).

The structural power of private sector industrialists derives from the very logic of the economy and the pivotal role that private sector capital plays in it. Simply put, when an economy is organized along capitalist lines, its health hinges on high levels of private sector investment. The state has an interest in fostering a healthy economy because it is essential to achieving other state objectives such as employment creation, improved living standards, and high tax revenues (Lindblom 1977, 173). The problem for the state is that it cannot simply order the private sector to invest. Instead, it must court the confidence of the business community by enacting policies that guarantee the community's interests (specifically, high and steady profits). The private sector's capacity to withhold investment (and/or undertake capital flight) endows private business with a "structural" mechanism for state domination. It enjoys something of a veto power over public policy even without having to organize itself polit- ically in any self-conscious way (Poulantzas 1972; Offe and Ronge 1975). By the logic of the economy, the state is obliged to serve the interests of the private sector.

The power that private sector industrialists enjoy thanks to this struc- tural mechanism is directly proportional to their contribution to capital formation. Where their contribution is relatively small, the threat of investment strike will lack force. In India, for example, Kochanek writes that the state in the 1970s did not "quake when business talk(ed) of a strike in the capital market" because most Indian businessmen received a large share of their funding from government credit agencies (Kochanek 1974, 269). Similarly, in Japan, the state was less than alarmed by the threat of capital strike in the 1970s, given the high debt-equity ratios that characterized Japanese businesses and the relatively small personal contri- butions that businessmen made to the capital formation of their firms (Kaplan 1972, 37). Evaluating the structural power of private sector industrialists thus depends on assessing their contribution to national capital formation.

But structural power aside, private sector industrialists command other routes to political influence. Students in the tradition of Hegel and Gramsci tend to focus on ideological mechanisms of domination available to the private sector. They argue that the controlling influence exercised by the private sector over cultural institutions such as the mass media and the educational system provides the business community with significant opportunities to shape the public's consciousness in the image of business preferences. This endows the private sector with one of its most effective sources of political power, for when successful, it invests business's preferences with the weight of popular will.

This route to power seems most plausible in countries where private sector businessmen do indeed exercise control over the media and edu- cation. In Mexico, for example, Camp (1989, 244–56) provides substan- tial evidence that most Mexican newspaper chains are controlled by leading entrepreneurial families. Similarly, in the United States, Bowles and Gintes (1976) provide convincing evidence of the business commu- nity's control over the content of education in American schools. Evalu- ating the ideological power of the private sector, then, depends to a large degree on assessing private business's role in such areas as education and the media.

But besides structural and ideological power, private sector industrialists possess a third route to political influence through instrumental relations with the state. Classic theorists of instrumentalism such as Miliband, Mills, and Domhoff argue that the private sector compels the state to serve its interests by participating actively in politics and intervening directly in the daily operations of the state. Three means of participation and intervention are typical. These include financing both political parties and candidates who champion private sector interests; occupying public office; and lobbying the state, either on a collective or an individualistic basis.[1] The private sector's superior economic resources and close social proximity to political elites privileges it in each of these efforts. Assessing the instrumental power of private sector industrialists rests on evaluating the capacity of industrialists to exploit each of these three routes to influence.

Autonomy

Besides power, the second factor that shapes the political position of private sector industrialists is *autonomy*. The term refers to the capacity of industrialists to conduct themselves independently in the political arena, even to the point of challenging the state in matters of public policy. The political independence enjoyed by private sector industrialists hinges to a large degree on their economic autonomy, that is, the degree to which their economic well-being is, or is not, *beholden to the goodwill of the state* (Rubio 1988). All things being equal, the more independent private sector industrialists are economically, the freer they will be to assert their interests, even against the state, in the policy arena.[2]

Economic autonomy is a complex concept and thus not easy to assess. Economic groups in modern societies are rarely either wholly autonomous or wholly dependent in their relationship to the state. Rather than resort to dyadic absolutes, it is better to conceive of autonomy as a spectrum, with intervening points of greater or lesser independence. The position of private sector businessmen on this spectrum turns on two questions: (a) To what degree is their profitability dependent on state intervention and support? and (b) To what degree is state support distributed on a discretionary basis? In both cases, autonomy is inversely related to the degree to which profitability is governed by political mediation rather than market principle.

Represented visually, the spectrum might be conceived in the following way:

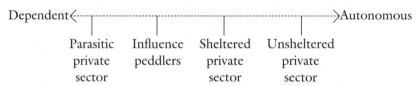

Dependent ⟵-------┬----------------------┬----------------------┬------------------┬-------⟶ Autonomous

Parasitic	Influence	Sheltered	Unsheltered
private	peddlers	private	private
sector		sector	sector

Positioned at the most "dependent" end of the spectrum is what an earlier generation of political sociologists called the "parasitic" private sector. These businessmen contribute little or nothing of value to the national economy and exist solely thanks to politically mediated subversion of the market. This politically mediated subversion is the product of special relations with state elites won through the exchange of bribes, friendship, and/or political support. In the Middle East, examples of parasitic businessmen include the "supply mafia" of Egypt—racketeers who use their personal connections within the state's ministries to commandeer supplies of scarce subsidized goods, which they then sell at exorbitant prices on the black market (Springborg 1989, 81–82). Also included in this category are the "commission entrepreneurs" of Saudi Arabia— businessmen who use their close relations with members of the royal family to snare positions as official "sponsors" of foreign companies. They act as go-betweens in the negotiation of state contracts but contribute little to the national economy beyond adding another state-mandated layer to the country's distribution circuit (Field 1984, 98). In both cases, these businessmen are utterly dependent on state-supported subversion of the market for their economic viability. Moreover, this subversion is mediated through personal relations (i.e., distributed by state elites on a discretionary basis), with disastrous implications for the political autonomy of the private sector.

Less dependent than the parasitic private sector but still far from autonomous are the "influence peddlers." This group is similar to the parasitic private sector in that close connections to state elites are essential to their profitability. They are different from parasitic businessmen in that influence peddlers do contribute something of value to the economy (though perhaps not as efficiently as they might, had they been forced to contend with pure market discipline). Well-known influence peddlers in the Middle East include Osman Ahmad Osman and Abbud Pasha of Egypt. Both were private contractors who parlayed close personal connections with leading political elites into hugely profitable contracting empires. In the process, however, they also supplied the country with roads, bridges, buildings, and dams (Vitalis 1989). Influence peddlers continue to be dependent on the state in the sense that good connections are an essential component of their economic success. Discretionary state support is a central assumption of their operations. Nonetheless, they enjoy a small measure of political autonomy (or at least, political leverage) vis-à-vis the state because they produce something of value to the state.

Next in the spectrum of autonomy is the sheltered private sector. This category includes all private entrepreneurs who enjoy boosted profitability thanks to state intervention and support but for whom that intervention and support is not subject to discretionary largesse on the part of the state. Wherever the state bestows its support on a uniform, nondiscretionary basis (e.g., standard, sector-wide rates of tariff protection or credit subsidies or tax concessions), the private sector might be considered "sheltered." The sheltered private sector is clearly dependent on the state in the sense that it owes at least a portion of its profitability to state support. But the fact that these benefits are granted on a uniform basis gives this sector a measure of political independence that mere "influence peddlers" do not enjoy. Examples of the sheltered private sector are many. In fact, in today's context, where "embedded liberalism" is standard operating procedure even in (or especially in) highly industrialized countries, sheltered enterprise is probably more the rule than the exception (Callaghy 1989). Many modern industries, ranging from the auto industry in the United States to high-tech firms in Japan, fall into the category of the sheltered private sector.

Finally, marking the most autonomous point on our spectrum are private sector entrepreneurs who receive no support or protection from the state whatsoever. These are the paragons of the liberal ideal for whom the market, not the state, determines the level of profitability. Economic enterprises (and especially industrial enterprises) so entirely self-reliant are relatively rare today. The United States, long the loudest advocate of this ideal, has protected its industrialists from the brutal vagaries of the market since the early part of the twentieth century (Bellon 1986). And the East Asian NICs (newly industrializing countries), long touted as models of market-led growth, clearly owe much of their success to persistent government intervention in and protection of industry (Deyo 1987). In fact, the most likely place to find self-reliant enterprises in many countries today is in the informal sector (which falls outside the purview of the state) or in areas (entire countries?) where the state apparatus has collapsed. The Magendo class in Uganda constitutes such an autonomous stratum (Rothchild and Chazan 1988; Kasfir 1984b). The category of the wholly autonomous private sector is a rare specimen but persists as an ideal type, and as such it rounds off our conceptual spectrum of autonomy and dependence for private enterprise.

Autonomy is a crucial political variable for the private sector. Without it, private entrepreneurs are reduced to the status of "eunuch capitalists," dependent on currying favor with the state to survive (Kasfir 1984a, 12). Under these conditions, private sector actors are less likely to be politically assertive, let alone challenge state elites in the policy arena. Gauging the autonomy of the private sector, in terms of its dependence on state support and the degree to which this support is distributed on a discretionary basis, is thus essential to evaluating the political potential of this stratum.

Analytic Distinction between Power and Autonomy

Autonomy and power do not necessarily go together for the private sector. In fact, the two can have entirely independent trajectories. For example, it is quite easy to imagine private sector actors enjoying substantial autonomy from the state while possessing little power over it. An independent business class such as the Magendo in Uganda might in no way be dependent on state support for its economic well-being. Nevertheless, it might lack the means and/or the desire to impose its preferences on the state. To the contrary, where the state is predatory, private entrepreneurs might want to keep as far away from the state as possible. Similarly, private sector actors might enjoy significant power over the state without possessing extensive autonomy. Many private sector enterprises exhibit substantial dependence on state support for their profitability. For example, the auto industry in the United States and the high-tech industry in Japan, not to mention ISI industries in many late-developing countries, all receive substantial state support in the form of either subsidized credit, export guarantees, or trade protection. Nevertheless, these enterprises often exercise significant influence over the state and state policy, thanks to their possession of multiple means to power (instrumental means, such as campaign financing; ideological means, such as media campaigns; and structural means, such as investment provision). Who would deny that the U.S. auto industry, whose profitability is clearly buoyed by a variety of state supports, wields significant political influence and clout in the American political system?

Even if political influence is possible in the absence of autonomy, clearly, the private sector that enjoys *both* autonomy and power is the best positioned to force its will upon the state. But as shown above, autonomy and power are quite distinct qualities, with independent trajectories for the private sector. To assess the industrialists' evolving capacity to influence state policy, each of these trajectories must be evaluated independently.

Evolving Power of Private Sector Industrialists in Tunisia

Have private sector industrialists in Tunisia managed to carve out political power in the context of state sponsorship? Disaggregation of the concept of power yields a mixed picture. Tunisian industrialists have been able to develop significant structural power as well as some instrumental power thanks to the increasingly important role they play in the Tunisian economy. However, other classic routes to private sector power (e.g., ideological and instrumental) still remain underdeveloped, due to factors largely unrelated to state sponsorship. Tunisia's institutional legacy, the size of its elite, and the relative youth of its industrial class, remain important obstacles to the exercise of private sector power.

Structural Power

As described above, the structural power enjoyed by private sector entrepreneurs is directly related to the contribution they make to national capital formation. Do private sector industrialists in Tunisia supply a large enough portion of capital formation to invest them with significant structural clout? At first glance, this does not seem likely. Tunisian investment codes set relatively low legal minimums for personal investment in industrial projects. Average investors are obliged to provide as little as 30% of their own funds to get industrial projects started (far below the 50% minimum that financial orthodoxy would normally require).[3] Entrepreneurs are allowed to establish firms under the FOPRODI framework,[4] investing as little as 10% out of personal funds.[5] Nevertheless, examination of actual dinars invested by the private sector paints a brighter picture. Although precise statistics on the share of industrial investment financed out of personal funds are not published by the Central Bank, API figures for 1983–86 suggest that personal funds represented a larger share of investment capital than legal minimums would suggest (Table 2.1).

As shown in Table 2.1, personal funds account for 35–42% of global industrial investment in Tunisia.[6] Moreover, for the vast majority of indi-

Table 2.1. Financing of Licensed Industrial Investment,
1983–1986 (in %)

	1983	1984	1985	1986
Personal funds	34.7	36.5	37.5	42.2
Bank credit	51.1	53	49.8	49.9
Other*	14.2	10.5	12.7	7.9

Source: Interview with M. Bel Habib, Agency for the Promotion of Industry (API), February 1988, and "Rapport d'activité de l'agence en matière d'agrément," API internal document.
*Primarily supplier loans.

vidual ventures, personal funds account for a much larger share of capital formation. For firms worth less than 500,000 dinars, a very rough calculation based on API figures for 1986 puts the average contribution of personal funds to start-up investment closer to 60%.[7] And for the countless tiny industrial firms that entirely escape API's count but make up Tunisia's vibrant informal sector, the entrepreneur's personal contribution to financing probably edges closer to 100%, since these small firms lack the guarantees and collateral necessary to secure bank loans (Sellami 1975).

From the above analysis, it is evident that the private sector accounts for a considerable share of industrial capital formation in Tunisia. To ensure healthy investment levels and economic growth, the state in Tunisia is indeed "condemned to seduce" private sector industrialists with policies that favor the interests of this class (Stoleru, cited in Warnecke and Suleiman 1975, 13). Business confidence acts as a constraint on public policy—a fact that is openly acknowledged by the state. Public officials routinely preface economic reform programs with the pronounced hope that reform will stimulate private investment. They regularly fend off labor's demands for a higher minimum wage with the claim that "business confidence will be lost" if wage increases are passed. The need to court private sector investment forces the state to anticipate even the unvoiced interests of the business community. In this way, the logic of the capitalist economy endows Tunisia's private sector industrialists with political clout even in the absence of conscious political organization.

The structural power of private sector industrialists, however, goes beyond their contribution to capital formation. As described at length in chapter 1, private sector industry accounts for ever-larger shares of job creation, export earnings, and GNP generation in Tunisia. In many areas it outpaces the contribution of the public sector, thanks to the initiative, energy, and management skills of private sector entrepreneurs. By the state's own recognition, Tunisia could not achieve its developmental goals without the private sector's contribution. The private sector's delivery on these goals has significantly boosted the structural power of its industrialists.

Ideological Power

Aside from structural power, private sector entrepreneurs can command political influence through ideological sources of power. Control over cultural institutions such as the mass media and the educational system provides them with an important opportunity to shape public consciousness in the image of business preferences. In Tunisia, however, this route to power seems less central to private sector influence. By and large, Tunisian businessmen have shown little interest in influencing school curricula. The electronic media remains, for the most part, the exclusive monopoly of the state (save for the European programming that appears on cable). Even the print media eludes the control of Tunisian businessmen. A fair number of Tunisia's leading journals and newspapers are published either by the state, parastatal organizations, or the ruling RCD Party.[8] Moreover, as one leading newspaper editor explained, the few independent journals that do appear in Tunisia do not owe their financial survival to business backing but rather to support from opposition parties, street sales, subscriptions, and/or subsidies from the state (interview, 10 December 1996).[9] Advertising revenues constitute only a small share of the journals' and newspapers' financial base (generally less than 30%), and a large percentage of the ads in the print media are placed by the state and public enterprises, not the private sector (80% of these ads, according to *Le monde diplomatique* [February 1997]). Hence, they do not constitute a significant route for private sector influence.

For the most part, Tunisian businessmen have shown little interest in shaping public opinion through the media or otherwise. To some extent, this indifference is a consequence of Tunisia's institutional legacy and the minimal political clout it vests in public opinion. In the absence of a truly competitive multiparty system and guaranteed civil liberties, politics remains, to a large degree, an elite affair, decided "among friends" rather than in consultation with the general populace. Hence, to the extent that businessmen consciously "propagandize" in defense of their interests it is through propaganda aimed at the elite, packaged in the form of "dinner-debates" and special business seminars hosted for public officials rather than through mass media campaigns aimed at the general public.[10]

Instrumental Power: Finance

The third route to private sector influence is through instrumental means such as financing political parties and candidates, directly occupying public office, and lobbying the executive. Finance is an especially powerful resource in countries where political competition is meaningful and where parties and candidates must raise private funds to sustain their political campaigns. Under these conditions, the capacity to finance lavish political campaigns becomes key to political success. Those with "deep pockets" are endowed with significant political influence.

In Tunisia, however, the institutional structure is such that finance has not constituted the royal road to political influence for the private sector. First, for most of the post-independence period, the Tunisian political system has *not* been characterized by competitive multiparty politics. The regime dropped any pretense of competitive politics in 1963 (Bourguiba outlawed the only significant opposition party in existence at the time— the Communist Party), and until 1981 political life was largely monopolized by one party, the Neo-Destour. The early 1980s saw some limited political liberalization in Tunisia with the legalization of several small opposition parties.[11] But even then, real political competition was stymied by the regime's extensive harassment of the opposition.[12] Ben Ali's rise to power in 1987 seemed to put Tunisia on track for a truly competitive political system. But within a few years the regime's harassment of the opposition, controls on media access, and passage of election rules that disfavored smaller parties all but eliminated any competitive electoral challenge to the ruling RCD Party.

The lack of true political competition in Tunisia means that election campaigns become occasions to rally mass support for the president and the regime rather than opportunities to compete for popular support. In the absence of truly competitive political campaigns, propertied Tunisians can hardly use their financial resources to play power politics. The absence of a competitive political system diminishes the power of finance in politics.

The political power of finance in Tunisia is undermined in a second way as well: by the fact that the ruling party has yet to develop financial independence from the state. The boundary demarking state budget and party coffers has always been fuzzy. The state has routinely built the party's office buildings, subsidized its journals, and paid the salaries of its staff. Such direct access to the state's treasury precluded the need to court financial support from Tunisia's propertied classes.

For a brief period in the late 1980s a breach in party-state relations seemed possible. Upon coming to power, Ben Ali promised that the separation of party and state would be part of his reform of the Tunisian political system. The intimation that state financing might be terminated set party chief Abderrahim Zouari scrambling for alternate funding for the RCD. Not surprisingly, well-heeled business elites constituted a promising target for the party leader. By late 1988 Zouari had begun courting businessmen throughout the country for financial and political support (*La presse*, 18 December 1988, 5; *La presse*, 21 December 1988, 4), hosting prestigious dinners to make the pitch that business support was indispensable to "the financial autonomy of the RCD" ("Confidentiel," *Réalités*, 4 November 1988) and garnering millions of dinars in pledges and in-kind donations from businessmen across the country.[13] Party reform suggested a new route to political influence for Tunisia's well-off businessmen.

However, this route to influence did not remain open for long. The new regime's initial enthusiasm for party reform soon waned, and by the early 1990s the party-state had settled back into "business as usual." Party and state were not severed as promised, and to this day the financial links between the two remain murky, suggesting continued party dependence. The state continues to finance RCD operating costs and political campaigns and even extends some financial support to the major opposition parties. As one leading businessman asserted, "All parties are paid by the state in Tunisia" (interview, 10 August 1993).[14] Businessmen still make small contributions to the ruling RCD (e.g., they may provide computers or cars or dinners for party functions), but as one Tunisian official stated, these contributions are the "cherry on the cake," not the essential financial base of the party (interview, 9 December 1996). As a result, finance has still not proven an important route to political influence for Tunisia's private sector.

Instrumental Power: Direct Participation

Besides finance, private sector entrepreneurs may be able to shape state policy either through direct occupation of elective or appointive public office or through the creation of a "power elite" (i.e., the creation of an interlocking elite that shuttles back and forth between employment in the public and private sectors, developing a common world view in the process and a common interest in defending private sector interests). Does direct political participation of this sort constitute an important route to political influence for private sector industrialists in Tunisia?

With regard to the question of a power elite, there is certainly some overlap between the governmental and industrial elite in Tunisia. As mentioned in chapter 1, a sizeable portion of Tunisian industrialists have begun their careers in government service and only moved to private sector industry after completing an "apprenticeship" in the public sector. This career path, called *pantouflage* in French, is by no means unique to Tunisia. In France, for example, Suleiman (1975, 35) observes that a stint in the public sector is "considered an essential element in the training" of future CEOs, resulting in a high degree of interpenetration between business and government.

The Tunisian case, however, is unusual in that pantouflage generally flows in one direction only. Government officials often leave the state to start industrial ventures in the private sector, but only rarely do private sector industrialists leave their firms to assume a position in government. The unidirectional character of pantouflage between government and industry has important implications for the notion of a power elite in Tunisia. The fact that many industrialists have served in state employ no doubt helps create a common language between industrialists and state officials. Moreover, the bonds of friendship that linger from years of employment together certainly facilitate communication between members of the two groups. However, the fact that industrialists and state officials do *not* shuttle back and forth between sectors means that, after some career settling, the two elites are, in the final analysis, quite distinct groups with rather divergent interests.[15] The notion of a unified "power elite" with a common world view and a common set of interests seems misplaced in the Tunisian case.

The infrequency of industry-to-government pantouflage is reflected in the fact that industrialists rarely occupy important government positions in Tunisia. A review of the professional biographies of Tunisian ministers turns up very few with industrial backgrounds (Larif-Beatrix 1988, 198–202). Tunisian industrialists are not well represented at the highest levels of political power. Moreover, Tunisian industrialists, by and large, do not seem drawn to direct participation in politics. Interviews with industrialists from various sectors and various firm sizes revealed a very low level of political engagement among them. Most of the industrialists interviewed had not registered as members of any political party, and those who claimed membership were usually little more than nominal card-carriers for the ruling party. Not a few industrialists displayed remarkable ignorance of political affairs (e.g., they were not able to identify the name of the RCD's party chief), a fact especially surprising since many of these interviews were conducted during a period of significant political change and heightened political awareness in Tunisia. When asked about their level of political activism, the industrialists gave varied responses. Some expressed indifference:

> I have no interest in politics; I focus all my energy on my business. (Interview, 9 August 1988)

Others expressed anxiety:

> There is still a problem of the party-state keeping dossiers on people. . . . Anyone of us can get caught on something (e.g., tax fraud) so we are afraid of getting into politics. I myself prefer to keep clear of it. (Interview, 21 July 1988)

Still others were apologetic:

> As a young man I was an activist but politics takes too much time. You can't run a business and be a politician at the same time. (Interview, 10 August 1988)

Very few industrialists claimed to be politically active on a regular basis.

This is not to say, however, that industrialists have been entirely excluded from the life of political parties in Tunisia. The RCD, for example, actively recruits industrialists to join its Social and Economic Council, and businessmen of all stripes participate in the formulation of the party's economic platform at its regular conventions.[16] Still, the number of industrialists so engaged in party activity remains quite small, as is their representation among the party elite. A review of the Destour's central committee in 1981 identified fewer than three industrialists among its eighty members; in 1988, the number had increased to only six out of two hundred members.[17] An official account analyzing the professional background of delegates to the RCD's national congress in 1993 listed none of the delegates as industrialists, although it did identify 4%, i.e., 57 of the 1,435 delegates as "commerçants" (*La presse*, 22 July 1993). A leading industrialist noted with pride that Tunisia's parliament counted thirty businessmen among the representatives of the RCD in 1996—the consequence, he explained, of a conscious choice on the part of President Ben Ali to assert the party's endorsement of the business community (interview, 14 December 1996). Still, these businessmen constituted only a small percentage of all the RCD members, suggesting the small role that businessmen (and industrialists, as a subset of businessmen) continue to play in party affairs.

How can this low level of political engagement and participation on the part of private sector industrialists be explained? To some extent, low levels of political activism may be a consequence of the youth of this class. Many private sector industrial firms are relatively small, first-generation enterprises, still scrambling to stay afloat. They do not have the "deep pockets" financially, managerially, or experientially, to devote significant resources to political engagement. In addition, low levels of private sector involvement in politics may also be a consequence of the regime's strategy of legitimation (and the private sector's acquiescence in this strategy). Ever since the independence struggle, the party-state has projected itself as a populist force, defending the "people" against "special interests." This populist image long excluded any public alliance with private sector business. If anything, it encouraged the state to distance itself somewhat from the business community. Consequently, even in an era of private sector encouragement, political activism for private sector entrepreneurs is not on everyone's agenda. RCD Party chieftains are not necessarily enthusiastic about being overrun by businessmen, concerned as they are to preserve the party's popular image and character (interview, 14 December 1988). And industrialists themselves do not always express eagerness to play a high profile role in party politics. Said one industrialist:

> The RCD must remain a mass party. Business should continue to finance it and try to influence its policies but it is in everyone's interests to downplay this. Spotlighting the role of businessmen in politics only gives ammunition to the populists . . . which might lead to a harmful reaction. (Interview, 28 December 1988)

The apparent conflict between attention to business interests and maintaining the state's populist image led this industrialist to argue that businessmen are better served by avoiding the political limelight and advocating their interests behind the scenes, in quiet consultation with state elites. For this industrialist, as well as for many others, *lobbying the executive*, not direct participation in politics, represents the most effective (and least provocative) route to political influence.

Instrumental Power: Lobbying

Lobbying the executive can be pursued on either a collective or an individualistic basis, and Tunisian industrialists have not had equal success with both. Lobbying on a collective basis has been especially stymied by obstacles ranging from the legacy of state institutions and the country's level of industrial development, to structural factors, such as the size of the elite. This hindrance is evident in the cases of three leading private sector lobbies and associations in Tunisia: the UTICA (Union tunisienne de l'industrie du commerce et de l'artisanat), the Tunisian Chamber of Commerce, and the IACE (Institut arabe des chefs d'entreprises).[18]

The UTICA

Of these organizations, the UTICA is the oldest and arguably the most important business association in Tunisia.[19] The UTICA was first organized by a small group of merchants and artisans in the mid-1940s to oversee the rationing of imported raw materials and semifinished goods made scarce by war blockades and postwar shortages. As the independence movement gathered steam at war's end, the UTICA also began to embrace a political role, providing organizational cover for the outlawed Neo-Destour Party, staging commercial strikes to protest colonial repression, and furnishing the Fellagha (guerillas) with arms and other supplies to fight the French. After independence, President Bourguiba rewarded the UTICA for its nationalist efforts by designating it one of only four legal national organizations established to manage relations between the state and important strata in Tunisian society.[20] As a national organization, the UTICA was assigned multiple missions: to communicate the interests of business to the state, to explain state policies to the business community, to promote business activity through the organization of fairs and expositions, to conduct educational seminars for its constituents, and, most important, to mobilize business support for the regime.[21]

During the early years of independence, relations between the UTICA and the party state remained largely harmonious. The UTICA's secretary general, Ferjani Bel Haj Ammar, was named a member of the Neo-Destour's Central Committee and, in the late 1950s, was even briefly appointed minister of the economy. The regime provided the UTICA with regular financial aid and in return the union delivered reliable public support for all government initiatives.

By the early 1960s, however, relations between the two began to sour as the regime embraced an etatist development strategy. Ben Salah's plan to promote the public sector and "rationalize commerce" directly contradicted the interests of UTICA's constituency.[22] When Ferjani protested these measures, Bourguiba summarily dismissed the veteran UTICA activist, replacing him with a more compliant candidate. Ferjani's protests that the UTICA was an autonomous organization, ruled by internal elections and not presidential whim, went unheeded. Bourguiba's will was accepted by UTICA officials, and although a number of the organization's executive bureau did resign in protest, no one resigned from the organization at large.[23]

The rest of the decade marked the eclipse of the UTICA. The regime, caught up in its enthusiasm for etatism, ignored the UTICA, which it considered an outpost of the private sector. Participation in UTICA activities fell off dramatically as businessmen sought other means to communicate their interests to the state.[24]

Only during the 1970s did the UTICA's fortunes began to improve. Ben Salah's fall from grace in 1969 and the regime's repudiation of his brand of etatism marked a new moment of opportunity for the private sector. The new prime minister, Hedi Nouira, came to office committed to championing the private sector in Tunisia and, to signal his support, he undertook a rapprochement between the UTICA and the Destour Party.[25] The UTICA was invited to take part in the negotiation of a pathbreaking social contract with the labor movement in 1977, and it joined in signing forty collective conventions between 1973 and 1979 that defined wages and working conditions for many sectors of the economy. UTICA officials were appointed to a wide spectrum of national councils (transport, credit, commerce, social affairs, labor conciliation) and participated in the Ministry of Plan's consultative commissions to help formulate the country's five-year plans. The union was also generously funded by the state: thanks to that support, the UTICA's permanent staff rose to more than 150 paid employees. It was able to publish as many as five regular publications and, in the early 1980s, was endowed with its own steel-and-glass highrise tower in downtown Tunis.[26] During the 1970s and 1980s, then, the union appeared better positioned than ever to defend the interests of the business community.

But despite this apparently favorable position, the UTICA fell far short of its constituents' expectations. Interviews with industrialists in the late 1980s turned up some very harsh criticism of the union. The UTICA, they complained, was "sclerotic," "a big zero," "a useless bunch of tea drinkers," "an empty structure," "an example of French mimetism—totally ineffective" (interviews, March–August 1988). And although individual chambers were occasionally singled out for praise,[27] by and large industrialists did not have much good to say for the union as a whole.

The question then is, Why, despite official recognition, adequate financial resources, and inclusion in many official policy-making bodies, did the UTICA fail to perform effectively as a lobby for the business community? The answer lies primarily in the union's failure to develop organizational autonomy from the state. Industrialists referred to the UTICA as "an extension of the government," "a parastatal," little more than "a transmission belt" for the administration, and "more at ease defending the economic policies of every government . . . to its constituents than critically appraising these plans and the means used to carry them out" (*Réalités*, 7 February 1988, 13).

The UTICA's lack of autonomy is attributable to two factors. First, it had long been permeated with Destour Party elites. Many leading lights of the UTICA were active members of the Destour, and their presence subordinated the business organization to the party's will. As a short-time UTICA president, Ezzedine Ben Achour, stated in 1964:

> The linkage between the party and UTICA is so solid and the number of Neo-Destour militants within UTICA is so high that [UTICA's] adhesion to the economic and social doctrine of the party is immediate and without reservation. (*L'action*, 11 November 1964, 4, cited in Chekir 1974, 83)

The party-state, moreover, took a direct interest in the internal affairs of the UTICA and routinely interfered in their conduct, most notably in the selection of the UTICA leadership. UTICA activists spoke of the ruling party's habit of circulating "informal" lists of its preferred candidates for election to executive posts in the union. Even nine years after the start of the "new regime" under Ben Ali, UTICA activists spoke of the regime's persistent policy of "consultation" with UTICA leaders when designating the composition of the union's executive board (interview, 20 December 1996). Furthermore, on the rare occasion when the UTICA's subordination was not forthcoming, the party-state did not hesitate to intervene and remove the offenders. Ferjani's dismissal from the presidency of UTICA in 1964 was only the most obvious case of such intervention. The presence of party-state loyalists in the organization meant that even egregious affronts to the organization's autonomy would not be protested in any significant way.[28]

Besides this sharing of elites with the party-state, the UTICA's autonomy has also been compromised by the union's means of finance. According to the UTICA's president, the association is primarily financed by a
small tax imposed on the *chiffre d'affaires* of local business.[29] This tax is
not turned over directly to the UTICA but rather is deposited in the state
treasury. The UTICA must then defend its budget to the state to attain
its annual funding. Clearly, financial dependence of this sort does little to
enhance the union's autonomy.

UTICA's indebtedness to the party-state at both the level of elites and
at the level of financing has two important consequences for the organization's character. First, it attenuates the vigor with which the UTICA
defends the interests of its constituents. The UTICA might try to modify
state policy *on the margin*, but rarely will it challenge the state's policy
direction as a whole, and never will it engage in a public test of wills with
the state. As one high-level UTICA official explained:

> The UTICA is forced to work *en douceur*. We must not be aggressive. The
> UTICA's way is not to conduct public discussion in the press or by demon-
> strations in the street but behind the scenes at the level of the elite. . . . The
> UTICA is cautious and wants to avoid confrontation. We don't want a
> powerful negative reaction so we move slowly. (Interview, 15 June 1988)

This cautious approach to the state explains the strong reaction UTICA
officials had to any portrayal of their organization as a lobby or pressure
group. UTICA officials rejected these terms because they implied too
much antagonism in the union's relation to the state. Not antagonism but
"collaboration is the rule between the UTICA and the state," said one
official (interview, 15 June 1988). In the judgment of UTICA leaders,
maintaining a nonconfrontational relationship with the state takes prece-
dence over, if it is not the key to, forceful defense of business interests.[30]

Besides attenuating UTICA's aggressiveness, the union's dependence
on the party-state also compromises UTICA's policy ambition and vision.
As industrialists and union activists have pointed out, the UTICA has
never promoted any coherent plan or project for the economy. For most
of the postindependence period, the organization has been entirely
absorbed with rearguard, defensive activities. In general, policy initiatives
were proposed by the state, and the UTICA scrambled to adjust them in
minor ways to suit the interests of its constituency. Thus, the union might
seek more generous subsidies for the canning industry or a more lenient
application of a new value-added tax, but it did not propose alternative
visions of the economy to those set forth by the government.[31] UTICA

officials confirmed this characterization of the union: its mentality, said one, has always been "to rectify rather than propose" (interview 15 June 1988).

Lack of autonomy has been a key reason for the UTICA's failure to be an aggressive, visionary defender of private sector interests in Tunisia.[32] Two other factors also undermine the development of effective collective lobbying on the part of private sector industrialists under the aegis of the UTICA. One concerns the size and maturity of most private industrial ventures in Tunisia. As described in chapter 1, most private sector industrialists in Tunisia preside over small-scale, underfinanced, highly repetitive, hand-to-mouth operations. These conditions tend to exacerbate the naturally competitive tendencies of private sector entrepreneurs, making them even more atomistic and mutually antagonistic. Organizing collective efforts in this context is a challenge. In addition, the straitened economic circumstances that characterize many of these ventures deprive many entrepreneurs of the luxury (of time and other resources) to participate in union activities. Consequently, participation rates in lobbies like the UTICA are lower than might be hoped.[33]

An additional barrier to effective collective action under the aegis of organizations like the UTICA derives from what is sometimes called "field size." Tunisia is a small country, and as is typical for such countries, the elite from all spheres tends to be small and its members well known to each other. The latter results in the personalization of problem solving, that is, members of the elite tend to resolve their problems by appealing directly to the appropriate *responsable* (the minister, the cabinet chief) rather than working through collective agencies.[34] As one olive oil manufacturer explained:

> In a small country like ours, once you get to be a certain size you have personal relations with the ministers. So rarely would you go through UTICA to deal, say, with a licensing problem. Rather, you would call your friend in the ministry and see how it might be resolved. . . . It is only the small merchants and artisans who rely on UTICA's mediation with the state to resolve problems that arise. (Interview, 3 January 1989)

An industrialist whose firms bridge many sectors of the economy corroborated this view:

> Large industrialists don't need the intervention of UTICA. They can go directly to the minister to discuss their problems. That's our custom. . . . In fact, the authorities seek out [industrialists] once they are large. (Interview, 27 December 1988)

Clearly, the business elite's ability to "go directly to the top" undermines the centrality of collective action as a means to mediate interests. Large industrialists, the most able to bear the costs of organizing collective efforts, have little interest in doing so. As a result, organizations like the UTICA and the chamber of commerce tend to be led by entrepreneurs with other interests at stake (e.g., personal political ambition), and this situation does not always make for the most effective representation of private sector preferences.

Tunisian Chamber of Commerce

Field size, institutional legacy, and lack of organizational autonomy undermine the effectiveness of the UTICA as a tool of collective lobbying on the part of private sector industrialists. Similar factors seem to be at work in undermining the effectiveness of the Tunisian Chamber of Commerce as well.[35] Created by legal decree in December 1957 (to replace the economic chamber that had existed under the French Protectorate), the Tunisian Chamber of Commerce was charged with the mission "to represent to public power the interests of commerce, industry, and artisanry." The law, however, was silent with regard to the chamber's financing, organizational structure, and election procedures, and this situation was not clarified for another thirty-one years. In the interim, the chamber was managed by "temporary commissions" appointed by the state in 1958 and not once reconstituted during the next three decades. The chamber financed itself through the sale of official documents necessary for foreign trade (e.g., certification for foreign commerce, certificates of origin, and visas for exportation); this income was supplemented by regular state subsidies. In terms of its mission, the chamber occupied itself with educational programs for the business community (especially outside the capital city) and the facilitation of foreign trade through providing official trade documents. It played virtually no role in the aggregation or communication of private sector interests to the state and was largely relegated to the back burner of Tunisian public life.

A gesture toward resuscitation of the chamber came in April 1981, with the publication of two decrees outlining election procedures for the organization, but the laws were never applied. Then, in the summer of 1988, President Ben Ali expressed an interest in reviving the chamber (originally to bypass the UTICA, which for a time he considered an ineffective link to the business community).[36] Two laws were decreed in May and June of 1988 outlining the chamber's operating procedures and mission. As before, the chamber was assigned the role of communicating and defending the interests of industry, commerce, and artisans to the state, in addition to promoting economic activity and fostering foreign trade by building contacts with chambers of commerce in other countries. Elections were declared open to any Tunisian businessman who paid the patent tax, although the state reserved the right to intervene in the choice of chamber officials if certain distributional requirements in terms of region and sector were not met by election results. Finally, the organization was to be financed primarily by the state. Every year, the Ministry of National Economy would approve an annual budget for the chamber.

Once again, compromised autonomy has proved most important in undermining the capacity of the chamber to act as an effective interlocutor for private sector interests. Financial dependence on the state has muted the assertiveness of the organization, as does vulnerability to state intervention in the selection of chamber's leadership. During the election of 1988, for example, state officials reviewed the twenty-five candidates elected to the chamber and chose the four *they* considered best suited for the job rather than leave the decision to a popular vote. Despite its formal resurrection, the Tunisian Chamber of Commerce has not proven an important voice for the private sector; its primary function seems to be to serve as yet another staging ground for business leaders with political ambition.

The IACE

Many of the factors that have undermined the capacity of the UTICA and the chamber to serve as effective lobbies for private sector interests seem less true for a third major business association in Tunisia, the IACE.[37] The Institut arabe des chefs d'entreprises was created in 1985 at the behest of a former finance minister-turned-banker, Mansour Moalla, in association with a number of university professors and private businessmen.[38] The mission of the institute was threefold: to create a center for education and reflection where entrepreneurs, academics, and public officials might meet to discuss issues facing private and public enterprise, as well as the state of the economy generally; to organize publications, conventions, and public fora that would promote a positive image of

enterprise, highlight the enterprise's contribution to national development, and stimulate the development of new entrepreneurs; and to create
a clublike environment where entrepreneurs might meet their business
colleagues, as well as leading administrators, academics, and others, in
a fraternal atmosphere (Moalla 1985). The founders were insistent that
their goal was to create neither "a syndicate nor a proprietor's assembly
nor an organism to defend corporatist interests nor a tool of combat"
(Actes des journées de l'Entreprise, IACE 1985, 10–12). Rather than duplicate the UTICA or the chamber, the IACE sought to supplement the
efforts of these organizations by establishing a clubby, intellectual center
for entrepreneurs.

To its credit, the IACE enjoyed considerably more organizational
autonomy than most other business associations in Tunisia. As noted
above, the initiative for the organization's creation came from the private
sector, not the state.[39] Its leadership was chosen by internal election and
was apparently free from party-state interference. Finally, the IACE supported itself through a combination of steep membership fees,[40] participation fees, and member donations.[41] It did not rely on state funding to
keep afloat financially.

Thanks to the prestige and dynamism of its founders as well as the
autonomy of its operations, the IACE experienced an auspicious beginning: membership doubled in its first two years.[42] IACE members hailed
from every sector of the economy.[43] The institute organized a steady
stream of seminars, dinner debates, and study groups that brought
businessmen and high-ranking government officials together to discuss
everything from Islamic banking, to Tunisian monetary policy, to the
development of Tunisia's stock market. The IACE also began a tradition
of organizing an annual three-day conference, "Journées de l'Entreprise,"
that attracted hundred of participants and developed into an important
social and educational event in the business community's annual calendar.
Finally, in 1987, the IACE began publishing an annual economic report,
analyzing the country's economic situation and publicizing the results
of a survey conducted with Tunisian entrepreneurs on the state of the
economy. The latter gave far-reaching voice to the opinions of Tunisian
businessmen. In this way the IACE achieved considerable success in
meeting each of its goals: education, reflection, promotion, and cadre-
building.[44]

But by the early 1990s, the IACE's star began to fade. The best explanation for its decline lies in the state's discomfort with frank public policy
confrontation—and the state's willingness to punish such confrontation

with all the means at its disposal. In 1993, Mansour Moalla, the driving force behind the IACE, angered state officials by making a public statement to the French journal *Le monde* chastising the Tunisian government for embracing a structural adjustment program that was too harsh and too obedient to World Bank/IMF interests (*Le monde*, 11 May 1993). Infuriated by this public censure of state policy (in an international forum, no less!), state officials decided to punish Moalla by attacking his position as president of BIAT Bank. Government officials ordered the withdrawal of state funds from the bank, spurring a run on BIAT and threatening its solvency. To save the institution from collapse, Moalla resigned from the BIAT presidency (*Jeune Afrique*, 3–9 June 1993; *Le monde diplomatique*, 23 July 1993). Shortly thereafter, he resigned from the presidency of the IACE as well.

Moalla's disgrace at the government's hand tarred the IACE by association. It also robbed the organization of one of its key draws: a prestigious and dynamic leader who could bridge the world of state and private sector.[45] But Moalla's departure did not mean the demise of the IACE. Three years later, the institute was still organizing conferences, publishing economic reports, and even contemplating the construction of a new center, complete with restaurant, in the fashionable Lac de Tunis neighborhood to reinforce the institute's "clubby" mission (interview, IACE leader, 16 December 1996). Still, by signaling the (limited) boundaries of state tolerance for public policy confrontation, the Moalla incident defined clear limits to the freedom and initiative of the institute. As one academic active in IACE conferences explained, although the IACE continues to operate, it necessarily functions as a less independent and dynamic force than was the case under its founding leadership (interview, 16 December 1996).

Clearly, then, effective collective lobbying on the part of the Tunisian private sector is, to a large degree, stymied by Tunisia's political and institutional legacy, its small field size, and the failure of most private sector associations to develop organizational autonomy from the state. But the case of the IACE demonstrates that even when organizational autonomy *is* successfully cultivated, collective lobbying organizations are undermined by the state's unwillingness to tolerate any *publicly confrontational* censure of its policies. The character of the state and, specifically, its unwillingness to guarantee civil liberties, such as freedom of association and freedom of speech, pose the most serious obstacle to effective collective lobbying on the part of all groups in Tunisian society, not least private sector industrialists.[46]

Lobbying by Individuals

Lobbying on a *collective* basis is not the most effective way for private sector industrialists to impose their preferences on the state in Tunisia. Instead, individualistic lobbying offers them a surer route to shaping public policy. Individualistic access to the state can be either *institutionalized* or *personalistic* and ad hoc. In Tunisia there are many provisions for institutionalized communication between individual businessmen and the state. For example, the statutes of the Central Bank stipulate that four members of the Administrative Council are to be chosen from among private sector businessmen.[47] The rules governing the Social and Economic Council (a purely advisory, but nonetheless prestigious, council to the state on social and economic affairs) reserve a certain number of seats for representatives of the business community. And traditions long observed at the Ministry of Plan reserve the presidency of several planning commissions to businessmen from the private sector (interview, 7 July 1988). These statutes and traditions provide for a regular, formalized pattern of access between individual businessmen and the state. The businessmen are chosen not for their ability to represent the business community in toto but rather for their stature and experience as leading businessmen in their sectors and the personal knowledge they can impart concerning economic affairs in Tunisia.

Besides such institutionalized access, individual contact with the state can be personalistic and ad hoc as well. Larger industrialists boasted of their easy access to state elites; they regularly called on ministers, cabinet chiefs, and Central Bank officials to discuss economic problems or lobby for specific public policy programs. For their part, public officials also acknowledged regularly consulting with business leaders before making public policy and routinely invited them to sit on committees at the Ministry of National Economy or Ministry of Plan. But in addition to this formal (if spontaneous) access to the state, businessmen also enjoy wholly casual, though nonetheless significant, contact with public officials. Such casual contact is the constant fare of dinner parties and social gatherings in a country with a numerically small elite. As many industrialists stressed in interviews, this casual contact with state officials should not be underestimated as a route to influence for Tunisia's business community, though its precise impact is difficult to gauge.

Trajectory of Private Sector Power

To sum up this analytic disaggregation of private sector power in Tunisia: private sector industrialists enjoy a fair amount of structural power owing to their growing contribution to capital formation, as well as their expanding role in employment creation and export earnings. The ideological power of private sector industrialists is limited by their failure to seize control of the country's leading cultural institutions. The state's monopolization of much of the media, along with the character of Tunisia's political institutions (the absence of guaranteed civil liberties and competitive politics), make investment in the media unattractive to the private sector. As for the instrumental power of private sector industrialists, the picture is mixed. Finance is not an important route to political influence in Tunisia, thanks again to the character of political institutions in the country: the absence of truly competitive multiparty politics and the failure to separate the financial operations of the ruling party and the state. Nor does direct participation in politics serve as an important route for impressing the policy preferences of industrialists on the state. The relative insecurity and infancy of many industrial ventures robs entrepreneurs of the luxury of participating in politics. The state's concern with preserving a populist image discourages such participation as well. Nonetheless, lobbying the state on an individualistic basis is a much-used and highly accessible route to influence, given the country's small field size, while collective lobbying is less successful, given the state's lack of tolerance for autonomous associations that confront the state in any publicly censorious way.

What is the trajectory of private sector power? By progressively "passing the baton" to the private sector for capital formation and investment initiative and by nurturing its growing role in the economy, the state has boosted the structural power of this stratum. The instrumental power and ideological power of private sector industrialists is likely to increase as the maturation and expansion of this class allows the diversion of some of its members into political participation and media dabbling. However, private sector power remains constrained by such factors as Tunisia's institutional legacy (the absence of multiparty competitive politics, the failure to guarantee civil liberties) and field size. Neither is given to easy remedy, and the fact of state-sponsored industrialization alone will not correct it.

Autonomy of Private Sector Industrialists in Tunisia

Small field size, an unfavorable institutional legacy, and the lack of generational depth pose obstacles to the expansion of private sector influence, but then so does the failure to develop autonomy. Where do Tunisia's private sector industrialists stand in the spectrum of autonomy? To what degree are industrialists dependent on state support for their profitability, and to what degree is that support distributed on a discretionary basis? Is the profitability of private sector industry governed largely by politically mediated subversion of the market rather than market principles?

With regard to the issue of dependence on state support, there is no question that the vast majority of industrialists in Tunisia have seen their profitability boosted by the battery of incentives and sweeteners provided by the state since the 1970s, if not earlier. Nearly every industrialist interviewed admitted to having been the recipient of state largesse in one form or another (e.g., subsidized bank credit, tariff protection, or price support). Some of the industrialists even went so far as to argue that state largesse had been too generous. "We are the spoiled children of [Prime Minister] Nouira," complained one textile manufacturer. "Tunisian industry," he argued, "would be better off today had it not received so much coddling from the state" (interview, 22 July 1988).

That said, it would be wrong to equate the dependence of Tunisian industry on state-boosted profitability with the utter reliance on state subversion of the market that characterizes the most autonomy-deprived end of our spectrum, the "parasitic" private sector. Unlike the supply mafia of Egypt or the commission entrepreneurs of Saudi Arabia, Tunisian industrialists do not exist thanks merely to state subversion of the market. The best evidence for this lies in the survival rate of industrial ventures in Tunisia in the face of recent economic reform. Since the mid-1980s, the Tunisian state has retreated from the wide variety of supports it once offered industrialists, among them price controls, quantitative import protection, and underpriced credit. This embrace of market reform, however, has not led to the demise of private sector industry. Although the years 1987–94 saw an average of 117 manufacturing enterprises declaring serious "economic difficulty" to the Ministry of Social Affairs (Ministry of Social Affairs, Service des statistiques, internal document), the overall number of private sector industrial firms in Tunisia did not decline during this period.[48] To the contrary, their number multiplied several times over, as demonstrated in chapter 1.

This performance suggests that private industry in Tunisia is not merely the creation of state subversion of the market. Much of it can successfully contend with market forces. Of course, the private sector continues to see its viability boosted by a variety of state measures. Many firms still enjoy protection from foreign competition in the form of substantial tariff barriers, and the state still provides "safety nets" and technical support for troubled firms that are judged viable in the long run. But state "sheltering" of this sort is hardly exceptional, even among industrial firms in the most advanced industrialized countries. Nor does it spell political self-effacement as evidenced by the assertiveness of such firms in the industrialized West (e.g., the Big Three in the U.S. auto industry).

Political diffidence might still be fostered among private sector industrialists, however, to the degree that state support is distributed on a discretionary basis. In the Tunisian case it seems clear that state elites *have* exercised a measure of discretion in the provision of incentives and sweeteners to the private sector. Moreover, close personal relations with state elites *have* been important in mediating access to state support. At least through the mid-1980s, many inputs essential to private sector operations (e.g., import licenses, operating licenses, product prices, and access to foreign exchange) were not automatically provided to all industrial ventures. Rather, they were the product of individual bargains wrested from the state by individual firms. Moreover, many benefits, such as input subsidies, underpriced credit, and extended tax holidays, were conditioned upon the state's subjective assessment of a firm's performance in, for example, its use of environmentally sound procedures or its level of integration into the local economy. State elites thereby enjoyed wide discretion in the distribution of benefits to industry. Finally, close personal relations with state elites often proved crucial to mediating this process. Nearly all the businessmen interviewed insisted that knowing someone "on the inside" of the state bureaucracy was essential to getting business done successfully in Tunisia.

Discretionary Support: Fatal to Political Autonomy?

At first glance, this situation may sound ominous for the autonomy of private sector industrialists in Tunisia. The fact that state support has been distributed on a discretionary basis and that personal relations with state elites have been crucial in mediating access to this support suggests that factors other than market performance (such as the capacity to "back scratch" or pay bribes, or to offer political support to political elites) might be most important in determining economic success in Tunisia. Were this the case, Tunisian industrialists would be thrust into the position of "eunuch capitalists" (Kasfir 1984a), forever focused on currying favor with state elites to guarantee their economic survival. Under these conditions, the political assertiveness and autonomy of private sector industrialists would clearly be compromised.

In fact, the situation for the autonomy of Tunisian industrialists is less dire than it first appears. Close examination reveals that personal relations with state elites have been important to business success in Tunisia not because state elites have governed the distribution of benefits with an eye to harvesting bribes or building a political base. If that were true, then the private sector's autonomy would be utterly undermined. But in Tunisia, personal relations with members of the state bureaucracy have been essential to business success because of the complexity, ambition, and inexperience of the state bureaucracy as well as an "information problem" that Tunisian bureaucrats face in governing economic affairs. While the discretionary nature of state support still counsels political caution on the part of Tunisia's private sector (e.g., not embracing provocative campaigns for democratization), it does not oblige total self-effacement.

How to understand the logic of cronyism in Tunisia? With regard to the nature of the state bureaucracy, Tunisia has long been plagued by an overly ambitious and overextended state. Taking the French state as its model (and perhaps as an inevitable consequence of early faith in planned development), the Tunisian state long attempted to impose its control on nearly every aspect of business affairs. It licensed, monitored, and regulated everything from prices to firm location to hard currency allocation. Such extensive regulation posed an extremely burdensome bureaucratic gauntlet for entrepreneurs to clear in order to get businesses started and keep them in operation. For example, in 1990, despite promises from the government that bureaucratic processes would be simplified, official permission to start a new enterprise still required more than forty different authorizations from different government offices (*Réalités*, 5 January 1990, 3). As a leading textile exporter, Mohsen Ben Abdallah, explained to Tunisia's minister of commerce and industry:

> To obtain an official license we [industrialists] are asked to provide the invoices from three suppliers not simply one. After that we are asked, and this is new, to provide the agreement from the bank that is going to finance the project. If this involves a development bank the agreement is not pro-

vided until after a formal review and the submission of all pro-forma invoices. All this must be reviewed at the level of the bank's board of directors which meets once every three months. Having obtained the pro-forma invoice and the agreement of the bank, one obtains the license of API after two months. All this means a lot of lost time. *Without a lot of good will and familiarity with the wheels of the bureaucracy, investment is a frightening venture.* (*Réalités*, 7 July 1989, 21)

Many industrialists voiced similar complaints in interviews. When asked to express their major grievance against the government, Tunisian industrialists most often mentioned neither high taxes nor heavy social security obligations but rather stultifying controls and endless paperwork imposed upon them by the state.[49] To make matters worse, the laws and regulations that govern business life are constantly in flux. Consequently, it proves extremely easy to get lost in the maze of state bureaucracy; a businessman's project might molder under a pile of dusty files in some bureaucrat's office for months simply for want of a single authorization. Knowing someone on the inside might help the businessman get his file read a little faster or make him better informed regarding the best supporting documents to submit with his file. One civil servant-turned-entrepreneur describes the situation as follows:

> It is very easy to get lost in the administration because it is so complicated. There is a lack of information—the rules of the game change constantly and are not written down systematically—but also there is the French heritage of state control and paperocracy.
>
> Knowing people and knowing the system—how many copies of which document go to which office—is a crucial advantage to not getting lost in the system. And if you know how to present a dossier, what papers are needed, what authorizations are necessary, it can make things move. (Interview, 8 July 1988)

Even the Tunisian state recognizes the importance of "knowing someone on the inside" of the state bureaucracy to getting business done. In recent years the state has actually institutionalized the provision of "insider contacts" to the private sector, first through the introduction of a generous furlough system, which encourages experienced civil servants to make the jump to the private sector and put their insider knowledge to work there, and second through the creation of a civil servant "loan program" (called "formal detachment") under which civil servants are lent to the private sector for a limited period of time to help shepherd specified economic ventures through the state bureaucracy.[50]

In this way the ambition and complexity of the state bureaucracy make personal contacts with state elites essential to business success in Tunisia.[51] But another reason personal contacts are important in mediating support from the state derives from an information problem that economic policy makers face in Tunisia. State elites often lack the technical data and/or the training necessary to assess the projects they are called on to approve. Under these conditions bureaucrats are often forced to fall back on the advice of "friends in business" to decide whether a project is viable or a borrower trustworthy. As one industrialist from the electromechanical sector explained:

> It's a question of lack of information. State bureaucrats often don't have enough proper information or proper training to decide objectively who should get the license or how much foreign currency really needs to be apportioned to a project. Often these *fonctionnaires* will call me about an electrical project and ask me—is this a worthy project? Should we support it? Then, if I know the fellow or the project of course it has a better chance. Conclusion: even with all the good will in the world, the lack of information makes objective decision-making impossible. Decision-making becomes arbitrary and to put an end to this arbitrariness we must do away with so much [administrative] control since the administration doesn't have the information or capacity to handle it." (Interview, 30 July 1988)

Cronyism is thus justified on the grounds that it helps solve an information problem. In this context it may be seen as abetting the rational allocation of economic resources rather than subverting it. As one Tunisian sociologist pointed out:

> Reliance on personal relations in making economic decisions is not all bad. Take credit distribution. Personal relations provide information regarding liability and risks. Certainly the quality of a project is foremost in deciding these issues but trust and credit worthiness has a personal aspect to it. Certainly copinage is bad when it leads to inefficient use of funds—for example, when projects are funded for reasons of friendship or politics rather than economic rationality. But social networks are relevant to the profitability of a project. A well-connected person can get things done faster. So don't overlook the relevance of personal networks to the economic performance of a project. (Interview, 1 July 1988)

In this way, cronyism is embraced because it helps entrepreneurs negotiate a complex bureaucracy and because it helps solve an information problem faced by state elites. The logic driving Tunisian cronyism, then, does not compromise private sector autonomy as much as one might think for two reasons: first, because (as is shown below) cronyism in Tunisia is not politicized in any essential way; and second, because it is not driven by corruption. Bureaucrats may fall back on cronyism to help them make informed decisions about the worthiness of a project for state support, but by and large their decisions are governed by a developmentalist ethos and not considerations of personal gain, political or economic.

With regard to the question of politicization, one industrialist explained that "relations with the state are *personalized* not politicized" (interview, 27 December 1988). Unlike the case in Iraq or Syria, it is not necessary to pass a political test or get the party's imprimatur to do business in Tunisia. Running the bureaucratic gauntlet is indeed a daunting process for entrepreneurs, but it appears equally daunting for entrepreneurs of all political stripes. One might say that, save for those entrepreneurs at the extremes of the political spectrum, the bureaucracy is largely politically neutral vis-à-vis businessmen. The clearest evidence for this neutrality lies in the fact that a good portion of the businessmen interviewed were not members of the Destour Party (and felt no economic obligation to join). Moreover, not a few successful businessmen were former political activists who, for one reason or another, had fallen into disfavor with former President Bourguiba. These men fled to the business world as a refuge from politics and, for the most part, were granted "the right to make money" free from politically motivated bureaucratic harassment.[52] Their success in business suggests the willingness of the state to forgo exacting political tests for private sector entrepreneurs.

Cronyism is not suffused with politicization, nor is it driven by corruption. Industrialists argued that one did not have to give officials a "cut of the action" in order to succeed in Tunisia; in fact, playing the pay-off game usually brought more harm than good to a businessman's fortunes. Interviewees insisted on making a distinction between cronyism and corruption and, more specifically, between cronyism and bribery, arguing that while cronyism was endemic in Tunisia, corruption and bribery were not. As one building contractor put it:

> There is no question that good relations with a minister can speed your dossier through the administration, get you your license faster, or smooth the credit acquisition process. Sure, good relations with the state helps *but good relations is not the same thing as "rashwa" [bribery]*. (Interview, 28 December 1988)

Tunisian industrialists rejected the importance of corruption to industrial success even when they admitted its presence on a smaller scale. A leading textile manufacturer described the situation as follows:

> Yes, there is corruption in Tunisia, but it's on the level of the *petit fonc-tionnaire*. The inspector comes to the firm before the holidays and asks to buy his kids some shirts at wholesale prices and you give it to him as a gift. But it's petty corruption and at least he offers to pay. At the higher levels, corruption is not significant. The biggest textile manufacturers . . . have not made their fortunes in this way. (Interview, 1 August 1988)

A large-scale truck manufacturer corroborates these views:

> Corruption exists at the lower levels, not at the top. Yes, Tunisia is a *république des amis*; there is some *copinage*, but not beyond a certain level. It's not the Middle East. Fortunes are not the result of clientalism. (Inter-view, 3 August 1988)[53]

Thus interview subjects repeatedly denied the importance of corrup-tion to industrial success.[54] They pointed out that the largest fortunes in the industrial community had been made in businesses that had no special relations, contractual or otherwise, with the state, whether referring to the case of Abdelwahab Ben Ayed of Poulina, Tunisia's poultry king, or Hedi Jelani of Lee Cooper Jeans, an export-oriented textile manufacturer, or Abdessalem Affes of STPA, a major couscous manufacturer. And although most admitted that petty corruption greased the wheel of nearly all business operations (e.g., the textile manufacturer's story of slipping a sample of free merchandise to the state inspector), interview subjects were unanimous in rejecting the view that shady relations with the state offered a primrose path to fortune. They dismissed any comparison to other Middle Eastern countries (where shady relations can prove essential to business success).

The latter became clear in the wake of the Hamila scandal. Hassine Hamila was a Tunisian entrepreneur who began his career in the Sudan as a sandwich vendor providentially situated near the officers' barracks that housed the future president, Gaffar Numeiry. Hamila eventually parlayed a close friendship with Numeiry into an enormous fortune by mediating supplies of arms, food, and transportation to the state. Ultimately, Hamila returned to Tunisia to conduct business and do good works. By 1988, however, he had been implicated in illegal trafficking in liquor, cigarettes, and imported furniture and was packed off to jail. According to the journal *Réalités*:

> Mr. Hamila didn't understand the difference between the working principles of [business affairs in] the Middle East, which are founded upon alliances with the political class, and those in Tunisia, where this is not always the case.

... [Hamila] believed he could buy everything with money. [This was] an error in judgement that risks costing him a great deal. ("Du casse-croûte au duty-free," *Réalités*, 18 November 1988)

So while cronyism is endemic in Tunisia, it is not essentially politicized or driven by the logic of corruption. The state bureaucracy may be cumbersome and inefficient but it is still largely governed by a developmental ethic rather than the logic of personal gain, political or economic. As many industrialists pointed out, insider contacts rarely got a truly worthless project approved; they simply helped good projects get approved faster. Moreover, insider contacts were not an absolute precondition of success. All the businessmen I interviewed affirmed that a good project could get through the bureaucracy by virtue of its merits alone, even without insider connections. The process would simply require greater patience and greater persistence on the part of the project's promoter.

Of course, the interesting question is why cronyism does not become politicized or infected with corruption in Tunisia, as has been the case in many other countries where state bureaucrats exercise discretionary power over the distribution of state benefits, for example, in Zaire (Callaghy 1984) and Senegal (Boone 1990). Why do state elites and the state bureaucracy in Tunisia remain committed to a developmental ethic and focused on a developmental course? The answer most certainly lies in avenues suggested by Kohli (1986) and Evans (1992). Surely, leadership plays a role: both Presidents Bourguiba and Ben Ali personally identified their prestige with the economic development of Tunisia. Further, the decent remuneration, secure employment, and specialized training enjoyed by Tunisia's higher civil service (Larif-Beatrix 1988, 229, 248; Camau 1978) have certainly provided the esprit de corps and security of tenure which analysts such as Evans (1992) suggest are crucial to the development of a professional, incorruptible state bureaucracy. New research in this area (Evans and Rauch, 1999) seems to bear out these hunches. The best guess is that fidelity to a developmental course lies in the character of the state and state leadership in Tunisia.

But no matter the explanation, the fact that the discretionary distribution of state supports is essentially not politicized and not infected with corruption in any substantial way has important implications for the autonomy of private sector industrialists. Because industrialists do not have to pass a political test or give state elites a "cut of the action" to succeed, and because they are honestly valued and rewarded for their contribution to the state's developmental goals, Tunisian industrialists are endowed with a measure of political leverage and political autonomy not enjoyed by private sector actors in most other countries where crony capitalism prevails. Cronyism and discretionary distribution of state support need not eliminate private sector autonomy so long as the state remains primarily driven by a developmental ethos.

Further fostering private sector autonomy in Tunisia is the state's progressive embrace of capitalist industrialization and especially market reform since the mid-1980s. Overall, the embrace of capitalist logic and market reform fosters increasing autonomy for private sector actors—at least for those who survive!—along two dimensions. First, it decreases the level of support extended to private sector actors (no more price control or underpriced credit), diminishing their dependence on the state for economic success. Second, the embrace of market logic means that state support is increasingly distributed on *a nondiscretionary basis.* For example, instead of individual firms cutting special deals with the state to secure price protection and import controls, the state now lets the local market set prices for domestic products but protects the market overall by providing sector-wide tariff barriers. Neither factor means that private sector dependence on state support is entirely eliminated or that discretion in the distribution of state support is entirely purged. Nevertheless, the trend toward less of both fosters more autonomy for private sector entrepreneurs.[55]

Measuring Influence over Policy

Having established the parameters of private sector power and autonomy in Tunisia, can we gauge the capacity of its industrialists to shape public policy in any precise way?

The political influence of any specific social group is notoriously difficult to measure because such influence is often exercised in an informal, "behind the scenes" fashion, making it very difficult to track. The problem of measuring influence is especially compounded in countries where electoral politics is not central to the design of policy (Haggard and Kaufman, 1995). Under these conditions an even larger portion of decision making is removed from public scrutiny and relegated to back-room bargaining, where it is difficult to chronicle. Many eminent political scientists have thrown up their hands at the prospect of measuring such influence precisely[56] but others have tried to approach the issue indirectly. The most common method involves the imputation of influence from policy.

Accordingly, the political influence of a given group is deduced from the sum of enacted policies that favor the interests of that group.

Careful reflection, however, reveals the error of this approach. To deduce influence from policy is to confuse class partiality on the part of the state with class capture—the inverse of confusing state autonomy with state neutrality (Dimassi 1983, 65). Actually, the state may choose a policy that favors a particular group in society thanks to an independent calculus of its *own* state interests; this policy may then simply coincide with the agenda of a particular group without necessarily being the political work of that group (Waterbury 1991).

Ample empirical evidence is available to support this analysis from countries as diverse as France, Mexico, and Korea. Ezra Suleiman's work on France (1978, 272–74), John and Susan Purcell's work on Mexico (1977, 198), and Jones and Sakong's work on Korea (1980) all found that a certain *coincidence of interest* developed between the state and private sector industrialists once the state in these countries identified economic growth as one of its highest priorities. To encourage their common objective, growth, the state enacted a series of policies favoring the interests of local industrialists. For example, under Mexico's alliance for profits strategy, the state subsidized business, controlled labor, and protected the profitability of the private sector in order to encourage private sector investment and growth (Purcell 1981; Maxfield and Montoya 1987). The legislation of such favorable policies cannot be taken as a measure of industrialists' influence, let alone their domination of the state's policy-making process. The best evidence for this lies in the fact that when the interests of the state diverged from that of the industrialists, the state did not hesitate to compromise the industrialists' interests. In the Mexican case, for example, when the interests of the state and the private sector diverged over the devaluation of the peso and private business "protested" through massive capital flight, the state did not hesitate to nationalize Mexican banks, despite the outrage of the private sector. Favorable policies thus are no indication of political domination by the favored group.

This certainly is the case for Tunisia's private sector industrialists. The favorable policies enacted by the state during the 1960s and 1970s were not the result of Tunisian industrialists clamoring for state favors, nor can they be taken as a measure of the political pressure brought to bear on the state by this group. Such a scenario would have been impossible since, as was shown in chapter 1, a class of private sector industrialists hardly existed in Tunisia prior to 1970. To the contrary, the state adopted these policies for its own reasons (largely due to recognition of its own financial and technical limitations);[57] in the process, it *created the constituency* for these policies. Rather than interpret these pro-private sector policies as the measure of private sector strength, these policies should be seen as a "gift" bestowed on Tunisian society without struggle. In this they are similar to the liberal personal status laws legislated during the late 1950s, which were not wrested from the state by a powerful women's movement but rather were handed down with paternalistic largesse by President Bourguiba to a still largely unmobilized female constituency.[58]

Tunisian industrialists have long been the beneficiaries of a coincidence of interest with the state in profitable private sector growth. Such a coincidence of interest makes it difficult to deduce political influence from policy because it forestalls any test of strength between industrialists and the state. This coincidence of interest masks the true driving force behind these policies (industrialists' interests? state officials' interests?) and eliminates policy as a clear indicator of their respective power.

Still, it is important to realize that the interests of the state and private sector industrialists are not always identical, and divergence between the two does create an opportunity to take the measure of the respective power of each. In recent years the interests of the state and private sector industrialists in Tunisia have diverged to some extent over the pace and purity of economic reform. Ever since the country's foreign exchange crisis in 1986, the regime's developmental ethos has led it to embrace the logic of economic reform prescribed by the World Bank and the IMF. With surprising alacrity and consistency, the regime has implemented recommended reforms ranging from devaluation of the dinar and tax reform, to budget and subsidy cutbacks and price liberalization. So faithful has Tunisia been in adhering to IMF/World Bank prescriptions that it has been hailed as a model adjuster by these agencies and held up as an example for other economically troubled countries to emulate (*IMF Survey*, 9 November 1992).

Nevertheless, the regime has compromised the logic of IMF/World Bank prescriptions in at least one important way. It has slowed the pace of trade liberalization, limiting the exposure of Tunisian industry to the full force of international competition. Nine years after committing itself to liberalizing reform, the regime still retains a relatively high level of tariff protection (43–75%) for those industries most likely to be hurt by foreign competition (i.e., finished consumer goods). And despite pressure from the World Bank to speed its progress at trade liberalization (World Bank 1996) the regime remains stubbornly committed to retaining tariff protection for local industry, for the medium term at the very least. For example, Tunisia's 1995 free trade accord with the European Union, allowed for a twelve-year delay in lifting tariff protection for Tunisian industry (EIU, *Country Report: Tunisia*, January–March 1996, 18–20).

The logic driving this policy decision is clear. The regime is concerned with protecting the vibrancy and confidence of indigenous private sector industry in Tunisia, even if this means violating IMF/World Bank prescriptions in the short run. This policy decision is important because it reflects the fact that state is not entirely free to make policy as it wishes. Left to its own developmental logic, the state might embrace the logic of structural adjustment and market reform (including trade liberalization) without reservation, just as it has in so many other policy areas. But recognizing that the private sector accounts for a major share of capital formation and growth in the economy (as well as the private sector's loudly voiced fears about rapid trade liberalization (EIU, *Country Report: Tunisia*, July–September 1995, 16), the state has been obliged to amend its logic in ways that foster the confidence and vibrancy of that sector. In other words, thanks to the structural power of private sector industry, the state is forced to accommodate preferences and logic other than its own in the making of public policy. This constitutes an important wedge in the policy autonomy of the state.

Naysayers may object to taking this policy decision as an indicator of private sector power, arguing that other factors contribute to the slow pace of trade liberalization in Tunisia as well. The state's concern for social stability and, more specifically, the prevention of massive job loss, also explains its reluctance to expose domestic industry to the full blast of international competition (and potential failure). The government's own 1995 study on trade liberalization predicted that as many as a third of Tunisian industrial firms and perhaps 120,000 jobs might vanish were tariffs on European industrial goods to be lifted immediately (EIU, *Country Report: Tunisia*, July–September 1995, 16). In a country already suffering from a 15% unemployment rate and where the creation of 60,000 jobs in the economy in a single year is reason for self-congratulation by the government, the loss of 120,000 jobs is likely to give the government reason to pause.

Similarly, some Tunisians, including a leading Tunisian banker interviewed repeatedly over six years, object to viewing the government's policy decisions as a measure of the specific power of any group in society. They argue instead that government elites, especially under Ben Ali's regime, make economic policy largely on the basis of "technocratic considerations" and that politics (weighing the power of any particular "constituency") only comes into play in a very general way (to what degree that constituency, if dissatisfied, is likely to undermine political stability in the country) (interview, 15 December 1993). Certainly, the rhetoric of the regime supports this view. At a recent IACE meeting, the minister of international cooperation and foreign investment, Mohamed Ghannouchi, restated the regime's consistent position on economic policy of recent years: namely, that it sought to take a "gradual and consensual" approach to the economy, in order to achieve growth *with* social stability. To realize this goal, the regime planned to undertake much consultation and discussion with all social forces and to take a gradual approach toward integration with the international economy. "Better to have a steady 5% growth sustained over 20 years," explained Ghannouchi, "than a faster growth rate for a few years that then explodes" (13 December 1996).

Of course, none of this gainsays the view that private sector industrialists *are* exercising structural power in the Tunisian economy and that the state *is* concerned with maintaining their confidence as a key means to social stability. Rather, it implies that slow implementation of trade liberalization should be taken as an indicator of the capacity of many different groups (labor, business, the unemployed) to limit state autonomy and influence the state in its choice of public policy. Nevertheless, given the state's extensive consultations with private sector industrialists on the matter of trade liberalization, there can be little doubt that the health and interests of this stratum weighs heavily in the state's decision making in this area.

Conclusion

The state's sponsorship of capitalist industrialization, undertaken with increasing enthusiasm since the early 1970s, has indeed led to the development of an important class of private sector industrialists in Tunisia. Over time, the progressive adoption of market reform has further enhanced the autonomy and power of these industrialists. Market reform has heightened the centrality of the private sector's role in the economy, augmenting its structural power. Market reform has also diminished the scope of state support and state discretion in the determination of private sector success, thereby augmenting private sector autonomy.

Still, there are significant barriers limiting the political influence of industrialists in Tunisia. The relative youth and inexperience of this sector combined with the country's small field size certainly work to undermine the instrumental power of private sector industrialists. But even more hobbling is the institutional context. The lack of a competitive political system and guaranteed civil liberties close off important routes to instrumental and ideological power for industrialists. The enactment of democratic political reform would clearly open some of these routes to influence for the private sector. Whether private sector industrialists are likely to use their newly found power and autonomy to campaign for democratic reform of the political system is explored in chapter 5.

CHAPTER 3

A Checkered Alliance:
State Sponsorship of Labor

State sponsorship of organized labor is a less straightforward affair than is the case with capital, for the coincidence of interest that characterizes the relationship between the developmental state and capital is more equivocal. Labor's economic agenda, specifically its quest for economic distribution, collides with the developmental state's logic of accumulation.[1] And labor's organizational agenda, which is to develop robust capacity for collective action, poses a direct threat to the developmental state's goal of keeping an uncontested grip on order. But labor's capacity to deliver organized political support endows it with potential value as a political ally, especially when the state's developmental policies are squeezing other groups in society and compromising its popularity. And labor's capacity to deliver social peace and wage restraint makes its organization a crucial asset that the developmental state often has an interest in sponsoring.

This motley coincidence and conflict of interests makes for a complex relationship with labor, one that can embrace both sponsorship and repression, even simultaneously. The state's competing economic and political logics may lead to the *inadvertent* embrace of both sponsorship and repression, such as when the state's economic agenda reinforces the size, concentration, and generational depth of labor, even as its political agenda calls for the repression of labor's organizational capacity. But the simultaneous embrace of sponsorship and repression may also be the *conscious* policy of the state, such as when it chooses a corporatist strategy that fosters labor's organization, through legal institutions and financial subsidies, but contains it too, through the control of elections and the vetoing of leaders. In choosing its mix of repression and sponsorship, the state must balance its multiple goals against its assets, weigh its desire for order and allies against its store of political confidence and economic latitude.

In the Tunisian case, these mixed motives, interests, and endowments have spelled a checkered alliance with labor. The state, driven by its own political and economic logic, has indeed played a major role in sponsoring the development of organized labor. In the early years of independence, the state's development strategy of state-sponsored industrialization fostered the structural conditions that empowered labor and favored the possibility of labor militance and collective action. At the same time, the state's political logic led it to pursue the disorganization of labor and its political neutralization through incorporation. In later decades, the state's embrace of a more market-driven strategy of capitalist industrialization undermined the structural conditions that favored labor's power. However, the state's political logic also led it to resurrect labor's organization, in an attempt to counterpoise organized workers as a populist ally against other mass-based threats to the state (e.g., the "Islamists").

Overall, the texture of labor-state relations in Tunisia can be mapped by assessing two key variables: the measure of the state's political confidence and the relative strength of labor's structural position. Charting these variables in a two-by-two matrix, we arrive at a rough periodization of labor-state relations in Tunisia, composed of four phases:

Organized Labor's Relation to State in Tunisia

	Labor structurally weak	*Labor structurally strong*
State politically confident	Null	Measured autonomy (1970s)
State politically insecure	Subordination/controlled cooperation (1960s, 1990s)	Repression (1980s)

Phase I, lasting from 1956–70, might be characterized as a period of labor's subordination. The political insecurity of the newly independent state made it averse to any show of organized political independence in society, especially that of mass-based movements like the national trade union federation. Nevertheless, the state needed to anchor itself in society through the cultivation of organized political allies. This dual objective led the state to forgo dismantlement of the labor movement in favor of its sponsorship and control through a strategy of subordination. The structurally weak position of labor made the trade union movement especially susceptible to this strategy.

Phase II, lasting from 1970 to 1977, might be characterized as a period of measured autonomy for labor. The state enjoyed increasing political confidence, thanks to its fifteen-year implantation in society and the flush state of the economy. Labor, for its part, began to exhibit greater independence and militance, thanks to its improved structural position. In response the state permitted the trade union movement a measure of autonomy, endorsing the movement with legal concessions and integrating it into the policy-making process through a variety of institutional innovations.

Phase III, lasting from 1978 to 1987, might be characterized as a period of state repression. A looming succession crisis and plummeting growth rates undermined the political confidence of the state and again made it nervous about nodes of political independence in society. Moreover, labor's increasing structural strength made trade union autonomy unmanageably threatening. These factors together spelled a period of harsh repression of the labor movement.

Phase IV, lasting from 1987 to the present, might be characterized as a period of controlled cooperation. With the ascension of President Ben Ali, the state regained a measure of political confidence, though this was soon compromised by the rising challenge from Islamists. The regime's need for a popular ally to countervail the Islamists led it to resurrect the labor movement, though under controlled conditions. Control of the movement was facilitated by labor's weakened structural position, the consequence of the state's switch in development strategies.

Chapter 3 elaborates this analysis. The chapter begins with a brief account of the labor movement's historical preeminence prior to independence. In contrast to capital, labor was not a creation of the Tunisian state but rather preceded it and even had a hand in creation of the state itself. This proved consequential for labor's postindependence survival as well as its subordination. The chapter proceeds with an account of the four phases of labor-state relations in Tunisia, documenting the measure and means of state sponsorship and repression in each period. Overall, the goal of the chapter is to trace the checkered nature of labor-state relations over the past forty years and to show that despite significant episodes of state repression, labor's survival and influence is to a large degree a consequence of the state's own making.

Pre-independence Origins

In contrast to capital, the labor movement in Tunisia does not owe a debt of origin to the state. Rather, both the creation of a class of "formally free" wage earners as well as its induction into the habits of trade union activism must be traced to European intervention. It was the arrival of European capital and its investment in mining, railways, and infrastructure that fostered the emergence of formally free wage earners in Tunisia. Prior to that, the vast majority of Tunisians had been ensconced in precapitalist relations of production in agriculture and/or handicrafts. And it was European workers who formed a significant core of Tunisia's fledgling working class. Native Tunisians resisted absorption into capitalist relations of production, and entrepreneurs were forced to fill labor shortages by recruiting workers from prison camps and abroad (Romdhane 1981, 86). By 1926, more than 40% of Tunisia's 110,000 workers were of European origin, and entire sectors of the economy were identified with foreign nationalities (Hermassi 1966, 15).

The large presence of European workers proved both a boon and bust for the development of organized labor. In some ways it endowed Tunisia's working class with a certain "precociousness" (Hermassi 1966, 17). European workers brought with them a tradition of trade union organizing that far exceeded what might have developed spontaneously in Tunisia at this time, given the country's delayed experience of industrialization and the small size of its working class. Tunisia's first trade unions (organized in the civil service, utilities, construction, and railway sectors) were the work of French and Italian laborers, inspired by labor movements back home (Dellagi 1980, 9; Sassois 1971). European workers brought with them legal traditions and legal assumptions that supported labor's organizing efforts. Thus, although the colonial regime did not officially sanction syndical activity until 1932, syndical liberties *had* been guaranteed by French law in France as early as 1884, and it became a ticklish matter for the regime to deny French citizens rights in the colony that they certainly enjoyed at home. Consequently, the colonial authorities unofficially tolerated the existence of French syndicates and thus provided a legal context more favorable to labor organizing than was typical in most (nonsettler-colonial) Middle Eastern states at the time.

But the presence of so many European workers also proved detrimental to labor's organization in one important way. It undermined working class solidarity by introducing intraclass stratification drawn along the lines of national origin. European workers enjoyed a privileged position in Tunisia. They were disproportionately recruited for better-paying skilled jobs and, even in unskilled jobs, enjoyed compensation rates significantly higher than Tunisian workers received. Wage discrimination based on national origin was officially endorsed by the colonial regime, which regularly published three different cost of living indices and salary grids for French, Italian, and Tunisian workers (Hermassi 1966, 18). European workers, for their part, proved quite jealous of their economic privilege. They clung dearly to their wage differentials and largely ignored Tunisian demands that equal wages be paid for equal work.

European workers failed to make common cause with their Tunisian counterparts in other ways as well. The European-led trade unions made only tepid gestures toward the inclusion of native Tunisians in the syndical movement, and when they did recruit Tunisians it was often for less than "disinterested" reasons.[2] Union meetings were generally conducted in French or Italian, excluding participation by Arabic-speaking Tunisians (Bessis, cited in Romdhane 1981, 90). And sectors that were primarily manned by Tunisian workers (e.g., docks and mines) went entirely unorganized (Hermassi 1966; Hamzaoui 1970). National cleavages divided the working class against itself and undermined the development of its full power potential.

But the infection of working-class politics with the politics of national cleavage did have *some* positive impact on labor's organization. Specifically, it was a sense of national consciousness and national grievance that spurred the creation of an *indigenous* trade union movement in Tunisia. This proved true in each of the three defining moments for indigenous labor organizing prior to independence. In 1924, Tunisian labor activist Mohamed Ali created the first cell of an exclusively Tunisian labor union, the Confédération générale de travailleurs tunisiens (CGTT), in response to the failure of French dockworkers in Marseilles to make common cause with Tunisian dockworkers around the principle of equal wages for equal work (Ahmed 1967). Colonial repression dissolved the movement a year later. In 1937, Belgacem Gnaoui made a second attempt to create an exclusively Tunisian trade union (the second CGTT), this time spurred by the failure of European workers to make common cause with Tunisian miners during a strike in 1936. Again, this movement met with colonial repression and dissolution (Ben Hammed 1980, 22). Finally, in 1944 Farhed Hached organized the founding kernel of Tunisia's present-day labor confederation, the Union générale de travailleurs tunisiens (UGTT), driven by the conviction that European-led unions did not take national grievances seriously enough. For a complex set of reasons, described below, this movement survived.

The primary advantage of giving syndicalism a nationalist cast was that it won the fledgling trade union movement a broad popular base within Tunisian society, well beyond the country's tiny working class. It also imbued the movement with enduring political legitimacy, thanks to its contributions to the country's independence struggle. By the late 1940s and early 1950s the UGTT was organizing strikes for the national cause, including general strikes to protest the arrest of Neo-Destour leaders. Abroad, UGTT leaders pressed the case for Tunisian independence in international forums such as the United Nations and ICFTU (International Confederation of Free Trade Unions). When the independence struggle turned violent, UGTT activists organized guerilla activity against colonial interests. And throughout this period the UGTT provided a cover for party activity, assuming a leadership role when the Neo-Destour was forced underground or its leaders arrested or imprisoned. The UGTT's contribution to the independence struggle was so central that it was ultimately cast in the role of "king-maker," serving as one of Tunisia's primary interlocutors in the Franco-Tunisian negotiations that led to independence in 1956.

But the association of the trade union movement with the nationalist cause carried with it two primary disadvantages. First, it tended to make the labor movement more of a target for colonial repression. Early incarnations of the indigenous trade union movement were dissolved by the colonial regime because they were perceived as vehicles for nationalist assertion and a "threat to public order" (Dellagi 1980, 9; Ben Hammed 1980, 22). Only in the 1940s, when Communist victory in the local French-led union (the CGT) fanned cold war fears, did the colonial regime welcome the creation of a counter syndical organization like the UGTT.

Second, the trade union's association with the nationalist cause made it more confused about its own professional mission and thus more vulnerable to incorporation by the larger nationalist movement. UGTT leaders were not always clear about whether the union's primary responsibility was to serve the interests of the working class or those of the nation as a whole. This confusion was abetted by three factors. First, the character of social stratification in Tunisia led to a certain conflation of nation and class. Here, as in many other colonized countries, the dominant class, composed of capitalists, landowners, and government officials, was overwhelmingly foreign. Class resentment was thus channeled along national lines, reinforcing nationalist sentiment and fostering the melding of national and trade union movements. Second, elite ideology also reinforced the conflation of class and nation. Both the leaders of the UGTT and the Neo-Destour were persuaded that class analysis was irrelevant to explain the exploitation and deprivation that most Tunisians suffered. Instead, they argued that in the context of underdevelopment the entire nation should be conceived as one class, united by its common experience of economic backwardness as well as its common struggle against the source of backwardness—colonialism (Ben Hammed 1980, 2; Belhassen 1977, 20). Third, the two movements shared leaders. Many of the syndical movement's leading lights (Habib Achour, Ahmed Tlili, Bechir Bellagha, and Ahmed Ben Salah) were originally Destourian militants who helped launch the UGTT because they saw it as part of a continuum of nationalist organizations that could contribute to the struggle against colonial domination. Both this melding of purpose and overlap in leadership muddled the clarity of trade union purpose and created a wedge for trade union domination by the Neo-Destour Party.

In short, the origins of Tunisia's trade union movement cannot be disentangled from the country's experience of European colonialism and the nationalist struggle waged against it. The trade union's alliance with the national struggle was a source of strength in the pre-independence period, conferring political legitimacy on the movement and expanding its popular base. At the same time, this alliance made the trade union movement vulnerable to political incorporation once independence had been achieved, as is demonstrated below.

Independence and UGTT Subordination, 1956–1970

With the achievement of independence the complex nature of the relationship between labor and the state became clear. The political logic of the new regime led it to support the survival of the trade union movement even as it sought to contain labor's independence through persistent interference in the union's internal affairs. At the same time the regime's economic logic reinforced labor's structural position and boosted the conditions for labor's power. The first decade and a half thus spelled organizational subordination for labor even as it planted the seeds for more vigorous self-assertion by labor later on.

The regime's inclination to sponsor and control labor simultaneously was largely the consequence of a "political confidence gap." One might have expected that, flush with the victory of independence, Bourguiba and his cohort would be almost cocksure in office. But although Bourguiba was the undisputed hero of the independence struggle, his grip on both society and party was not entirely secure. The Neo-Destour Party, while still vibrant, had suffered organizationally from years of repression and clandestine operation under the colonial regime. And within the party, Bourguiba faced a significant challenge from a culturally conservative coalition of religious leaders, Djerbans, and landlords from the South.[3]

But these challenges did not reduce Bourguiba's ambition. The "supreme combatant" had grand plans to revolutionize Tunisia, culturally, socially, and economically, and make it a "modern" country in the image of Western Europe. The gap that emerged between his political confidence and ambition planted in Bourguiba a desire for political control that spurred him to stamp out any node of autonomy and dissent in society.

Bourguiba's political ambition put him on a collision course with the trade union movement. Of all organizations in society, the UGTT was in the strongest position to challenge Destourian hegemony. It had a large popular base, counting nearly 180,000 members at independence (Hermassi 1972, 155). Its nationalist credentials rivaled that of the Neo-Destour Party, owing to the central role it had played in the independence struggle. Its organizational structure was robust after years of organizing under the relatively generous syndical liberties granted by the colonial regime. And it was blessed with dynamic leadership, including a charismatic former university professor, Ahmed Ben Salah, whose vision for radically restructuring the economy captured the imagination of many.[4]

The UGTT's political preeminence at independence was certainly clear to Bourguiba. The union confederation had already been cast in the role of kingmaker twice: in negotiations with France, when the UGTT had served as one of the official interlocutors that oversaw the state's creation; and at a crucial party congress in 1955, when UGTT support had defeated the conservative challenge to Bourguiba. In fact, the UGTT's decision to throw its support to Bourguiba during that fateful congress ultimately secured the president's rise to power. Bourguiba remembered the UGTT's services, but he was not necessarily grateful.

On the surface, Bourguiba acknowledged the UGTT's preeminent position and offered the trade union an executive role in the newly created state. He assigned a generous share of the seats in the National Assembly to UGTT activists and conferred at least four ministerial positions to members of the trade union executive (Azaiez n.d., 230–35, 170–77). But in reality Bourguiba was intent on emasculating the trade union, turning it into just one more state-controlled "national organization" that would serve as an arm of the state rather than a node of autonomous power in national politics.

In his ambition to subordinate the UGTT, Bourguiba was abetted by three factors: the UGTT's own confusion about its mission in national politics; the enormous overlap in members and leaders shared by party and union;[5] and the personal rivalries and unsated ambitions that divided the UGTT's leadership. These factors provided both a wedge for Destourian interference in union affairs and enabled Bourguiba to root out any trade union leader with a taste for autonomy, as is evident from three instances of confrontation between the UGTT and the party-state during this early period.

The first instance of confrontation between union and state came in 1956. That year, the secretary general of the UGTT, Ahmed Ben Salah, proposed the merger of the trade union movement and the Neo-Destour Party to create a single political force in the image of Britain's labor party. Ben Salah argued that the UGTT ought to shed its class-specific character because an exclusive focus on workers' interests was inappropriately divisive in a poor, underdeveloped country.[6] Instead, the union should act as vanguard for the entire nation, attacking the root of its common deprivation: an antiquated social and economic structure.

Now in theory Bourguiba should have welcomed Ben Salah's initiative. After all, Bourguiba's oratorical trademark had always been the denial of class conflict in the Tunisian context, the rejection of corporate interest group representation, and the insistence that Tunisians stand united to overcome their common foes of colonialism and economic backwardness. But the theoretically unobjectionable proved politically inadmissable. Given the relative strength of the UGTT in the mid-1950s, Bourguiba feared that a merger between the Neo-Destour and the trade union would spell his party's subordination (Dellagi 1980, 11).

To avert political eclipse, Bourguiba sought to prevent a merger and discredit Ben Salah. Relying on tactics that would become paradigmatic for his maneuvers in the years to come, Bouguiba played on personal rivalries and unsated ambitions within the union leadership to split the union movement and "pluralize" it organizationally. Specifically, he encouraged one of Ben Salah's leading trade union rivals, Habib Achour, to form a new union, the UGTT. Bourguiba immediately endorsed the break-away union even as he criticized it.

Faced with the fragmentation of the trade union movement, the UGTT "caved." Destourian loyalists within the UGTT used their majority on the union's administrative council to remove the troublesome Ben Salah and vote in his place a Destourian party loyalist—Ahmed Tlili.[7] Shortly thereafter, Achour dissolved the rival union and rejoined the UGTT. The threat to Bourguiba's power—a trade union led by independent-minded Ahmed Ben Salah—had been eliminated.

The second instance of confrontation between state and union was to come just a few years later. At first, Ahmed Tlili acceded to the union's role as a "national organization" and subordinated the corporate interests of labor to "the greater good of the national whole."[8] But by 1963 the trade union leader began to chafe under Bourguiba's domination. Tlili became suspicious of the regime's grand scheme to expand the state's role in the economy, and he resisted Bourguiba's attempt to tighten his grip on the political scene. He spoke out from the trade union pulpit, calling for more open debate about political and economic alternatives for Tunisia and championing further "democratization" of the political system (Ahmed 1967).

This stance proved too defiant for Bourguiba's tastes. Once again, he used the overlap in membership between the party and union to bring the union under his control. In 1963, at the UGTT's Ninth Congress, Bourguiba instructed all Neo-Destourians in the trade union to withdraw their support from Ahmed Tlili. The conference subsequently voted to remove Tlili from his post as secretary general, replacing him with the perennial claimant to UGTT leadership (and presumably loyal Destourian), Habib Achour.

A third instance of trade union–party confrontation came a year later, in the wake of an IMF-inspired economic reform. In 1964 the IMF counseled Tunisia to devalue the dinar by 25% to help correct the country's trade imbalance. This devaluation threatened a significant loss in earning power for Tunisian workers. The latter had already suffered real wage losses of 11% between 1955 and 1960, owing to a combination of wage blockage and inflation, and worker discontent had already boiled over in several spontaneous strikes during the period 1961–62.

Up to that point the UGTT had stuck to its policy of counseling wage restraint and opposing strike activity. But to continue ignoring worker discontent in the face of devaluation risked irrevocably alienating the rank and file from the union leadership. Consequently, Achour decided to make his support for the devaluation policy contingent upon a commensurate raise in workers' salaries, to compensate workers for the inflation that was certain to follow devaluation.

This demand infuriated Bourguiba. It represented an unacceptable act of political independence and defiance on the part of the UGTT. Bourguiba denounced Achour and his supporters as "khobzists," bread and butter unionists who put narrow class interests above national welfare (Ahmed 1966, 172, 185). The president then moved to silence the union. Initially, he had Achour imprisoned on trumped-up charges.[9] His next move was to organize an extraordinary UGTT congress to elect a pliant Destourian loyalist as Achour's replacement. The new trade union chief, Bechir Bellagha, came to office committed to submitting the trade union movement to Destourian party control. At his first press conference he announced that the UGTT's orientation was "identical to that of the party," and he promised full collaboration between party and union during his term (*Annuaire de l'Afrique du Nord* [*AAN*] 1965, 169).

These three moments of confrontation between party and trade union reflect the underlying political logic of the Tunisian regime at this time: namely, subordinate all nodes of political autonomy and opposition in society to party control, including the UGTT. But even as the regime subordinated the trade union movement, it did not seek to eliminate the union. The regime needed a popular base in society, and the trade union movement offered it an organized alliance. Consequently, the regime sponsored the UGTT through a variety of means. Financially, it fostered the union's solvency through a system of automatic "check-off" that guaranteed dues from the public sector and civil service. Legally, it maintained a framework that endorsed labor's right to organize collectively, if not strike. Politically, it conferred prestigious posts on trade union leaders, including appointments on the National Planning Commission, the Social and Economic Council, and the Neo-Destour's executive board, the bureau politique, as well as seats in the National Assembly. None of these positions gave the union decisive executive power in the regime, but they did reward union leaders with status and something of a consultative role in government. All together, the goal was not to eliminate the trade union but rather sustain it and harness it to the regime's political and developmental objectives.

Thanks to this mixture of carrot and stick, the UGTT abandoned any contestatory role in Tunisian politics. It renounced strike activity and counseled a policy of wage restraint so as not to compromise national

Table 3.1. Industrial Disputes, 1961–1969

Year	Number of Disputes	Workers Involved	Days Lost
1961	23	885	1,234
1962	11	393	1,272
1963	7	405	629
1964	—	—	—
1965	—	—	—
1966	5	306	469
1967	—	—	—
1968	1	350	88
1969	1	400	1,200

Source: International Labor Office, Yearbook of Labor Statistics, 1971.

productivity. Between 1955 and 1962 the UGTT made no wage demands, even though the cost of living had risen 11% by 1960 (Ahmed 1967). Wages remained largely frozen throughout the 1960s, save for a brief reprieve in 1965.[10] In addition, strike levels remained extremely low throughout the 1960s (Table 3.1):[11] To retain the loyalty of workers, the trade union focused on projects that would advance workers' welfare without inflating wage levels, such as the development of literacy programs for working people, the creation of worker vacation colonies, and the organization of producer and consumer cooperatives to help reduce the cost of basic commodities for workers (Dimassi 1983, 188).

By the mid-1960s, then, it was clear that the party-state had succeeded in domesticating the trade union movement. Under the stewardship of the party faithful, the UGTT gave itself over to being little more than the party-state's transmission belt, popularizing and defending the government's policies to the working class rather than aggregating and communicating the interests of workers to the state. Organizationally, the trade union slid into a period of decline. Membership dropped off dramatically (Dellagi 1980, 11). The political logic of the regime triumphed in the subordination of the UGTT.

But even as the political logic of the state worked to weaken the UGTT, the economic logic of this developmental state worked in unanticipated ways to shore up the structural power of Tunisia's working class and favor the development of a stronger labor movement in the country. This was true in a number of different ways. Prior to independence, the development of Tunisia's labor movement had been handicapped by the small size of the county's working class, its cultural heterogeneity, the low educational levels of Tunisian workers, and their relatively shallow roots in the working class. Romdhane (1981, 75) guesses that at independence Tunisia could count only 150–200,000 people as salaried workers; that is, not more than 15% of the population could be considered workers. The working class continued to be extremely heterogeneous culturally until relatively late. Even in 1953, Europeans still constituted 30–40% of all workers employed in the larger enterprises (Liazu 1979, 119). Literacy levels among workers remained extremely low. A survey conducted in 1968 found that 44% of workers were still completely illiterate (Dimassi 1983, 487). And most workers in the 1960s were "first-generation" proletariat, with only shallow roots in the working class. A survey conducted in 1964 found that only one fifth of all workers had fathers who had been workers as well; nearly half of all workers were of peasant or artisanal origin (Dimassi 1983, 485). All these factors worked to undermine the solidarity and combativeness of the working class as well as the development of a strong labor movement in Tunisia.

But the state's developmental policies changed many of these conditions and worked to shore up the strength of the working class. The regime's strategy of state-led industrialization led to the mushrooming of the working class—by 1974 the number of workers totaled 500,000, or 33% of the active population (Romdhane 1981, 75). The regime's conscious policy of "Tunisification," especially in state-owned enterprises and the civil service, made for a more homogenous working class as native Tunisians were hired to replace departing and aging Europeans in the workforce. In addition, the regime's ambitious program to provide universal primary schooling to all Tunisians bore fruit in rising levels of literacy in the general population and a better-educated core of young workers entering the workplace. Finally, the regime's commitment to industrialization lengthened the country's experience with industry and made second-generation workers less of a rarity (Bedaoui 1986). In short, even as the political logic of the regime led it to stamp out the autonomy of organized labor, the developmental logic of the regime led it to foster those very conditions that would reinforce organized labor's strength and militance. This strength and militance would become evident in the next phase of labor-state relations, the phase of "measured autonomy."

Measured Autonomy, 1970–1978

The 1970s saw a remarkable rise in worker militance and trade union assertiveness, especially when compared to labor's quiescence and subordination during the early independence era. The ascendance of labor during this period was in large part a consequence of the state's own making. A shift in economic development strategy led the state to embrace a new political rhetoric as well as institutional innovation that fostered labor's rise. At the same time, the state's prior pursuit of economic development yielded the unintended consequence of a structurally empowered working class. These factors together with such conjunctural factors as various economic windfalls and a rise in the state's political confidence, led to a brief golden period for Tunisian labor. The state proved willing to tolerate and even sponsor a measure of trade union autonomy, and labor was structurally strong enough to demand it. The result was a significant rise in labor activism and the realization of important wage gains for much of the decade.

To explain labor's ascendance we must look first to the shift in the state's development strategy. As described in chapter 1, the fiscal crisis and economic stagnation plaguing the country by the late 1960s led the regime to exchange its etatist development strategy for one in which the private sector was encouraged to take the lead in stimulating national growth. This shift in strategy was accompanied by ideological and institutional innovations that had important implications for labor.

In terms of ideology, the regime's shift in strategy was accompanied by a renunciation of the rhetoric of socialism and unanimity so prevalent during the 1960s. Gone was the collectivist imagery of the Ben Salah era and the rigid conception of national unity that it implied. Tunisians were no longer presumed to be bound by a "mechanical solidarity," that is, an identity of interests imposed by the overriding importance of the common foe of underdevelopment. Instead, the new prime minister, Hedi Nouira, embraced the rhetoric of liberalism that permitted a more pluralistic vision of Tunisian society and acknowledged a legitimate diversity of interests among groups in society (*AAN*, 1974, 368–70). The UGTT could now be encouraged to voice the specific concerns of the working class without fear of accusation of betrayal to some larger national cause.

Besides this ideological innovation, the regime embraced institutional innovations as well. Recognizing the diversity of interests in society, but wanting to assure the "social peace" necessary for successful private sector–led development, the regime sought to create an institutional context for the peaceful negotiation of differences between business and labor. Specifically, the state sought to a create a "structured partnership" between the two, with representatives of each side to meet regularly to negotiate wages, working conditions, and productivity norms. For this corporatist policy to work, however, the state was obliged to sponsor, first and foremost, the creation of credible representatives for both sides.

In the case of labor this meant the resuscitation of the UGTT. To foster the trade unions' revival, the state permitted the reinstatement of the trade union's last independent-minded secretary general, Habib Achour.[12] In addition, it endowed the trade union with new legal rights (most important, the right to bargain collectively for wages)[13] while it reaffirmed established labor rights (such as workers' right to strike).[14] The regime also invited the UGTT to participate as a full-fledged member, along with representatives of the UTICA and the state, in a series of high-profile conventions designed to set the course of business-labor relations throughout the decade. These conventions negotiated the terms of worker-employee relations, established the principle of a minimum wage (the SMIG), and defined the salary grids for 80% of Tunisia's non-agricultural labor force.

Of course, this resuscitation of the UGTT took place in a corporatist context. While the regime sought to make the country's national organizations "more dynamic, open, and respected" (Nouira, cited in *AAN*, 1973, 516), it also expected these organizations to "structure their social partners." That is, in exchange for a monopoly of representation and a chance to participate in the policy-making process, these national organizations were expected to contain the aspirations and moderate the demands of their constituents in a way that would make compromise possible and deliver the social peace and stability that economic development required. Thus, even as the state resuscitated the trade union movement though official endorsement, legal innovation, and extensive inclusion in the policy-making process, it intended to set limits to trade union assertiveness.

The state's endorsement and inclusion of the labor movement was facilitated first, by a confluence of windfalls—plentiful rains, good harvests, and the rise in world commodity prices for Tunisia's main exports of olive oil, phosphates, and petroleum (Central Bank, *Annual Report*, 1970–74). Historically high growth rates were the result, with annual averages clocking in at 8% in real terms between 1970 and 1977 (Central Bank, *Annual Report*, 1971, and *Statistiques financières*, November 1977). This expanding pie made for less of a zero-sum game between business, labor, and the state and made labor's accommodation possible. Second, the regime enjoyed unusual self-confidence during the early 1970s. Bourguiba's hold on power was secure (the succession crisis had not yet accelerated), the ruling party was well rooted throughout society, despite some criticism that it had degenerated into a rigid machine; and no serious contender for power had emerged, despite the obvious failure of the regime's etatist policy. The regime's confidence was evident in its sudden endorsement of political debate and liberalization (*AAN*, 1970), and this too created space for labor's self-assertion.

Conscious state policy explains part of the UGTT's ascendance at that time. But labor's assertiveness was also the unintended consequence of the state's development policies. As shown above, the state's commitment to industrialization, Tunisification, and universal primary education served to expand, deepen, and educate the working class. These developments favored the reinforcement of working class identity and fostered the conditions for labor militance. The deepened sense of working class consciousness among the rank and file was evidenced by the fact that the vast majority of strikes carried out during the 1970s were *not* the work of the trade union leadership but rather were initiated by workers at the base. Typically, strikes would erupt spontaneously, staged by workers aggrieved over abusive dismissals or poor wages. Trade union officials would then have to scramble to catch up with events, intervening to mediate the dispute and/or declare the strike legal.[15]

The surge in labor's assertiveness during the 1970s, however, was not solely the consequence of state sponsorship, advertent or inadvertent. Two other factors also fueled labor's militance: blocked wages and changing political conditions.

Save for a brief reprieve in 1965, wages for Tunisian workers had remained largely frozen throughout the first decade and a half of independence. This blockage became increasingly difficult for workers to bear as inflation levels rose (Mahjoub 1978, 559). The freeze on wages proved especially galling, because it persisted during a period of rising prosperity for the country as a whole. Workers balked at being excluded from this general good fortune. The regime's change in rhetoric only fueled workers' impatience. In the past, the regime's collectivist rhetoric had justified wage blockage as part of the common sacrifice Tunisians had to make for the sake of national development. But the regime's new liberal rhetoric no longer cultivated the image of common burden sharing, and workers resisted being singled out to shoulder the cost of development.

The triumph of material interest over self-sacrificing nationalist sentiment within the labor movement was given vivid symbolic expression in the way workers changed their wording of Tunisia's national anthem. As one veteran trade union leader in the mining sector explained to me, during the 1950s and 1960s, striking miners generally draped their collective action with patriotic cloth by singing Tunisia's national anthem during trade union meetings and demonstrations. One phrase from the anthem, "namūtū namūtū, wa-yaḥyā al-waṭan" (we shall die, we shall die, but the homeland will live on!) was especially resonant for trade union activists, since the labor movement had sacrificed so many martyrs to the national cause during the struggle for independence. During the mid-1970s, however, the miners continued to sing the anthem on occasions of collective action but did so with one minor change. The stirring phrase "namūtū namūtū wa-yaḥyā al-waṭan" was altered to "na'ishū, na'ishā, wa-yaḥyā al-waṭan" (we shall live, we shall live, and the homeland shall live on). The alteration signaled the miners' belief that the days of the working class's supreme self-sacrifice for the sake of the homeland were over, and the time had come for workers to "live," that is, to get their fair share of the country's growth (interview, 17 November 1988).

Besides the matter of blocked wages, labor's combativeness during the 1970s was also fueled by changing political conditions. The failure of the regime's etatist development strategy constituted the first publicly acknowledged breach in the "omniscience" of Tunisia's supreme leader. As such, it created a context in which contestation and debate suddenly seemed more legitimate. Many groups jumped at the opportunity to contest, from a "liberal caucus" in the ruling party that lobbied for more intraparty democratization to students who demonstrated for more student union autonomy. This atmosphere created political space for workers to protest long-suffered wage blockage. Further, the trade union movement became a lightning rod for many of the politically discontented who were eager for an institutional base from which to contest the regime (Karoui and Messaoudi 1982; Dellagi 1980). The UGTT was attractive to them because it was relatively well endowed with important political resources: a press, an autonomous financial base, numerous seats in parliament, and an international forum at the ICFTU and the ILO. Many student activists "graduated" from campus politics to trade union politics, especially in the white-collar unions (civil service, education, banks, and Post, Telegraph, and Telephone [PTT]). These unions spearheaded the movement's trend toward radicalization in the 1970s and provided an ideological grounding for the rank and file's increasing militance.

This confluence of conscious state sponsorship, increasing structural strength, general economic prosperity, and brief political opening fostered an upsurge in labor militance that stood in stark contrast to the quietism of the 1960s. The latter is evident from strike statistics for the decade (table 3.2). Strikes proved increasingly frequent and of longer duration

Table 3.2. Industrial Disputes, 1970–1979

Year	Number of Disputes	Workers Involved	Days Lost
1970	25	5,887	6,104
1971	32	2,623	3,587
1972	150	18,458	31,589
1973	409	18,473	49,653
1974	131	21,000	8,197
1975	363	40,671	11,750
1976	372	67,386	27,500
1977	452	88,335	140,201
1978	178	21,433	36,938
1979	240	22,430	35,287

Source: International Labor Office, *Yearbook of Labor Statistics*, 1980.

Table 3.3. Inflation-Adjusted Minimum Wage (SMIG), 1971–1977

Year	Cost of Living	Nominal SMIG	Real SMIG
1971	100	100	100
1974	111.2	125	112.6
1975	121.6	139.4	114.6
1977	136.7	185.6	135.8

Source: Jaziri 1980–81, 29.
Note: Relative values using 1971 as base rate. SMIG stands for Salaire minimum industriel garantié.

during the 1970s. That many of these strikes gripped sensitive nerve points in the Tunisian economy (i.e., the railways, tramways, bakeries, mines, and the PTT) meant they were quickly felt throughout Tunisian society.

The surge of worker militance during the 1970s won the Tunisian working class important gains, especially in the realm of wages. Workers at nearly every level saw their salaries increase. The minimum wage was augmented four times during the seven-year period 1970–77 (compared to only two times during the entire first fourteen years of independence (1956–70). These increases were relatively generous even when adjusted for inflation (table 3.3).

In real terms, then, minimum wage workers enjoyed more than a 35% increase in their wages between 1971 and 1977. The average worker also saw significant salary increases, estimated at somewhere between 23 and 46% in real terms (depending on one's source). Statistics on annual

Table 3.4. Average Annual Salaries in Tunisia, 1970–1977

Year	Declarations to the Caisse Nationale de Sécurité Sociale	Census of Industrial Activities
1970	100	100
1971	100.2	105
1972	100.4	108.8
1973	103	106.5
1974	112.2	113.5
1975	127.1	119.4
1976	139	120.3
1977	146.6	123.6

Source: Romdhane 1981, 445.
Note: Relative values using 1970 as base rate. Salary data excludes civil service workers.

average wage levels for the period reported by two different government sources are presented in table 3.4.

To some extent, these wage gains were facilitated by the "fat years" that Tunisia enjoyed, especially during the first half of the decade. Still, it is doubtful that these concessions would have been forthcoming without labor militance. Respectable growth rates during the 1960s, averaging 5.2% per year in real terms (Elmanoubi 1993, 15), had not translated into commensurate wage gains when labor was quiescent.[16] Moreover, the timing of these wage gains suggests that these raises were the fruit of increased worker agitation. Wage gains tended to follow surges in strike action. For example, the first major increase in the minimum wage came in 1971—only after the country saw a 25-fold increase in strike activity during the previous year. And Prime Minister Nouira's commitment to fathering a "social contract" between business, labor, and the state (that would guarantee "socially just wages for workers") came in July 1973, only after another year in which strike levels rose another 5-fold. The remainder of the decade was punctuated by regular volleys of strike activity followed by wage and contract concessions, until finally, in 1977, the desire for social peace prompted state and business elites to embrace a social pact that introduced the notion of indexing wages to inflation (Jaziri 1980–81, 30–33).[17] Thus, labor disruptiveness did prove effective in eliciting important wage and contract concessions for labor during much of this decade. In retrospect, the material gains won as well as the space permitted for worker activism made this period the "golden years" of trade unionism in independent Tunisia.

Repression, Resurrection, Repression, 1978–1987

For most of the 1970s, then, the state's own economic and political logic helped develop an increasingly assertive, empowered, and financially rewarded working class. The triumph of labor might have continued well into the 1980s had not two other factors intervened. First, a downturn in the economy increasingly put the economic agenda of state and labor at odds. Second, a succession crisis sapped the tolerance of the ruling party elite for trade union autonomy, especially when the union leadership presented itself as a contender for the helm. The persistent assertiveness of the labor movement, itself a consequence of rank and file militance as well as the leadership's political ambition, put the trade union movement on a collision course with the regime. Nearly a decade of UGTT repression ensued, save for a brief reprieve midway, when the regime's need for political allies temporarily outweighed its other concerns.

Tunisia's economic downturn was felt as early as 1977 and only worsened in the mid-1980s. Stagnation in the real value of petroleum production between 1975 and 1978, combined with exceptionally poor rains and poor harvests in 1977, led to a sharp drop in Tunisia's annual growth rate (Central Bank, *Annual Report*, 1977; Central Bank, *Statistiques financières*, November 1977, September 1981). In the 1980s the economy took an even more serious plunge, owing to a succession of poor rains and harvests, in 1982, 1983, and 1986; a decline in world petroleum prices (*halved* in 1986); a decline in tourist revenues due to regional disturbances; and stagnation in worker remittances, because of economic recession in Western Europe (Central Bank, *Annual Report*, 1981–86; Elmanoubi 1993, 94–95). Average annual growth rates dropped from 4.1% in 1977 to 2.8% in real terms between 1982 and 1986, with the years 1982 and 1986 both registering negative growth rates (Central Bank, *Statistiques financières*, September 1987, September 1989). In the context of this shrinking pie, the state's accumulation imperative and labor's distributive imperative came to be seen as zero-sum goals. In addition, the state's economic development strategy, ever more reliant on private-sector led investment, required a context of social peace and distributive restraint; this, too, put labor and the state at odds.

Labor-state relations were further compromised by the regime's declining political self-confidence. The country's sorry economic state certainly played a role, but even more important was the aging of Tunisia's leadership and the succession crisis it sparked. By the mid-1980s, Bourguiba was in his eighties, and the scramble over possible succession made the elite of the ruling party even more suspicious of competing nodes of political autonomy in Tunisian society. Their suspicion was especially aroused by an organization with nationalist credentials, a broad popular base, and a dynamic, ambitious leadership that could credibly claim the national mantle, namely, the UGTT.

Not helping matters was the UGTT's increasingly assertive stance in the public arena, fueled to some extent by the rising militance of the base. The old guard of the UGTT felt forced to embrace this militance for fear of drifting into irrelevance or falling victim to an internal putsch by "young Turks" clustered in the white collar unions. Consequently, the older leadership endorsed an increasing number of strikes mounted by the rank and file. They also invited militant leftists to join the union central and take control of the union paper, *Al-Sha'b*.[18] By the late 1970s, political ambition led union militants to propose that the UGTT form an independent political party to advance the interests of the working class. Union leader Habib Achour began to take provocative steps, such as meeting with declared enemies of the state like Libya's president, Muammar Qaddafi, to assert the UGTT's autonomy in public affairs. The assertiveness of the trade union challenged the hegemony of the party-state and soon provoked the full force of state repression (Kraiem 1980a).

The first act of this repression came in 1977. With unusual violence the state put down a major strike in Ksar Hellal (Tunisia's textile hub), calling in the army to repress the strikers. Soon after, a party activist voiced death threats against UGTT leader Habib Achour. The party created the "Force ouvrière tunisienne," an ultimately ephemeral organization designed to duplicate, if not supplant, the UGTT. It stepped up a media campaign to denounce the trade union but eventually turned to more violent tactics as well, dispatching party thugs to sack UGTT locals across the country. Local police did not intervene. Finally, in early 1978, the party called on the UGTT to hold new elections under the auspices of "neutral" authorities and submit their finances to government control (*AAN*, 1977, 542–44; Kraiem 1980a).

Besieged in this way, the UGTT leadership decided to call a twenty-four-hour general strike. The trade union's goal was to protest the propaganda and violence waged against it as well as assert trade union autonomy. Trade union activists gathered at union locals around the country, and rioting soon erupted in Tunis, Sousse, Sfax, Gafsa, and Tozeur.[19] The rioting provided a pretext for the state to intervene with the army.

In the melee that ensued at least 46 people were killed (nonofficial estimates put the number at somewhere between 150 and 300), and several hundred were wounded. UGTT headquarters in Tunis and in other major cities were occupied by state security forces. Eleven out of thirteen members of the union's executive committee were placed under arrest (including Achour), and hundreds of other union leaders and rank and file members were jailed as well. A state of emergency was declared for the entire republic, and a curfew was imposed on Tunis along with its suburbs (*AAN*, 1978, 411; *Le monde*, 1 January 1978; *ILO-RCFA* 61 [1978]: 163–72). "Jeudi Noir," as that fateful Thursday in January was called, marked a dark turning point in trade union history.

Political subordination of the trade union movement was the regime's primary goal. Within a week of the general strike, the state orchestrated the imposition of a more pliant leadership on the UGTT. A new, provisional executive bureau was appointed, composed of the Destourian party faithful found within the trade union's ranks. The new executive was confirmed by a somewhat irregular trade union congress held a month later.[20]

Tunisian workers branded the members of the new executive *fantoches* (puppets), to be distinguished from the *légitimes* (those legally elected in 1974 and now, for the most part, under arrest). And so began the trade union's decline. With the legitimacy of its leadership in question, the trade union's membership dropped off.[21] Payment of dues fell off as a result, jeopardizing the viability of the union. The government was ultimately forced to provide a direct financial subsidy to the UGTT to ensure the trade union's survival (interview, 16 December 1988). Both the increasing financial dependence of the trade union as well as the fact that the union's leaders were being handpicked by the regime made clear the UGTT's renewed subordination to the party-state.

The sorry state of the UGTT might have persisted had not three factors intervened to amend the political calculations of the regime. These factors heightened the regime's desire for popularly grounded political allies and inspired a brief reversal in its repressive policy toward the union.

First, in January 1980 a sixty-man guerrilla unit of Tunisian nationals, trained in Libya and entering from Algeria, attacked Tunisian army, police, and National Guard posts in the southern town of Gafsa, hoping to spark popular insurrection against the regime. In fact, the raid elicited no popular response in Tunisian society, and the commandos were quickly suppressed by the army. But the raid suggested the waning popular legitimacy of the regime in regions like the underprivileged South and prompted the regime to seek ways to reinforce its popular base.

Second, in 1980 Prime Minister Hedi Nouira fell victim to a stroke and was replaced by a relatively unknown figure, Mohamed Mzali. A secondary-school teacher by profession, Mzali was the political creation of Boruguiba. Mzali realized that he could not survive the machinations of Tunisian politics without an independent base of his own, and so he cast about for a constituency, ultimately settling on the UGTT. Building bridges with the trade union had the potential to provide him with a powerful popular base of support, and this persuaded him to rehabilitate the trade union movement.

Third, contrary to the regime's hope, repression of the UGTT légitimes did not lead to a decline in working class combativeness. Rather, after a brief dip in 1978, strike levels soon regained their high 1970s level, as statistics from the period show (Table 3.5). State elites were committed to restoring social peace to Tunisia, essential as it was to the success of the country's development strategy. To many leaders of the party-state, the best prospects for restoring social peace lay with the resurrection of a legitimate trade union movement that might be able to bring workers under control and deliver popular restraint in exchange for corporatist bargains.

For these reasons, the state briefly sought to restore the UGTT. The party created the National Syndical Commission to oversee the reformation of the UGTT and the election of new UGTT leadership. Because most imprisoned activists were pardoned prior to the election campaign (save for Habib Achour, who remained under house arrest, forbidden any role in public life), the légitime wing was able to win the major share of leadership posts (*Jeune Afrique*, 18 February 1981). In fact, in a striking move for trade union autonomy, the UGTT chose as its new secretary general a trade union activist who had never been a member of the Destour Party.[22]

Table 3.5. Industrial Disputes, 1976–1980

Year	Number of Disputes	Workers Involved	Days Lost
1976	372	53,011	130,378
1977	452	88,335	150,933
1978	178	21,433	36,938
1979	240	22,430	34,287
1980	346	51,027	83,781

Source: Ministry of Social Affairs, internal document.

Besides endorsing the organizational resurrection of the UGTT, the regime also sought to renew its alliance with the trade union movement by granting generous financial concessions to workers. The generosity of these wage concessions was especially evident in setting the official minimum wage, as shown in Table 3.6.

These wage hikes were warranted neither by productivity gains registered by Tunisian workers nor rapid growth in the economy overall. To the contrary, the Tunisian economy registered a negative growth rate (−0.5 in real terms) in 1982, the very same year that Mzali decreed a 32% increase in the minimum wage (Central Bank, *Statistiques financières*, September 1987). Moreover, these wage concessions directly contradicted the stated logic of the regime's own Sixth Plan, which called for annual salary growth not to exceed 17.5% during the plan period (*AAN*, 1982, 659). Rather, the wage gains granted by the regime constituted what one Tunisian economist called a "political wage." They were driven not by economic rationality but by political concerns—Mzali's desire to guarantee social peace and build himself a political constituency in the working class (interview, 12 October 1988).

But this politically driven reconciliation between state and union soon came to an end, largely because the UGTT's resurrection did not accomplish the political goals the state had sought.

First, restoration of the legitimate UGTT leadership did not deliver social peace. Despite the return of the légitimes to trade union leadership, militance on the part of the rank and file remained high, matching and even surpassing the levels of combativeness achieved during the turbulent 1970s (Table 3.7). This rising combativeness, moreover, was not limited to the rank and file. The UGTT leadership proved increasingly willing to support the base's strike initiatives, as evidenced by the growing number

Table 3.6. Minimum Wage (SMIG) Increases, 1980–1983

Year	SMIG (dinars)	Nominal Value of SMIG*	Cost of Living*	Real Value of SMIG*
1980	45.586	100	100	100
1981	55.586	121.9	109.3	111.5
1982	75.586	165.8	133.8	123.9
1983	83.906	184.1	144.5	127.4

Source: Calculated from Central Bank, *Statistiques financières*, 1984; various plans.
*Relative values using 1980 as base rate.

Table 3.7. Industrial Disputes, 1976–1983

Year	Number of Disputes	Workers Involved	Days Lost
1976	372	53,011	130,378
1977	452	88,335	150,933
1978	178	21,433	36,938
1979	240	22,430	34,287
1980	346	51,027	83,781
1981	575	115,528	242,324
1982	530	101,331	187,120
1983	570	132,983	231,959

Source: Ministry of Social Affairs, internal document.

Table 3.8. Number of Strikes, 1980–1983

Year	Strikes with Warning	Strikes without Warning	Total Number of Strikes	Percent with Warning*
1980	16	330	346	5
1981	50	525	575	9
1982	56	474	530	11
1983	86	484	570	15

Source: Ministry of Social Affairs, internal document.
*Percentages are rounded.

of strikes that received the formal sanction of the UGTT central (see Table 3.8). Such formal sanction endowed the strikes with legal status. Strikes were increasingly orchestrated by the union leadership with careful attention to legal forms, specifically the observance of the ten-day warning period. Such support for strike action came in marked contrast to the diffidence trade union elites showed toward much rank and file combativeness during the 1970s.

Second, not only did resurrection of the UGTT not deliver social peace, it also did not secure Mzali's place in politics. To the contrary, restoration of the UGTT fostered the emergence of an important political rival to Mzali, one best positioned to challenge him in the succession crisis. In the mid-1980s, President Bourguiba finally released trade union activist Habib Achour from house arrest. The old trade union lion immediately rejoined UGTT politics and got himself elected president of the union (serving alongside Secretary General Taieb Baccouche). Once in office, Achour set about building his political base in the working class. Given his historic role in the independence struggle and his strong popular base in the UGTT, Achour constituted the most important challenge to Mzali's ultimate hold on power.

Finally, resurrection of the UGTT did not deliver a reliable, loyal social base for the ruling party. If anything, the UGTT leadership was vigilant in asserting its distance and autonomy from the party-state. In 1981, the UGTT's National Council voted to forbid trade union members from holding positions of authority in both the party and the trade union simultaneously (*Le Maghreb*, 5 December 1981). In 1982, the trade union decided not to participate in the government's popular "consultations" over the Sixth Plan (arguing that it had not been consulted early enough to affect the content of the plan), and it instructed its parliamentary deputies to withhold their approval from the plan's ratification at the end of July. Finally, in 1983, the UGTT decided to forgo participation in the government's Social and Economic Council,[23] arguing that a 7 June law reasserting the government's right to designate council members by decree compromised the union's autonomy to an intolerable degree (*L'avenir*, November 1983, 20–21).

But perhaps the most blatant evidence that the UGTT's resurrection would not deliver a loyal base of support to the PSD came once Achour was again securely at the helm of the UGTT. In classically authoritarian fashion, Achour set about dismissing those members of the Executive Bureau most supportive of an alliance between trade union and party. Seven "Frontists" were banished for supporting the formation of the National Front in the 1983 elections. (Achour, still under house arrest at that time, had opposed the creation of such a front.)[24] The dismissal of the Frontists led to a devastating schism in the trade union movement and the rise of a parallel trade union, the UNTT (Union nationale de travailleurs tunisiens).[25] But what was more important, the Frontists' dismissal made clear the UGTT's eagerness to divorce itself from any loyal partnership with the ruling party and, hence, the political unreliability of the trade union to the party-state.

The failure of the UGTT's resurrection to deliver on any of the political goals sought by the party-state put the union on a collision course with the government. This tension was only heightened by the economic difficulties the country faced in the mid-1980s. In this context, generous wage concessions were unlikely to be forthcoming. By 1985, Prime Minister Mzali had announced his intention to hold down wages by linking all future wage augmentations to increases in *productivity* rather than increases in the *cost of living* (a departure from the policy of the 1970s).

Anything less, he argued, would fuel inflation and further degrade the workers' standard of living (*IEA*, no. 144 [April 1985]).

In short, by the mid-1980s, state and union were once again on a collision course, given their contrary economic and political agendas. The years that followed saw a significant resumption of state harassment and repression of the UGTT.

At first, the state limited itself to taking advantage of the internal schism in the trade union movement. Although this schism had not been engineered by the state, as had been true in the case of earlier trade union schism in 1956, it *was* the object of opportunistic exploitation. The state took steps to prop up the renegade UNTT (which supported a closer relation to the party-state), initially through symbolic means (public endorsement of the UNTT by both President Bourguiba and Prime Minister Mzali) (*La presse*, 22 February 1984; *Réalités*, 27 July 1984). Later, financial measures were also taken. In 1984 the state declared its intention to *end the automatic check-off* of 1% of public sector salaries, which had traditionally been turned over to the UGTT's treasury and which had constituted the major share of the UGTT's financial base (*Jeune Afrique économique*, 12 April 1984). Henceforth, workers would have to specify in writing that they wished to designate a portion of their salaries for union dues. In addition, they were required to identify the union they wished to support. This measure weakened the UGTT by undermining its financial foundation at the same time that it gave the UNTT a financial base of its own.

The regime's contraction of trade union rights accelerated in the next few years. In 1984, in the wake of an upsurge of strikes led by the UGTT, the regime prohibited trade union meetings at the workplace (*AAN*, 1984, 991). Later that year, in reaction to heavy strike activity concentrated in the public sector, the regime dismissed more than two thousand civil servants and imprisoned several hundred (*Le monde diplomatique*, December 1985). In 1985 the regime suspended the trade union's journal, *Al-Sha'b*, for six months following its publication of an "offensive" editorial.[26] That same year the regime reiterated its ban on trade union meetings at the workplace and ended any form of check-off for trade union dues.[27] It also voided the system of "syndical detachment," under which the government had paid the salaries of public sector workers elected for permanent assignment to the UGTT.[28] Finally, it sequestered UGTT bank accounts and removed UGTT enterprises (including the Amilcar Hotel and the Insurance Company Al-Ittiḥād) from trade union control. All the while the government-controlled press conducted a propaganda campaign against the UGTT's leadership, accusing it of deviationism, antipatriotism, and corrupt management.

But the state's offensive did not end there. In late 1985 the regime also began to take direct action against UGTT locals, occupying trade union offices in the provinces, locking out and, in many cases, dismissing and/or arresting legitimately elected trade union representatives. These representatives were forcibly replaced with Destourian party loyalists (*Le quotidien de Paris*, 23 January 1986; *Le monde*, 2 October 1985; ILO report 243: 194–95). On 7 November the government placed Habib Achour under house arrest on trumped-up charges.[29] By the end of November, government courts condemned him to a year in prison for mismanagement of a UGTT cooperative. When the trade union movement refused to disavow Achour, the party-state took its harshest move against the UGTT. On 21 January 1986, police forces invaded the UGTT's central headquarters and deposed the trade union's legitimately elected officials. The regime replaced them with "provisional syndical committees" composed of Destourian loyalists, later referred to by the government as the Shurafā or "honorable ones."

The imposition of the Shurafā marked the nadir in trade union history and confirmed the view of many activists that the 1986–88 syndical crisis was more profound (if less bloody) than that of 1978 (interview, 3 November 1988). At least in the 1978 repression, the government had imposed a leadership on the UGTT that possessed legitimate trade union credentials, even if they hailed from the union's Destourian wing. The Shurafā, on the other hand, were Destourian loyalists who lacked any trade union credibility, and their imposition turned the UGTT into "a parody of a union" (*Réalités*, 31 January 1986). The imposition of this leadership, along with the dismissal and arrest of many trade union activists, the prohibition of trade union meetings at the workplace, and the dismantling of the trade union's financial base dealt a fatal blow to the institutional underpinnings of trade union autonomy and guaranteed the movement's near-complete emasculation.

Over the next two years the government made a few attempts to bolster the credibility of the union. It organized an extraordinary national trade union congress to confirm the installation of the Shurafā with the hopes of giving this leadership the appearance of popular election rather than government appointment. It later engineered the reunification of the UGTT and the UNTT, restoring to the movement "one powerful, united, and independent trade union organization which combines all forces and trade unionists of good will" (ILO, report 246, 107). Nevertheless, the

Table 3.9. Number of Strikes, 1984–1987

Year	Strikes with Authorization	Strikes without Authorization	Total Number of Strikes	Percent with Authorization*
1984	142	403	545	26
1985	46	267	391	12
1986	0	170	170	0
1987	15	226	241	6

Source: Ministry of Affairs, internal document.
*Percentages are rounded.

Table 3.10. Minimum Wage (SMIG) Increases, 1984–1987

Year	SMIG (dinars)	Nominal Value of SMIG*	Cost of Living*	Real Value of SMIG*
1984	83.906	100	100	100
1985	83.906	100	107.8	92.8
1986	93.066	110.9	114	97.3
1987	105.040	125.2	122.2	102.4

Source: Calculations based on Central Bank, Statistiques financières, 1988, various plans.
*Relative values based on 1984 as base rate.

emasculation and subordination of the trade union movement remained clear. Leadership of the movement continued to be chosen by the party-state.[30] And the state-dominated trade union maintained a near-categorical refusal to sanction strikes. The latter is evident from the number of strikes the trade union central authorized during 1986–87 (Table 3.9). The emasculation of the trade union movement permitted the state to persist in its policy of wage blockage. The official minimum wage stagnated in real terms throughout this period (Table 3.10). As a result, the trade union rank and file continued to feel estranged from the official trade union. Workers around the country organized petitions rejecting the Shurafā and declaring their loyalty to their properly elected representatives (Réalités, 25 April 1986). Deposed leaders from the Sixteenth Congress continued to organize covertly, lodging complaints with the ILO and staging a "shadow" congress of legitimate trade union leaders to protest the government's treatment of the movement (Jeune Afrique, 25 February 1987). But the government responded to such activism with further repression. By February 1987, more than 350 trade union activists had been dismissed from their jobs as punishment for syndical activities (*Jeune Afrique*, 25 February 1987). The state confiscated the passports of many union activists and subjected them to a multitude of petty harassments. By late 1987, then, the future for autonomous trade union activity appeared extremely bleak.

Controlled Cooperation, 1988–mid-1990s

The year 1987 marked the beginning of a new era in Tunisia. In November Bourguiba was deposed on the grounds of senility and replaced by Zine Abdine Ben Ali. Unfortunately, the factors that fueled confrontation between the state and the UGTT during the decade of repression (1978–87) did not vanish with the removal of Bourguiba. To the contrary, the economic and political agenda of Ben Ali's new regime suggested persistent collision between state and union and made continued repression of the UGTT seem all but inevitable. Contrary to expectation, however, the UGTT enjoyed a surprising resurrection. In somewhat improbable fashion, the state itself took the initiative to restore the UGTT, driven as it was by new political concerns. Thus, just when the state's economic and political logic seemed to spell the emasculation of the UGTT, the trade union movement received a new lease on life, thanks to the state's own hand.

The UGTT's restoration was improbable for several reasons. First, the political logic of the state under Ben Ali continued to be at odds with the UGTT's ambition to assert itself as an autonomous force on Tunisia's political stage. Although Ben Ali came to power on a wave of promises to democratize and liberalize Tunisian politics, within a short time of assuming office he proved just as enthusiastic as his predecessor about establishing uncontested control of Tunisia's political helm. Twenty years in the security apparatus had not cultivated an abiding appreciation of free-wheeling contestation in Ben Ali. Rather, in the name of order, he was soon engineering a determined retreat from the cautious political opening he began in 1987 (Gasiorowski 1992; Bellin 1993). All nodes of autonomous contestation in society were crushed; piously promised civil liberties were repudiated. None of this augured well for the UGTT, long the most independent-minded contestatory force in Tunisian society and one that relied on protected civil liberties (e.g., freedom of association) for its power and influence.

The economic logic of the state was equally inauspicious for organized labor. As described in chapter 1, the state had embraced a more market-

driven strategy of capitalist industrialization in 1986, in hopes of sur-
mounting fiscal and foreign exchange crisis. As part of this strategy, the
state committed itself to subjecting ever-larger portions of the economy
to the logic of the market, shrinking the bloated public sector, and relying
more heavily on private sector forces, foreign and domestic, to drive economic growth. The strategy put even more emphasis on the importance
of social peace and wage restraint as two preconditions for growth, since
the strategy's success rested, to a large degree, on the country's capacity
to attract private investment. The logic of this strategy thus collided
with the goals of organized labor, suggesting the likelihood of labor's
continued repression.

Furthermore, the state's choice of development strategy worked to
weaken labor structurally. During the early decades of independence
the state's development strategy (public sector–led industrialization) had
strengthened the position of labor by fostering the growth, concentration, and generational depth of the working class. But with the embrace
of ever more market-driven capitalist industrialization, the state espoused
measures that potentially undermined the structural position of organized
labor. Emphasis on private sector–led growth meant that industrial growth
tended to be centered in firms that were smaller and more scattered than
had been the case under state-led growth; this led to the dispersion
and deconcentration of workers, a hindrance to workers' organization.
Reliance on international investment to spur growth forced Tunisian
workers to compete for potential investors with wage-poor countries in
Asia and Eastern Europe, a strategy that exerted significant downward
pressure on wages. Finally, the state's intention to contract the public
sector threatened to shrink those very enterprises and agencies where the
UGTT had always found its broadest base. In short, the state's new economic agenda put the interests of labor and state at increasing odds at the
same time as it compromised the structural underpinnings of labor's
strength. The state's economic and political ambitions suggested that
repression and emasculation of the trade union movement would
continue.

But contrary to expectation, these years actually saw the resurrection
of the UGTT, thanks to the state's own initiative. In 1988, President Ben
Ali committed himself to the restoration of a legitimate, representative
trade union movement in Tunisia. To this end he freed all trade union
activists from jail, decreeing a general amnesty for all persons sentenced
for offenses committed while engaged in trade union activism. He expe-
dited the reinstatement of *all public sector* workers dismissed from their

jobs for syndical reasons;[31] he also encouraged the private sector to reinstate their activists. Most important, he oversaw the organization of new
trade union elections at the local, regional, and national level that were
conducted, by and large, in a free and fair fashion.[32] These elections
handed large victories to activists from the old légitime wing of the union
(*Le Maghreb*, 2 December 1988) and thus restored legitimate leadership
to the UGTT.[33] In the next two years, the president rescinded the ruling
that had prohibited trade union meetings at the workplace, restored trade
union property (such as the Amilcar Hotel and the Al-Ittiḥād Insurance
Company), cancelled some $5 million in UGTT debt, and once again
permitted publication of the UGTT's weekly newspaper, *Al-Sha'b* (U.S.
Dept. of Labor, *Foreign Labor Trends: Tunisia*, 1989, 4; 1991, 4). Moreover, the regime brought the UGTT back into policy discussions, expanding trade union representation on the advisory Economic and Social
Council, and calling on the UGTT to participate in extensive negotiations
to redefine the collective conventions that govern wages and working conditions in much of the Tunisian economy (*Foreign Labor Trends: Tunisia*,
1991, 4). In this way, by the early 1990s, the UGTT had been restored
to a place of influence on the Tunisian political scene.

How can this restoration of the UGTT at the state's initiative be
explained? Clearly, the economic agenda of the state still called for the
restraint of the trade union movement. Rather, it is the political logic of
the regime that explains state support for revival of the UGTT at that
time. The initial drive for resurrecting the UGTT came from Ben Ali's
brief flirtation with democratic reform. The former army general came to
power without any substantial popular base of his own. To build support
for his new regime he draped his rise to power with the mantle of democratization. Restoring syndical rights to the country's legitimate trade
union was in keeping with this general strategy. But, as described above,
the president's commitment to democratization proved short-lived. What
must be explained, then, is why the regime *persisted* in sustaining and
endorsing a "legitimate" UGTT, even once its moment of democratic
enthusiasm had passed.

Again, the best explanation focuses on the political logic of the regime
and specifically, the new political challenges it faced. From the moment
Ben Ali came to power, the strongest threat to his regime was posed
by Islamist forces. Although Islamist movements had been virtually
insignificant as a political force in Tunisia during the early decades of political independence, they began to gather steam in the wake of the Iranian
revolution. During the late 1970s and early 1980s they built a broad base

of support in Tunisian society by playing on popular alienation from the state elite's Europhilic and Francophone cultural orientation. The Islamists also exploited popular disaffection with the regime's economic performance, specifically, the persistence of poverty and blocked career opportunities that plagued many in society. The Islamists soon began to pose a significant threat to the hegemony of the Destourian regime (Burgat 1988). In fact, it was Bourguiba's continued tangling with the Islamists during the 1980s that most jeopardized the "old combatant's" hold on power. And it was an imprudent clash over Islamists that proved most immediately responsible for Bourguiba's deposal and Ben Ali's rise to the presidency (Hermassi 1989, 300; Bellin 1995, 133). Thus, when Ben Ali came to power, the Islamists constituted an important force on the Tunisian political scene. By this time the Islamist movement could count among its many strengths a broad popular base, a widely read journal (15/21); a charismatic leader, Rachid Ghannouchi; and an effective organizational structure, complete with a clandestine coercive apparatus (Burgat 1988; Hermassi 1989).

Ben Ali clearly felt threatened by the Islamist challenge but was evasive in his early treatment of them. In his first years in office he hinted at the possible inclusion of Islamists in his new regime. But by 1989 the president chose to deny the leading Islamist movement legal status as a political party, thereby officially excluding them from the political game. Exclusion gave way to "open warfare" between Islamists and the regime. Leading Islamists denounced Ben Ali, and the most extreme wings of the Islamist movement organized violent attacks against the government. The latter, for its part, began a vigorous campaign of repression against Islamists. This campaign involved mass arrests of Islamists, expulsion of some of the movements leading figures, and general harassment of citizens visibly supportive of the movement.

But Ben Ali's strategy to combat the Islamists did not focus on repression alone. Among his other tactics was the cultivation of support in popular movements likely to be free from Islamist influence. This logic explains Ben Ali's support for the UGTT's restoration. Like labor movements elsewhere in the Middle East (e.g., in Egypt, Turkey, and Syria), the UGTT had remained largely secular in orientation and less taken with Islamist enthusiasm than most other associations in civil society. Certainly, Islamist sentiment had made some inroads into the trade union movement.[34] But by and large the Islamists' influence in the trade union remained relatively contained.[35] In the UGTT, then, Ben Ali saw the possibility of cultivating a popular ally that might countervail the Islamist threat. It was this political logic that drove the state's resurrection of the UGTT. As one perceptive observer noted, the Islamist movement is, in many ways, the UGTT's "most strategic ally" (Alexander 1996, 307) because its persistence explains the state's continued support for the trade union movement.[36]

Of course, there is no need to exaggerate the resurrection of the UGTT under Ben Ali's regime. As ever, the Tunisian state is still driven by its political goal of political dominion over Tunisian society, and so it has not reinstated many of the syndical rights essential to trade union independence and combativeness. For example, Ben Ali's regime did not restore the system of automatic check-off that in the past had guaranteed the UGTT 1% of the salaries of nearly all public sector workers. Instead, the burden shifted to workers willing to take the initiative to declare their membership and commitment to paying union dues in writing. In addition, the regime set a ceiling on fees that might be transferred through check-off at twelve dinars per year in the public sector and six dinars a year in the private sector (interviews, labor activists, 10 December 1996, 12 December 1996. This reduction in transferable dues (combined with falling membership levels) has led to a serious weakening in the financial base of the union.[37] Today, the UGTT is increasingly dependent on subsidies from the state (reputed to be 100–120,000 dinars per month, paid directly to the Executive Bureau by the CNSS (Caisse nationale de sécurité sociale) (interview, labor activist, 18 December 1996), and this financial reliance clearly compromises the trade union's autonomy.

Besides undermining the financial base of the union, the state took other steps to rein in the UGTT. For example, though the state lifted its ban on union meetings at the workplace in 1989, it did not endorse this practice as a syndical right. Instead, holding such meetings remained a matter of the "rapport des forces" between managers and workers in each sector and enterprise, making activism at the level of the base more difficult to organize (interview, labor activist, December 1996). In addition, the state regularly interfered in local and regional elections, consulting with UGTT leaders in their composition of candidate lists and "coincidentally" arresting activists (primarily Islamists but also leftists) at election time to prevent the election of the latter to office (interview, labor activist, August 1993; interview, U.S. Dept. of Labor attaché, 3 August 1993). The state also overlooked the flouting of democratic procedure by the top UGTT leadership when this meant the removal of independent-minded activists from the union;[38] it also actively harassed labor activists who sought to establish independent labor organizations.[39] Finally, the regime never unequivocally endorsed civil liberties, such as freedom of speech and association—liberties that are essential to the vitality of the trade union movement.

For this reason, many old-guard trade union activists complained that the UGTT in the mid-1990s had lost its militance of old. Instead, they argued that its leadership had succumbed to co-optation by the state. But even if the state's controlling measures had prevented the UGTT from being the focal point of contestation, as it had been in the 1970s, the UGTT's persistent contribution as defender of the interests of Tunisian workers remains undeniable. Because President Ben Ali proved eager to court the support of the UGTT (all in the name of "social stability"), workers gained a number of important victories, most notably regular wage increases granted throughout 1990–96, despite significant economic pressures to withhold these raises. In short, the UGTT had been organizationally restored in Tunisia, endowed with a largely legitimate trade union leadership and empowered, within limits, to defend the interests of working people in Tunisia. This resurrection, moreover, was the state's own work, carried out at the state's own initiative, a consequence of the state's own political logic.

Conclusion

Organized labor was not a state-created constituency in Tunisia, as was private sector industry; the trade union movement preceded the creation of an independent state in Tunisia and ultimately played a central role in the creation of the state itself. Nevertheless, once independence was achieved, the state did play a dramatic role in shaping the development of organized labor, though the changing political and economic logic of the state often shaped labor's fortunes in conflicting ways. During the early decades of independence, the state's political logic drove it to subordinate the UGTT politically, purging its independent-minded leaders and repressing its activists. At the same time, the state's economic development policies worked to bolster the depth, concentration, and solidarity of the working class in ways that would foster labor's militance and defiant independence. During later decades, the economic development strategy of the state, specifically its emphasis on private sector–led, market-driven, internationally integrated development worked to undermine the structural position of labor. But surprisingly, at labor's weakest moment, the state stepped in to resurrect the trade union movement, to establish a popular ally that might serve as counterpoise to the political threat presented by the Islamists. In short, throughout the five decades since independence, the fortunes of organized labor in Tunisia have been shaped in conflicting ways by the state, with its revival today in large part a consequence of the state's own strategy for political survival. Whether this social force has proven able to carve out sufficient power and autonomy to shape the state's policy-making process is another matter, as chapter 4 demonstrates.

CHAPTER 4

Influence under Constraint: The Trajectory of Labor's Power and Autonomy

Can labor carve out policy influence in the context of a checkered alliance? Does the project of sponsored industrialization reinforce labor's position to the point of eroding the state's capacity to dictate policy unilaterally?

Clearly, the relationship between the state's developmental project and labor's influence is less triumphal than is the case with capital. A switch in the state's developmental strategy, specifically from inward-focused, public sector–led industrialization to export-oriented, private sector–led growth, can chisel away at the structural underpinnings of labor's power. And the collective, public nature of labor's power makes it more subject to state discretion, undermining labor's autonomy. Still, state sponsorship of labor in the early stages of development can create a lasting cultural and institutional legacy that persists even after the conditions that originally generated it have changed. Moreover, the dual nature of labor's power assures workers a measure of influence even when their political alliance with the state is strained. These factors, together with the state's evolving political needs, can spell significant influence for labor in the shaping of public policy.

Chapter 4 elaborates this argument. The chapter begins with a brief discussion of the dual sources of labor's power and the special challenges that labor faces in preserving its autonomy. The chapter then turns to the Tunisian case, exploring the trajectory of labor's power and autonomy in the context of state-sponsored industrialization. Finally, the chapter explores the influence labor has been able to exercise over public policy. In Tunisia, labor, like capital, personifies the state's developmental paradox—a social force nurtured by the state's own logic that ultimately erodes the unilateral power of that state.

Power

What is the source of labor's power? Private sector industrialists are said to command three routes to power: the capacity to provide or withhold investment capital, the capacity to control cultural institutions that shape society's preferences, and the capacity to influence government operations through campaign financing, office holding, and social proximity to public officials. Labor typically commands two. S. E. Finer writes that labor's power derives primarily from its capacity to vote and its capacity to disrupt (Finer 1973). Both routes, in combination or individually, help workers impose their preferences on the state and state policy.

Finer's analysis derives from his work on organized labor in Western democracies. Extrapolating this analysis to less-developed countries requires some adjustment, especially with regard to the power that labor derives from the capacity to vote. In many LDCs the vote is a less compelling source of power for labor both because the organized working class is relatively small (it does not command the numbers that might make its voice in elections decisive) and because the overarching political system may be less than democratic, making the control of votes less decisive in shaping the fate of a regime. Nevertheless, labor can still exercise political leverage in this context, thanks to its capacity to deliver organized popular support to the regime (e.g., through supportive rallies and demonstrations). Both the regime's need for populist legitimation as well as organized labor's special capacity to deliver it endow workers with a key source of power even where the regime is less than democratic and workers' numbers are proportionally small.

Besides this source of "political power," labor also derives power from its capacity to organize disruptive collective action. Typically, labor's disruptive repertoire includes strikes, go-slows, and lock-outs. The power of this repertoire is most enhanced when organized labor dominates sectors that are indispensable to the economy. Where labor can organize disruptions in infrastructural sectors such as transport (or in export-oriented industries in countries where hard currency is in short supply), its preferences are likely to carry most weight with the regime.

Labor's capacity for disruption is shaped by its militance and sense of collective solidarity. The factors that shape this capacity have been the subject of much analysis. They include structural variables in the economy, statist variables, institutional variables, leadership, and culture. To assess the impact that state-sponsored industrialization might have on labor's power, we must analyze its impact on these intervening variables. A brief account of each variable follows.

Structural Variables

Without lapsing into vulgar economism or mechanistic determinism, it is possible to argue that structural variables in the economy, such as employment levels and occupational structure, shape the mind set and behavior of working people. Although consciousness and combativeness should not be deduced unproblematically from the structural position of workers, since structural factors do not constitute a *sufficient* condition for the development of working class consciousness, they nevertheless constitute a necessary or at least *highly facilitating* condition for the emergence of such consciousness (Lockman 1991, 12). With that proviso in mind, one can identify four structural factors that condition labor militance.

The *level of worker concentration* is an important factor that conditions labor's solidarity and militance. The concentration of workers in ever-larger factories nurtures solidarity and militance, so much so that Marx predicated on it the rise of a revolutionary working class movement. By contrast, small-sized enterprises retard its development in at least three ways. Small enterprises often sustain a "family feeling" between workers and owners, permitting employers to maintain a paternalistic relationship with their employees and blunting a sense of alienation and class conflict between them (Kerr et al. 1960, 150; Zakarya 1977). Small enterprises tend to individualize conflict with employers, since the conflicts are not corroborated by replication in large numbers, a condition that undermines workers' militance. Finally, workers in small firms are hobbled by their expendability (a striking work force of ten is much more easily replaced than one of ten thousand), and this too discourages the combativeness of workers.

Labor scarcity is another structural variable that conditions labor's consciousness and behavior. Again, Marx anticipated the importance of this factor, pointing to the debilitating impact that a "reserve army of the unemployed" had on efforts to improve conditions for the working class. Indeed, working class power has historically been associated with the attenuation of this reserve army; workers' greatest gains have been made in the context of full employment (Panitch 1981). With replacement workers scarce (and hence costly), workers face less risk of dismissal for misconduct. In this way, one of the most important bridles on working class militance is weakened.

The *skill level* of the workforce is a third variable that conditions labor's capacity for collective action and combativeness. Where workers are skilled, their replacement costs are high, making employers loath to dismiss them. The extra measure of job security enjoyed by skilled workers makes militancy less risky and hence more likely (Vellinga 1980, 328).[1]

Finally, labor's solidarity and militance is conditioned by the *workers' commitment to the labor force*. Where such commitment is temporary, as in the case of the "birds of passage" studied by Michael Piore (1979) or the "part-time proletariat" studied by Gates (1979), the hopes for developing organized solidarity are slim.[2] Temporary workers lack the time commitment to their jobs necessary to justify the sacrifices demanded by union organizing. These workers are also more likely to put up with conditions of work and pay that a long-term labor force would not tolerate (Arrighi and Silver 1984, 196).[3]

Structural variables like concentration, scarcity, skill level, and workforce commitment tend to be associated in predictable ways with different strategies of industrialization. Some scholars thus link labor's capacity for militance and mobilization with choice of development strategy. For example, a strategy that emphasizes the development of heavy and consumer durable industries, such as that adopted by Brazil and South Africa in the 1970s and 1980s, is said to "manufacture militance" because of those sectors' heavy reliance on *skilled and semi-skilled workers* and the *shortage* of skilled workers that results from their rapid growth (Seidman 1994). Similarly, an export-oriented strategy of industrialization, as opposed to an import-substituting strategy, is said to retard militance because it universalizes the "reserve army" to worldwide proportions and because, historically at least, this strategy has been focused on the development of light consumer industries that employ *low-skilled* workers (Deyo 1984). Identifying a country's choice of development strategy can go far in predicting the militance, solidarity, and hence power that labor commands.[4]

Statist Variables

Besides structural variables in the economy, the character of the state and its institutions also plays a central role in structuring class formation and interclass relations (Evans, Rueschemeyer, and Skocpol 1985). Most important, the state shapes labor's capacity for collective action and combativeness by defining the legal context in which workers operate (Cohen 1989). This legal context, also known as the "labor regime," determines whether workers enjoy the right to organize, to bargain collectively for wages, and to carry out strikes. Analyzing the content of labor legislation thus offers key insight into the state's role in shaping the position of labor. Equally important is an analysis of the state's *application* of this legislation, that is, the degree to which the state actually abides by its own legal codes (Collier and Collier 1979, 969–70).

Leadership, Culture, and Trade Union Institutions

Much of the comparative literature on labor focuses on the role that labor leadership, working class culture, and the organizational structure of the labor movement play in shaping labor's capacity for collective combativeness. Labor leadership, depending on its dynamism and political autonomy, can stir or suppress workers' impulse to militance. Family structure, religion, art, and other means of "discursive contestation" shape, express, reinforce, and/or undermine working class consciousness (Sofer 1980, 175; Lockman 1991, 17). The organizational structure of the trade union movement, specifically the degree to which it is centralized or decentralized, democratically organized or not, financed from above or below, shapes the degree to which the trade union will be responsive to the concerns of the rank and file and willing to embrace and/or mobilize their discontent (Bates 1971; Sandbrook and Cohen 1972; Lipset, Trow, and Coleman 1956).

Autonomy

Power, whether derived from the capacity to deliver political legitimation or the capacity to disrupt, is one factor that shapes labor's ability to impose its preferences on the state. Autonomy is another. As in the case of capital, labor's ability to conduct itself independently in the political arena turns on the degree to which its well-being is beholden to the good-will of the state. In contrast to capital, labor's well-being proves to be doubly vulnerable to state discretion, both because of the economic logic of the developmental state and because of the public nature of labor's route to power.

The central role played by the developmental state in the economy significantly constrains labor's autonomy. Often the state serves simulta-neously as employer, distributor, arbiter, and adjudicator of the working class. The state may be the largest single employer in the country. State-led wage commissions may set wage scales. State-led labor boards may rule on the fairness of contracts and arbitrate labor disputes. State labor inspectors enforce negotiated contracts and labor law. This dependence on the state's goodwill encourages labor leaders to embrace a measure of voluntary restraint in their conduct of labor activism. They have an incen-tive to renounce combativeness for the sake of staying in the state's good graces.

The embrace of more market-driven development strategies does not necessarily remedy this constraint on labor's autonomy (again, in contrast to the case of capital). For although a market-driven strategy might con-tract the state's role as economic entrepreneur, it is less likely to reduce the state's role as adjudicator, enforcer, and regulator of labor's rights. Furthermore, the embrace of market-driven strategies often compromises the structural underpinnings of labor's strength by concentrating growth in precisely those sectors where labor is dispersed, poorly skilled, and less committed to the labor force.[5] Under these conditions labor is likely to look to state intervention to compensate for its own weakness and thus becomes even more dependent on the state's goodwill to protect its inter-ests (Ahmed 1966, 146–47; Roddick 1980, 249; Petras and Engbarth 1988, 104).

But labor's autonomy is also vulnerable to more constraint due to the public nature of labor's route to power. In contrast to capital, whose power is exercised through activities that are primarily private (the deci-sion to invest or not, to run for office or not, to hobnob with public officials or not), labor's means to power is much more public—the con-sequence of workers' capacity to organize collectively in the public arena. As such, labor's power is uniquely hostage to state tolerance and the state's willingness to grant labor political space to organize. Is freedom of asso-ciation guaranteed? Is collective bargaining a legal right? Especially where democratic institutions are absent, the state may enjoy a fair amount of discretion in its embrace and enforcement of such collective rights.

Relationship between Autonomy and Power

Even in the face of compromised autonomy, labor can still exercise power over the state. The explanation lies in the multiplicity of the routes to power enjoyed by this, and other, social forces. The importance of multiple routes to power has already been suggested in our discussion of capital and the case of the automotive industry. Companies like Chrysler exercised significant political influence in the United States even though their economic well-being was long dependent on government subsidies and protection. While such dependence compromised the companies' structural clout, their continued capacity to undertake media campaigns, finance political parties, and hobnob with socially proximate public officials assured them continued influence over government policy. Similarly, in the case of labor, the fact that workers command two routes to power assures them influence even when dependence compromises one of them. If lack of autonomy undermines workers' capacity to disrupt, at least they still retain the leverage that comes from the capacity to deliver organized popular support to the regime. In this way even highly dependent labor unions can win substantial concessions from the state, at least so long as the state values the union's political alliance. The impressive benefits enjoyed by organized labor in Mexico for much of the twentieth century (despite the unions' corporatist dependence on the state) constitute just one clear case of this phenomenon.

Labor can exercise political power even in the face of compromised autonomy. But as in the case of industrialists, organized labor is best positioned to impose its preferences on the state when it enjoys the concatenation of both these properties rather than endowment with just one. To assess the trajectory of labor's influence over state policy, both properties must be evaluated independently.

Evolving Power of Organized Labor in Tunisia

The trajectory of labor's power in Tunisia has not been unilinear. The state's strategy of sponsored industrialization has fostered some conditions that favor labor's power but has undermined others. Its industrialization strategy authored the *structural* conditions for labor's militance, especially when this strategy was inwardly focused and public sector led. However, once the state switched to a more export-oriented, private sector–led approach, the strategy of industrialization chiseled away at the structural foundation for labor's militance. The developmental logic of the state led to gradual liberalization of the state's labor code, enlarging the space for legal collective action by labor. But implementation of this code by the state proved increasingly spotty as economic conditions (not to mention high politics) put the state's agenda progressively at odds with labor's ambition. The state's developmental projects helped build the foundations for a culture of labor solidarity. But it had indifferent impact on the character of trade union leadership and institutions. Overall, the state's embrace of sponsored industrialization nurtured labor's militance and solidarity, especially in its early stages. But even when the state switched to a more market-driven, externally oriented strategy of development, the imperative of this new strategy for social peace and the heightened need it generated in the state for political allies reinforced labor's power and influence in the public arena.

Structural Variables in Tunisia

Tunisia's embrace of state-sponsored industrialization during the early decades of independence created structural conditions conducive to the development of working class solidarity and combativeness. Central to the state's strategy at this time was the creation of large, primarily import-substituting public enterprises in industrializing industries that were to intended to serve as poles of development for the national economy. Especially during the Ben Salah period (1962–69), the state focused on creating huge industrial units in heavy industry and consumer durables, such as the El-Fouledh complex (steel) in Bizerte, the STIA (automobile assembly) in Sousse, and the ICM (basic chemicals) in Gabes. Under the state's stimulus, the size of the industrial working class mushroomed, growing from somewhere under 100,000 in the early 1960s to 188,000 in 1971 and then to 343,000 in 1982 (Zeghidi 1990, 20).[6] The creation of large industrial enterprises led to the dramatic concentration of workers in the industrial poles of Bizerte, Gabes, and Sousse. The establishment of these poles served to anchor permanent working class communities that were soon two, even three generations deep (Bedaoui 1986). In short, Tunisia's embrace of state-led, import-substituting industrialization nurtured the size, concentration, and commitment of the labor force, all of which fostered working class solidarity and combativeness. This burgeoning solidarity and combativeness was given concrete expression in the explosion of strike activity that marked the 1970s. That this militance was driven by the rank and file (often despite opposition from the trade union's leadership) stands as further proof that combativeness and solidarity had taken root at the very base of the working class and was not merely an artifact of passing elite politics.[7]

By contrast, the development strategy proclaimed by the state in the early 1970s, and most enthusiastically implemented in the 1980s and 1990s, led to a shift in the structural conditions governing labor. First, the state's decision to transfer responsibility for the country's industrialization away from public enterprise and into the hands of the private sector spelled the decreasing concentration of workers in the workplace. Private sector enterprises in Tunisia tended to be smaller than public sector firms, thanks to both the smaller reserves of start-up capital available to private entrepreneurs and the strategic calculation on the part of these entrepreneurs that smaller firm size might better serve their economic and political interests.[8] In addition, the new private firms tended to be increasingly dispersed geographically as an ever-larger number of private entrepreneurs set up small factories in the countryside, attracted by the prospect of a docile, disconnected workforce as well as by governmental inducements to develop employment opportunities in rural areas.[9]

Second, the state's embrace of a market-driven approach led its industrialization strategy to be not only increasingly export-oriented (given the small size of Tunisia's domestic market) but also increasingly focused on the development of light, labor-intensive, low-tech industries (e.g., textiles and electronics assembly). The strategy intended to exploit Tunisia's comparative advantage in abundant, lower-cost labor (lower cost at least in comparison to the price of labor in Tunisia's targeted West European markets). As a consequence, the Tunisian state did not follow the path of large NICs like South Africa and Brazil, that is, it did not focus on developing heavy and consumer durables industries that utilize increasing numbers of skilled and semiskilled workers.

Third, an industrialization strategy that relied on low cost, low-skilled labor led industrialists to value labor discipline and docility over long-term job commitment on the part of their workforce. As a result, entrepreneurs in such export-oriented industries as textiles and electronics assembly preferred to recruit the lion's share of their workers from among young female workers "in the interlude between childhood and marriage" (Birks 1980, 271).[10] Hence, it is no surprise that the national population survey conducted in 1989 found that women constituted 76.5% of all workers in the textiles/leather sector and that 75% of these women were under the age of twenty-five (National Institute of Statistics 1989, 119, 390).

Zeghidi found that 55% of these women were also unmarried (Zeghidi 1990, 23).[11] As one trade union organizer explained, these workers are extremely difficult to organize, since they lack any long-term commitment to their jobs and "are in this to build their trousseaus" or, at most, to supplement their family's income on the occasion of a special event or crisis (interview, 21 November 1988). Investors seemed to prefer young female workers for this very reason: they were believed to be more docile than men.

Of course, none of this suggested the complete structural undoing of labor in Tunisia. Workers in many sectors of the economy (e.g., metallurgy, chemicals) remained highly concentrated, highly skilled, and deeply committed to the workforce. In these sectors, as well as in certain non-tradeable sectors like transportation and banking, the structural conditions for worker solidarity and militance remained strong. Nevertheless, the state's choice of development strategy meant that the fastest-growing sectors of the economy would be precisely those sectors where workers were likely to be dispersed, low skilled, and less than wholly committed to the workforce. In addition, the continued wage pressure implied by Tunisia's progressive integration into the world economy,[12] along with continued high levels of unemployment and underemployment in the country,[13] spelled structural conditions that curbed workers' militance and compromised their propensity for collective action. Thus, while this strategy might not utterly disempower organized labor, the anticipated trajectory of growth would clearly chisel away at labor's structural position.[14]

Statist Variables

Tunisia's labor regime had a mixed impact on the development of labor's power. In purely textual terms, the country's labor code is relatively liberal, at least by the standards of the region. The state endorsed the principle of "syndical rights" from the moment of independence and progressively expanded these rights over time, spurred in part by its own developmental logic. In terms of implementation, however, the state's performance has been less sanguine. The state has regularly violated its laws whenever economic constraint and/or high politics put its goals at serious odds with labor's agenda. Overall, the state's labor regime has had enormous if variable impact on labor's capacity for combativeness and collective actions. On the one hand, the liberal code and the state's relative adherence to it during the first two decades of independence built the foundation for a large and active trade union movement. On the other hand, the state's routine violations of the code in the late 1970s through the late 1980s chiseled away at the edifice of the UGTT, leaving it much more diminished and tentative by the 1990s.[15]

Textually speaking, Tunisia's labor code has gone through three stages. In its first stage, at independence, the regime endorsed syndical rights, but only in the vaguest of terms. The new constitution *did* contain an article asserting that "syndical rights would be guaranteed." And the state *did* ratify two ILO conventions (nos. 87 and 98) in 1957 affirming the protection of syndical liberties as well as workers' right to negotiate collectively. In 1959, moreover, the government revised the old colonial law that had governed syndical life in Tunisia, ending the government's right to dissolve trade unions by administrative fiat. But many basic rights were still denied to labor. Workers did not have the right to strike,[16] nor were they permitted to bargain collectively for wages.[17]

The second stage of Tunisia's labor regime came in 1966, when the state enacted a full-fledged labor code for the first time. This law explicitly guaranteed workers the freedom to form occupational associations for the sake of defending workers' economic and social interests. It established an exceptionally liberal protocol for the creation of trade unions.[18] It required that workers be represented collectively in all firms with more than twenty employees (though no provisions were made for smaller firms). It provided explicit protection for trade union activism, forbidding employers to penalize workers for trade union membership and threatening employers with fines should they dismiss workers "abusively" (i.e., for reasons of trade union activism). And, finally, it endorsed labor's right to strike. Nevertheless, the labor code still fell short in two important ways. First, it hedged workers' right to strike with a variety of bureaucratic constraints. These constraints were not insubstantial;[19] failure to respect them deemed a strike illegal, punishable by serious fines and imprisonment.[20] Second, the code continued to withhold from workers the right to bargain collectively for wages.

The third stage in Tunisia's labor regime came in 1973. Here it was the developmental logic of the state, and specifically Prime Minister Nouira's decision to abandon an etatist development strategy in favor of a more liberal one, that spelled the liberalization of the labor regime. Nouira's desire for a credible bargaining partner led the state to endorse labor's right to collective wage bargaining in 1973. The General Collective Agreement effected that year decreed that wages would henceforth be set "by common agreement." A tripartite commission composed of representatives of business, labor, and the state was established to determine the official minimum wage. Similar committees were established to set wage ladders above the minimum wage, on a sector-wide basis. At the same time that the state made this concession, however, it also imposed new constraints on labor's right to strike. In 1976 an additional condition for legality was appended to the labor code requiring workers to give the state ten days' advance notice of any planned strike activity for the strike to be considered legal (article 376 bis). Moreover, in the 1973 agreement, the government reasserted its right to invalidate strikes and requisition workers in cases where it judged the strikes to be prejudicial to vital national interests (article 389).

Overall, the texts of Tunisia's labor regime saw gradual liberalization, getting one boost in 1966 and a second in 1973. Less sanguine for labor, however, has been the state's record in terms of its *implementation* of these texts. Although by the mid-1970s Tunisian labor law explicitly endorsed workers' right to organize collectively, conduct strikes, and bargain collectively for wages, the state repeatedly violated each of these rights at different times during the next twenty years. As described in chapter 3, in the late 1970s and again in the mid-1980s, the state did not hesitate to occupy trade union offices, chase out legitimately elected trade union officials, and impose its own leadership on the UGTT when the state's political interests so dictated. Similarly, in the mid-1980s, the state tolerated as well as instigated the abusive dismissal of hundreds of UGTT militants from their jobs. Interviews with labor leaders turned up countless tales of government harassment committed during the late 1970s and mid-1980s. The record shows that the government has routinely ignored Tunisian labor law and resorted to repression when political expedience so demanded.

None of this is to say that the labor regime's legal rubric was of no importance in Tunisia. Even during moments of extreme confrontation with the trade union movement, such as in the late 1970s and mid-1980s, Tunisian political elites never formally renounced trade union rights. To the contrary, they often went to great lengths to maintain a façade of legality in their attacks on the UGTT. Although this concern for legality rarely dissuaded Tunisia's political elite from resorting to trade union repression when political interests strongly mandated it, still, this attention to legality reflected the regime's belief that sustaining the appearance of workers' rights was an essential component of its formula for domestic and international legitimacy. This endowed the labor movement with some political leverage over the state, at least on the margins of political exigency.

Given the mixed nature of Tunisia's labor regime (liberal in terms of texts but mercurial in terms of implementation), the regime's impact on labor's capacity for collective action (and hence power) has also been mixed. Clearly, the country's relatively liberal labor code has favored the development of collective solidarity and combativeness on the part of Tunisian workers. The size and reach of Tunisia's trade union movement, large and pervasive by the standards of the region (only Turkey compares favorably) owes much to the state's official tolerance for collective organizing.[21] And strike levels would never have reached the highs of the mid-1970s, early 1980s, and early 1990s had the Tunisian regime denied workers the right to strike (as do, for example, the regimes in Syria and Egypt).[22] At the same time, the state's mercurial fidelity to its own labor laws *has* undercut labor's capacity for cohesion and collective action repeatedly over the past two decades. Government repression in 1978 and again in 1985 resulted in plummeting strike levels. The year 1978 saw a 60% decline in strikes over the previous year; 1985 and 1986 saw a 30% and 70% decline in strikes when compared to 1984 levels. Government repression also sparked dramatic declines in UGTT membership rates. Adhesion to the UGTT plummeted in the wake of the repressions of 1978 and 1985, and while membership rates recovered from the first repression in just a few years, they had yet to recover from the second by the mid-1990s (interview, labor activist, August 1993).

The state's economic logic is partly responsible for the evolution in the country's labor regime. The state's commitment to a more liberal development strategy in the 1970s explains the liberalization of labor code enacted then. And the state's violation of its own codes in the late 1970s and mid-1980s was driven in part by economic constraints spelled by a more externally oriented development strategy. But clearly this is not the whole picture. High politics played a key role in shaping Tunisia's labor regime, specifically the state's fluctuating sense of political confidence and preoccupation with political control. The labor regime was liberalized when the party-state felt politically secure. Three such periods stand out: the mid-1960s, when the Destourian regime had established its hegemony over all national organizations; the mid-1970s, when the regime enjoyed a unique moment of conjuncturally driven prosperity; and the late 1980s, when Ben Ali came to power flush with the legitimacy of overturning Bourguiba's sclerotic rule. By contrast, the labor regime turned repressive when the state felt weak and politically threatened, for example, in the early years of independence, when the party-state's control over Tunisian society was not yet secure, and in the late 1970s and mid-1980s, when economic recession and a looming succession crisis made the state elite feel besieged and insecure. The evolution in labor's capacity for militance cannot be explained by focusing on the state's economic logic alone.

Culture, Leadership, and Trade Union Institutions

Working class culture, trade union leadership, and trade union institutions have all proven significant in shaping labor's capacity for militance and collective action. Although there is as yet little systematic research into the discursive content of working class culture in Tunisia, there is no question that cultural factors such as high rates of literacy and a relatively high degree of cultural homogeneity,[23] as well as long experience of shared struggle,[24] have distinguished Tunisia's working class in the region and account for its strong sense of solidarity and militance. The militance of this class is best evidenced by the ability of Tunisia's rank and file to sustain impressive rates of strikes and other forms of organized activism, even when formal trade union structures have been repressed.[25] No doubt, the developmental logic of the state has contributed to the evolution of this working class culture. For example, the state's project of promoting universal literacy certainly expanded the reach of trade union organs like *Al-Sha'b*. But many other dimensions of working class culture that have played a role in fostering this militance and solidarity, such as cultural homogeneity and shared experience of struggle, either precede or exist despite the state's intentions. They cannot be directly linked to the state's developmental project and so do not concern us much here.

The same may be said for trade union leadership and institutions. Both play a key role in shaping the combativeness and militance of the working class. That the UGTT's early leaders saw themselves as the vanguard of both the nation and the working class often led them to prioritize the state's developmental project and restrain labor militance. This was true well into the early 1970s. By contrast, the rise of a new generation of trade union leaders who came of age during the postindependence period and earned their stripes in either the radical student movements of France or Tunis, the shop floor struggles of Tunisian factories, and/or the prison cells of the Tunisian state proved more committed to embracing the specific interests of labor and more willing to chart an independent (and at times even militant) course for the trade union movement. Leaders from this generation were instrumental in spearheading the strike movement of the 1970s and 1980s.

Similarly, the organizational structure of the trade union movement also shaped labor's capacity for militance, albeit in a primarily regressive direction. The centralized nature of control in the UGTT[26] and the union's primary dependence on financing from above,[27] as well as its failure to uphold democratic procedure,[28] have made the trade union vulnerable to Michels' Iron Law of Oligarchy (Michels 1962). Consequently it has drifted away from responsiveness to the concerns of the rank and file and metamorphosed into a vehicle for the advancement of the trade union elite.

But important as these factors are to determining labor's capacity for militance and collective action, their evolution does not seem to be related in any clear unidirectional way to the process of state-sponsored industrialization in Tunisia. The development of autonomous UGTT leadership is largely a consequence of a generational shift in trade union leadership and the emergence of trade union leaders with professional origins outside the party-state. The organizational structure of the trade union has remained relatively constant during the past four decades despite important variations in the country's development strategy. As such, these factors do not serve as a conduit linking the state's development strategy to the power and autonomy of social forces in Tunisia.

The Power of Alliance

The evolution in labor's power is in part a consequence of labor's changing capacity for disruptive collective action. But equally important is labor's capacity to deliver organized popular support to the regime. The state's developmental project has amplified the importance of this capacity due to its generation of disaffected social groups who increasingly pose a political challenge to the regime. Although Tunisia has enjoyed impressive growth over the past forty years, the country's development strategy has widened the gap between the haves and have-nots and left significant portions of society disadvantaged. The disaffection of those left out has helped fuel opposition to the regime, led by the Islamist movement. The development of this threat has boosted the value of a reliable popular ally for the regime and led regime elites to court labor as a countervailing force. Chapter 3 elaborated this trend in the Tunisian case. Thus, even as

Tunisia's development strategy has chiseled away at some of the structural and statist underpinnings of labor's power, compromising labor's capacity to disrupt, the development strategy has also reinforced labor's clout by reflating the value of labor's alliance.

Evolving Autonomy of Organized Labor

The autonomy of organized labor has long been under attack in Tunisia, and recent shifts in the state's development strategy have only compromised it further. The central role played by the state in the economy has cast it in the position of chief employer, regulator, and adjudicator of labor since the early 1960s. Thus, the *economic* well-being of workers has long been subject to the state's discretionary goodwill. More recently, Tunisia's embrace of an export-oriented, market-driven strategy of development has only magnified labor's dependence on the state's benevolence because this strategy has concentrated growth in sectors where labor is structurally weak. Labor has been forced to look to the state to shore up its wage and working conditions beyond what either its market position or disruptive capabilities might yield on their own.

Labor's autonomy has also long been compromised by the state's inconsistent commitment to the basic rights of labor, as reflected in its mercurial labor regime. Labor's *organizational* well-being is thus also subject to state discretion. The magnitude of this discretion is amplified by the absence of democratic institutions that might force the state to be accountable to its own laws. In recent years the state has exercised its discretion to contract the labor regime as the shift to an export-oriented, market-driven development strategy has put the agenda of labor and state increasingly at odds.

The Tunisian state has played a central role in managing the economy and governing labor affairs ever since the early independence period. The state is labor's largest single employer, providing work for a major share of the labor force in the civil service and public sector enterprises. State-led wage commissions set intersectoral wage scales as well as the minimum wage. State-led advisory boards rule on the fairness of collective conventions and arbitrate labor disputes. State labor inspectors enforce negotiated contracts and labor law. The state thus plays a crucial role in determining the quality of life for many working people.

Given this dependence on the state's goodwill, trade unions have been known to renounce combativeness and to sacrifice trade union autonomy for the sake of maintaining good relations with state elites. This has been most evident in the willingness of trade union activists to consider state preferences in its selection of trade union leadership. In the early 1980s, for example, trade union leaders blocked the appointment of left-leaning radicals to leadership positions in the UGTT in compliance with state preferences. Similarly, in the late 1980s, the trade union leadership blocked the ascent of Islamist militants in the UGTT hierarchy, again in compliance with state wishes (interview, labor activist, August 1993).

The shift in the state's development strategy toward more export-oriented, market-driven industrialization has not diminished labor's dependence. Although this strategy has contracted the state's role as economic entrepreneur, it has not reduced the state's role as adjudicator, enforcer, and regulator of labor's rights. Further, the switch in strategy has tended to concentrate growth in precisely those sectors where labor is dispersed, poorly skilled, and less committed to the labor force, that is, where organized labor is structurally weakest. Labor in these sectors is likely to look to state intervention to compensate for its own weakness. Dependence on state intervention has been evident in the course of national wage negotiations. In both 1990 and 1993, for example, workers in the textile sector—one of the sectors most afflicted by dispersed, low-wage, low-commitment workers—relied heavily on state intervention to bolster their bargaining position. As Alexander (1996, 305) reports, it was "widely acknowledged" that the wage concessions won were made possible thanks to considerable pressure exerted by the government on textile owners. They far exceeded what textile workers might have been gained on their own given their relatively weak market position and their structurally compromised capacity for militance and collective action.[29]

The state's mercurial commitment to labor rights has been explored above. Although the juridical texts of Tunisia's labor regime ostensibly guarantee labor the rights essential to organizational vigor, the state has been inconsistent in its observance of these texts, routinely limiting labor's freedom of operation whenever its political interests so prescribed. The state has proven quite adept at reining in trade union autonomy, relying on means that have ranged from the exertion of informal influence over internal trade union politics and the unilateral revocation of liberal labor codes, to naked repression of the trade union movement, in blithe disregard of existing labor law. Relying on these various means, the state has at different times controlled the choice of trade union leadership, undermined the trade union's financial independence, and in general circumscribed the range of trade union activity.

Evidence of such intervention is legion. As described in chapter 3, the state has routinely interfered in the UGTT's choice of leaders, at first relying primarily on informal means to influence leadership selection but later resorting to the use of outright coercion. During the first two decades of independence the state controlled the appointment and removal of four trade union secretaries general (Tlili in 1956, Achour in 1963, Bellagha in 1965, and Achour again in 1970), relying on Bourguiba's enormous prestige as well as the significant overlap in members and mission of the party-state and union to control trade union elections. In later years, the state removed independent trade union leaders, relying on straightforward coercion, as in 1978 and in 1985, forcibly replacing them each time by Destourian loyalists.

The state has also intervened in various ways to undercut the financial autonomy of the UGTT. In the early years of independence the state provided the UGTT with the basis for a surprising degree of financial independence, thanks to its endorsement of a system of automatic dues check-off that paid 1% of all public sector and civil service salaries directly into the coffers of the UGTT. In addition, the state permitted the UGTT to supplement its income through the ownership and operation of various commercial and industrial ventures as well as through the sale of UGTT membership cards to private sector workers. By 1985, however, the state undercut this autonomy, unilaterally ending the system of automatic check-off of dues. A year later the state also sequestered UGTT bank accounts and seized control of UGTT enterprises, such as the Amilcar Hotel and the Al-Ittihād Insurance Company. Henceforth, the financial health of the UGTT hinged on direct subsidies from the state.[30]

The state has also exercised enormous discretion in setting boundaries to labor activism. The state unilaterally amended the labor law to suit its preferences (e.g., bureaucratizing labor's right to strike in a 1976 amendment). When even this amended labor law proved too liberal, in 1978 and again in 1985, the state simply responded by repressing any labor activism it found too threatening.

In short, the state has enjoyed a fair amount of discretion in shaping the operations of organized labor. The absence of effective democratic institutions has only compounded the state's discretionary power. Without the capacity to impose precise political accountability on the state, citizens are powerless to prevent the state from changing labor law or ignoring it whenever interest so dictates. Equally inauspicious for labor, the embrace of an export-oriented, market-driven development strategy has fueled the state's inclination to restrain labor's autonomy. Labor and the state find their agendas increasingly at odds, since concessions to labor more directly undermine this strategy's logic of growth. Moreover, this strategy places an increasing premium on labor discipline—a further incentive to the state to circumscribe trade union autonomy.

Despite this assault, the autonomy of the labor movement has not been entirely erased. The development of working class culture at the level of the base has sustained rank and file militance even when the state has imprisoned trade union leaders and compromised the union's financial base. The resurgence of strike activity instigated by the base during the late 1970s and again in the 1980s suggests a streak of persistent independence within labor that the state cannot ignore. Moreover, the historic weight of trade union institutions has invested these institutions with a legitimacy that makes it very costly for the state to eliminate them completely. Every time the state has clashed with the trade union movement it has been forced to step back from the precipice of elimination, as was evident in 1978 and 1985. Working class culture and institutions have staying power that prevents the state from entirely subjugating labor. But there is no denying that labor's autonomy has suffered for the past two decades, and the future does not look rosier.

Indicators of Influence?

Given this mixed picture one might be tempted to conclude that in the case of labor, the state's developmental project has *not* given rise to a social force capable of imposing its preferences on the policy-making process. But while the current trajectory indeed counsels against triumphalism for labor (the picture is significantly brighter for private sector industrialists), it is premature to discount labor's influence over policy. In fact, in Tunisia there is significant evidence to indicate that organized labor *has* been able to circumscribe state autonomy and make the state accountable to labor's preferences on many important issues over the past twenty-five years.

The clearest evidence can be found in the dramatic wage concessions won by labor in the 1970s and early 1980s. Of course, as discussed in the case of capital, it is hazardous to deduce influence from policy, since a wide variety of factors beyond the influence of any single social force comes into play in determining policy outcomes (e.g., the ideological preferences of the political elite, or larger contextual factors, such as the health of the economy).[31] Nevertheless, there is much to suggest that the wage concessions won during these years were indeed an indicator of labor's influence. First, the ideological disposition of state elites did not spell generous concessions to labor. The 1970s marked a shift of the Tunisian elite away from a socialist ethos of collective responsibility and common burden sharing and toward the embrace of a frankly liberal world view, less responsive to working class appeals for equity and social justice. Second, the timing of the concessions, which for the most part followed rather than preceded labor militance, suggests that they came in response to labor activism. Third, while the robustness of the economy clearly played a role in favoring generous concessions to labor, that role can only be seen as permissive and not determining. Tunisia had experienced respectable growth rates during the 1960s and yet this growth had not translated into respectable wage concessions to workers so long as labor was quietist. Only when labor took an activist bent, expressed in the skyrocketing strike rates of the 1970s, did robust economic growth translate into generous wage concessions for workers. It was labor's demonstrated capacity for militance and collective action that motivated the government to change its policy and accommodate labor's preferences in the form of significant wage concessions.

Since the mid-1980s, labor's position has looked somewhat less bright. Dramatic wage concessions have not been forthcoming; at best, the average wage rate in Tunisia held constant (in real terms) between 1985 and 1993, while the minimum wage (again in real terms) actually suffered a small regression (−1.6%) (Institut d'études quantitatives 1994, internal document). Moreover, during this period the state undertook many policy initiatives (most notably, the embrace of structural adjustment and privatization) that did not reflect the preferences of labor. Clearly, labor has not enjoyed comprehensive veto power over public policy in Tunisia. Economic recession, persistently high levels of unemployment, the erosion of labor's structural position (brought on by the embrace of an export-oriented, market-driven development strategy) have all taken their toll on organized labor, diminishing its assertiveness in the political arena. The UGTT no longer boasts of being a leading point of contestation in Tunisia. Rather, it has proclaimed its "partnership with the state" in managing Tunisia's development (interview, labor activist, 15 December 1996; U.S. Dept. of Labor, *Foreign Labor Trends: Tunisia*, 1994).

Partnership, however, does not mean powerlessness. Even during this period of trial for Tunisian workers, organized labor has continued to exert influence over state policy, in three key areas.

First, in the area of wage policy: although the regime did not endorse dramatic wage gains for labor at this time, the three cross-national triennial wage negotiations conducted in 1990–96 each granted wage gains that ranged between 5 and 10% in current terms, sufficient to keep pace with inflation (Central Bank, *Annual Report*, 1996). Although this might not seem to be an enormous victory for labor, the protection of Tunisian wage levels, which are relatively high by international standards, and which were sustained despite the downward wage pressure exerted by integration into the international economy, nonetheless represented a significant accomplishment for Tunisian workers.

Second, in the area of structural adjustment, and more specifically with regard to privatization, the state has taken a go-slow approach (despite World Bank/IMF pressure to the contrary) to respond to labor's concern about the protection of jobs. In the name of "social peace," the state has actively managed the transfer of public enterprises in ways that preserve the most jobs, and it has slowed the process of transfer overall (World Bank 1996).

Third, in the area of labor code reform, for more than a decade the Tunisian state has been hectored by a chorus of voices coming from the private sector (both domestic entrepreneurs and foreign investors) as well as from international agencies like the World Bank and the IMF calling for the reform of Tunisia's labor law. The law, they argue, makes the hiring and firing of workers too onerous, both financially and bureaucratically, and denies Tunisian firms the flexibility necessary to respond to fluctuating business opportunities efficiently.[32] Given the state's far-reaching embrace of IMF/World Bank development prescriptions as well as its championing of the private sector, one might have expected it to adopt this reform with dispatch. But surprisingly, the state has proven extremely cautious in dealing with the reform question. For five years the regime procrastinated, raising the issue of labor law reform for public discussion but never actually going through with formal change of the law.[33] Finally, in 1996, the regime enacted modest reform, endorsing the notion of indefinite term contracts (i.e., hiring workers on a temporary basis) and placing ceilings on the fines that businesses would be required to pay for dismissing workers (EIU, *Country Report: Tunisia*, October–December 1996). But even then, at the insistence of the UGTT, the regime placed hedges on the reform, for example, workers employed on a "temporary basis" for three consecutive years would automatically be made permanent. Moreover, the reform fell far short of private sector and World Bank recommendations in that it did not endorse the principle of "freedom of hiring and firing." Employers wishing to fire employees, for whatever reason, must still obtain approval from the National Commission of Dismissal.

In short, the state has proven extremely cautious in carrying out labor code reform, and the best explanation for this caution lies in the unstinting opposition of the labor movement to such reform. For all the weakness of organized labor, the state has been loath to "take it on" and jeopardize social peace. Thus, despite political pressure and ideological convictions to the contrary, the state has felt constrained to proceed cautiously on labor reform and thus avoid the direct confrontation with labor that a precipitous change would invite. This "go slow" approach constitutes important evidence that even though organized labor appears besieged, the state still feels constrained to consider its preferences when making public policy.

Labor, then, does exercise influence in the policy-making process in Tunisia, even if the future trajectory for that influence appears to be flat in the near term. The structural conditions for working class combativeness persist in many sectors; vibrant working class leadership and culture have established themselves; even the state's embrace of export-oriented, market-driven development, so corrosive to labor's position in some ways, has created incentives for the state to bolster organized labor, specifically by fueling the need for a popular ally to countervail the Islamist challenge. Still, major obstacles to labor's influence remain. Slow growth, persistent unemployment, and a development strategy that concentrates growth precisely where labor is likely to be weakest all work against organized labor. But even were economic conditions to improve, labor would still face an enormous obstacle to consistent influence, namely Tunisia's problematic political institutions. The lack of liberal democratic institutions, such as guaranteed civil liberties and competitive elections, deprive labor of the organizational conditions essential to its power, namely freedom of speech and association as well as accountability of the state to its own laws (labor laws among them). To safeguard labor's rights and create the conditions for consistent influence, Tunisia must make progress toward the establishment of irrevocable liberal democratic institutions. Whether labor is likely to champion this effort, however, is the subject of chapter 5.

CHAPTER 5

Capital and Labor:
Agents of Democratization?

State-sponsored industrialization has indeed given rise to social forces that can shape public policy in Tunisia. In recent years both private sector industrialists and organized labor have imposed their preferences on the state in important policy areas such as labor code reform, trade liberalization, wage rate determination, and privatization. But the want of liberal democratic institutions still closes off important routes to political power for both social forces and checks their policy influence. Confronted by this obstacle, are industrialists and labor likely to champion democratic reform?

The Tunisian case makes clear the *democratic paradox* of sponsored growth. The very same factor that works to empower industrialists and labor, enabling them to make the state responsive to their interests, also discourages them from becoming advocates for democratization. For while state sponsorship nurtures the power of industrialists and labor, it continues to undermine their autonomy. Both social forces still find their fortunes beholden to the goodwill of the state, and this dependence, combined with other factors such as fear, for capitalists, and "aristocratic position," for organized labor, makes them diffident about democratization. As a consequence, capital and labor do not marshal their forces behind a democratic agenda. Instead, they contribute to a syndrome of "stalled democracy" whereby the state is stunted halfway between autocracy and fully accountable government, responsive to a few privileged interests but hardly accountable to society as a whole.

Chapter 5 explores this argument in the Tunisian case. The chapter begins by establishing capital and labor's coolness toward democracy, evidenced by their detachment from the regime's democratic project launched in 1987 and by their muted response to the regime's authoritarian retreat in the early 1990s. The chapter then explores why capital and labor are diffident about democratization. The chapter also reflects on why this diffidence might be more common among industrialists and labor in late-developing countries and why their experience diverges from the expectations of many classic works of political economy. Finally, the chapter identifies the political consequence of this diffidence—stalled democracy—and the state's failure to move beyond limited responsiveness to the privileged few.

Democratic Diffidence of Private Sector Industrialists

Private sector industrialists in Tunisia displayed a marked lack of enthusiasm for democratization both at the height of the country's democratic reform in 1987–88 and again during the period of authoritarian retreat in the 1990s. In 1987, when President Zine Abdine Ben Ali announced the start of a "new era" that would embrace political pluralism, civil liberties, and progressive democratization, private sector industrialists manifested their diffidence for the reforms by their resolute political passivity. At a time when many activists scrambled to take advantage of this window of legalized pluralism (six legal opposition parties were formed within a year of Ben Ali's new presidency), the private sector showed no interest in mobilizing a party to defend business interests. Nor did the private sector take advantage of the regime's promise of expanded civil liberties. No new business mouthpiece emerged in the aftermath of the 1987 change, nor did any new business associations emerge to promote the business point of view. Instead, members of the private sector retained a studied aloofness from politics. Asserted one industrialist, himself a leader of the community: "Businessmen should not make politics. It's not their métier" (interview, December 1993). Another entrepreneur explained: "We businessmen are not political. We leave politics to the politicians. Our national service is to create employment . . . jobs and bread" (interview, August 1988).

To the extent that members of the private sector were politically energized in the "new era," it was largely to reaffirm their loyalty to the ruling party. Industrialists provided material support to the RCD, offering both cash and in-kind donations.[1] A dinner held by the RCD party chief in 1988 brought in more than one million dinars' worth of pledges to the ruling party from the business community. That sum swelled to six million in just a few weeks as additional businesspeople joined the fund-raising bandwagon (interview, 14 December 1988). In-kind donations in the form of cars, computers, and food for the party's use were also provided by the private sector. At the party's youth conference held in 1988, for example, a number of industrialists outfitted conference participants with uniforms and tennis shoes, free of charge. Similarly, the refreshments served at the party's national congress, held during the summer of 1988, were supplied by private businesses, gratis.

Besides material assistance, the private sector also showed its support for the ruling party by running candidates in the RCD lists during national parliamentary elections. By the mid-1990s, thirty businessmen could be counted among the representative of the RCD in parliament (interview, 14 December 1996). Although small in terms of percentages, this number nonetheless constituted a departure from the past, when few businessmen served publicly in RCD lists.

But aside from modest expressions of support for the ruling party, the private sector limited its engagement in politics. Most important, it steered clear of any behavior that smacked of the defining right of democracy—contestation. Chariness of contestation was most clearly demonstrated by the private sector's relation to the Tunisian Human Rights League (LTDH). In the absence of a truly independent fourth estate in Tunisia, the Human Rights League has served the function of democratic watchdog, challenging the state to live up to its promises to defend human rights, civil liberties, and democratization. It has been the most valiant champion of contestation in the country, and in this capacity it repeatedly clashed with the state and suffered significant repression. But while the league counted among its supporters Tunisians of every stripe, from free professionals and former labor union activists to Islamists and students, tellingly, no businessperson of note served on its board. Nor did the private sector provide financial support to the league (interview, 5 March 1997). In all, private sector business showed a marked disinterest in supporting the institution that was leading the drive for democratization in Tunisia.

But the expression of diffidence about democratization went beyond studied aloofness from formal politics. More telling was the private sector's response to the regime's relapse into authoritarianism. The business community expressed no dissent at this development. To the contrary, business leaders stood by President Ben Ali and actively voiced their misgivings about democratization in countless interviews. Many admitted the democratic deficiencies of the Tunisian regime but dismissed these failings. They argued that Tunisians were not ready for democracy and that authoritarianism was necessary for the country's economic prosperity. Said one banker:

> Yes the regime is not perfectly democratic . . . but our goal now is stability. . . . The people need to focus on the person of Ben Ali. . . . That is what unites the country. . . . Otherwise we will descend into tribalism. So I support the regime . . . for the stability necessary to foster development and growth. (Interview, December 1993)

Said an entrepreneur in the electronics sector:

> Liberty is good . . . but is not for "les gosses" [kids]. It's for adults. Democracy is a goal, it's not where we start. . . . It's better to have one person rule well than for one thousand imbeciles to rule badly. If the masses are not well-educated, not educated to think long term, we will head toward the abyss like some other countries in the region. (Interview, December 1996)

Distrust of democracy was further fostered among Tunisia's business elite by the descent of neighboring Algeria into civil war after that country's brief flirtation with democratic opening. Again and again, businessmen stressed that Algeria was a cautionary tale for what might happen in Tunisia should democracy be embraced too precipitously. As one leader in the cosmetics industry explained: "We have a democracy . . . as much democracy as we can afford and manage. What would you prefer, some security? Or people getting killed in the street? We don't want to be like Algeria" (interview, December 1996). For the sake of stability, security, and prosperity, Tunisia's business leaders were content to forgo democratization and embrace an authoritarian regime with a "firm hand." Their response to Tunisia's relapse into authoritarianism was not resounding silence so much as outspoken assent. Tunisian businesspeople were clearly willing to exchange the right to vote (meaningfully) for the right to "make money."

Democratic Diffidence of Organized Labor

The private sector, however, was not alone in its diffidence about democratization in Tunisia. Organized labor also proved less than energetic in its embrace of political reform. Although rhetorically the UGTT asserted its commitment to civil liberties, rule of law, and other political institutions essential to accountable government, in terms of concrete action aimed at promoting democratization, the union's role was limited.

This restraint was evident in several ways. Like the business community, organized labor did not seize the opportunity to make good on the regime's offer of political pluralism. Labor neither organized its own party to defend labor's interests nor threw its support to any of the opposition parties. As an organization, the trade union movement remained aloof from competitive politics, officially endorsing none of the parties, not even the ruling RCD.[2] The UGTT's official explanation for such aloofness stressed the trade union's desire to retain its political autonomy and neutrality, as well as to avoid the political fragmentation of the rank and file. Nevertheless, this commitment to neutrality did not prevent the UGTT from mounting an active campaign in support of President Ben Ali's re-election bid in 1994. Maintaining good relations with the regime and avoiding any hint of public confrontation seemed as important a political goal for the UGTT as retaining trade union autonomy and unity.

The UGTT's reluctance to embrace contestation was evident in other ways as well. Like the business community, the UGTT kept its distance from the Tunisian Human Rights League. The trade union provided no financial support and no official endorsement to the league. To the contrary, the UGTT was adamant about maintaining its distance from the league to the point where the union's newspaper, *Al-Sha'b*, refused to publish any of the league's official communiqués describing the regime's human rights abuses and civil liberties violations. As one union activist explained: "*Al-Sha'b* wants no part in criticizing the government." Trade union leaders excused this tendency, arguing that formal confrontation with the regime would only bring down the government's wrath and "get *Al-Sha'b* closed down" (interviews, December 1996).

Beyond this, UGTT activists time and again expressed their reluctance to spearhead the drive for democratization in Tunisia or condemn the regime's return to authoritarian ways. As one labor leader said:

> We must go gently to avoid cut-off or closure. The UGTT was always a force for the opposition during the sixties, seventies, and eighties . . . but now this is not our role. . . . This is the role of . . . opposition parties. . . . Our responsibility is not to be the sole force contesting the regime. (Interview, December 1996)

Similarly, another labor activist emphasized the union's incapacity to lead the opposition:

No, the UGTT does not give support to the Tunisian League of Human Rights. But what support could the UGTT give? It is simply too weak. (Interview, December 1996)

Thus, while the trade union movement may have served as a pole of opposition and a progressive political force in the early decades of the regime, by the 1990s the UGTT had clearly retreated from any directly confrontational political role.

Why This Diffidence?

How might we explain the reluctance of capital and labor to embrace the cause of democratic political reform in Tunisia? State sponsorship of their development is certainly an important factor, especially when combined with other conditions such as fear, in the case of capital, and aristocratic position, in the case of labor.

In the case of capital, state sponsorship has spelled compromised autonomy for the private sector and, hence, political timidity. Beyond owing their origins to state largesse, delivered in the form of subsidized start-up capital, subsidized infrastructure, and protected markets, many private sector industrialists find that their economic well-being continues to be beholden to the goodwill of the state. Trade protection and fiscal concessions still buoy the profitability of many firms, and spot subsidies and support programs distributed by the state on a discretionary basis have helped many firms restructure to face foreign competition on a firmer footing. The state's adoption of a more market-driven strategy of development has diminished the role of discretion in the provision of state support to the private sector but has not yet eliminated it. Friendly collaboration with state elites, not public contestation, continues to be important to private sector success. Entrepreneurs have good reason to remain aloof from campaigns for democratization, since their embrace would be interpreted by regime elites as provocative and confrontational.

Second, state sponsorship has lessened capital's incentive to champion institutionalized accountability—one of democracy's defining characteristics and, presumably, one of its key selling points. As described in chapter 1, the state has long identified its own economic interest with the prosperity of the private sector. It played a central role in nurturing the development of the private sector and especially the development of private sector industrialists. It anticipates private sector interests when making public policy and regularly consults with business leaders to assure this end. Even when fiscal crisis forced the state to cut back on supports and sweeteners to the private sector, business elites still asserted that the state was "à l'écoute" to private sector interests, providing whatever support it could muster to viable business projects (interview, December 1996).

Given the state's persistent solicitousness of the private sector, the latter's disinterest in democratic reform is less than surprising. So long as the state generally anticipates private sector interests, why should capital feel compelled to create formal mechanisms to *ensure* state accountability? To the contrary, the private sector stands to lose from the creation of such institutions because they broaden the constituency to which the state must give ear and dilute the impact of capital's privileged access.

But a third factor dampens the private sector's enthusiasm for democracy as well, and that is fear. Private sector capital everywhere is concerned, first and foremost, with protecting property rights and securing the long-term profitability of its investments through the guarantee of order (Payne 1994). But where poverty is widespread and the poor potentially well mobilized (say, by Islamists), the mass inclusion and empowerment associated with democratization threatens to undermine the basic interests of many capitalists. At best, such inclusion threatens to flood politics with the "logic of distribution" rather than the "logic of accumulation" (Callaghy 1994, 243). At worst, it potentially confers upon the property-less the means to overturn the social order.

In Tunisia, the private sector's fear of democratization seems to stem less from concern that mass empowerment will lead to a direct attack on their property rights (Islamist movements, which are the best-organized popular force, typically respect the sanctity of private property even as they advocate social justice) but more from fear that democratization will empower radical Islamists and potentially spark civil war. The association made among democratization, Islamist empowerment, and instability is drawn from the Algerian experience; mistakenly, one might argue, since it was the exclusion of Islamists from democratic opening, not their inclusion and empowerment, that actually fueled the outbreak of civil war in Algeria. But for most Tunisian businesspeople, the association between democratization and chaos is clear. Thus, they prefer the continuation of an authoritarian regime capable of maintaining a firm grip on public order to the introduction of democracy. If the cause of democracy is endorsed, it is relegated to some distant future when Tunisia's prosperity is secure and the economic frustration that currently fuels revolutionary movements has dissipated.

As for organized labor, a similar set of factors keeps the UGTT ambivalent about pressing for democratization. State sponsorship may sound too benign a term to describe the state's relationship with the UGTT, especially given the brutal repression that the trade union has repeatedly suffered at the hands of the state for the past two decades. Nevertheless, in recent years the trade union *has* benefited organizationally from state-sponsored resurrection, as described in chapter 3. And trade union members have benefited economically from state-brokered labor contracts. During the 1990s, when multiple factors such as high levels of domestic unemployment and the wage pressure imposed by integration into the global economy ought to have spelled wage regression for labor, organized labor enjoyed surprising success in negotiating wage levels (Alexander 1996). This success was not the consequence of labor's market power but rather of its political value to the state. In exchange for labor's political alliance, and its commitment to supporting the political and economic status quo, the state shored up labor's position and brokered wage concessions that far exceeded what workers might have won without such political intervention. As a result, organized labor continues to see its interests best served by a collaborative as opposed to confrontational relationship with the state. Labor's desire not to upset the applecart of state patronage prevents it from outrightly embracing a campaign for democratization.

Another factor dampening organized labor's enthusiasm for democratization is its aristocratic position, that is, the degree to which it is privileged vis-à-vis the general population. Where organized labor enjoys a privileged stance, it is likely to exhibit a degree of "dis-solidarity" with the unorganized masses in the informal sector and agriculture. Under such conditions, and especially where labor's aristocratic position is a consequence of political intervention rather than a reflection of true market power, labor will perceive its interests to be better served by maintaining a cozy relationship with the state, even if the institutional arrangements are authoritarian, rather than by championing institutions that make the state accountable to mass interest (i.e., democracy).

In Tunisia, organized workers are much better off than the vast majority of their unorganized compatriots. Workers in the informal sector enjoy none of the benefits that organized labor commands in terms of wage and working conditions, social security benefits, and job security. Yet their share of the workforce is growing at twice the rate of employment in the formal economy, and they account for more than one third (34.9%) of total urban wage earners (World Bank 1995b, vol. 2, annex C.2). The unemployed in Tunisia are also economically disadvantaged and their number is growing too, officially clocking in at 15.3% of the active population but reaching a level of 42.7% for 18–24 year olds seeking their first job (World Bank 1995b, vol. 2, annex C.1). In short, the economically privileged position in Tunisian society that organized labor enjoys creates a disjuncture between their material interests and that of the vast majority of poorer Tunisians. Workers do not necessarily see their interests served by mass empowerment, and they have less incentive to join forces with other subordinate strata to make the state more accountable to mass interest. To the contrary, labor's dependence on state propping for its aristocratic position encourages the UGTT to husband its privileged relationship with the state, even if that means bolstering an authoritarian regime.

Defying the Expectations of Political Economy

Capital and labor's diffidence toward democratization in Tunisia defies the expectations of many classic studies in political economy. Both liberals and Marxists writing in this tradition have long identified the protagonists of capitalist industrialization as the historical agents of democratization, although they differ over which protagonists played the leading role. Drawing primarily on the historical experience of Western Europe, these scholars fall into two schools.

One school, led by Moraze (1968), Hobsbawm (1969), and Moore (1966), identifies the *capitalist class* as the class agent of democracy. Western European democracy, they argue, was the consequence of capitalists colliding with the absolutist state over the feudal restraints it posed to their advance. Motivated by the desire to eliminate these barriers, rising capitalists marshaled their economic power to create parliamentary institutions and impose parliamentary control on the state.

By contrast, a second school, led by Marshall (1950), Thompson (1963), Bendix (1964), Therborn (1977), and, most recently, Rueschemeyer, Stephens, and Stephens (1992) identifies not rising capitalists but rather the *working class* as the class agent of democracy. Capitalists, they argue, were primarily interested in establishing liberal forms of rule, not democracy. While capitalists supported the introduction of representative government and the protection of civil liberties, they opposed the extension of political rights to the lower classes—the true mark of democracy (Rueschemeyer, Stephens, and Stephens 1992, 8, 58). Instead, it was the working class, organizationally empowered by capitalist development and motivated by the desire to seek political redress for its economic subordination, that fought to extend suffrage to all. As such, the working class was the true champion of democratization in Western Europe.[3]

But no matter their differences, both schools agree on at least three central verities of democratic transition: democracy is the product of struggle in which *social classes* play a central role; *interest*, not enlightenment, drives regime change; and among the panoply of interests that animate people politically, *material* interests trump all others. All told, this analysis suggests that social forces are most likely to champion democracy when their economic interests put them at odds with the authoritarian state.

Why do capital and labor in Tunisia fail to conform to the expectations of this analysis, declining their designated role as the agents of democratization? This phenomenon reflects not so much a flaw in the logic of the political economy analysis as a change in socioeconomic conditions that inform the calculations of capital and labor. In Tunisia, as in many late-developing countries, such factors as the late timing of industrialization and the problem of generalized poverty foster collaborative rather than confrontational relations with the authoritarian state. They also reinforce the problem of fear on the part of capital and the aristocratic status of labor. Both discourage capital and labor from championing democracy.

Late timing refers to the fact that late-developing countries like Tunisia embark on the process of industrialization in a world already industrialized, commercially integrated, and highly competitive. These conditions tend to drive both private sector capital and labor into the arms of the state. Private sector capitalists typically need help with capital accumulation, since the start-up capital for late industrializers often exceeds the capabilities of individual, first-generation entrepreneurs. In addition, fierce international competition leads these entrepreneurs to seek state intervention in the form of tariff barriers, import quotas, and the like to protect their operations from foreign rivals. As for labor, late timing means the importation of industrial technology that tends to be capital rather than labor intensive. Reliance on capital-intensive technology exacerbates the problem of labor surplus and weakens the market position of labor. In addition, industrialization at this late date generally involves integration into the international economy, a process that globalizes the "reserve army" of labor. This undermines labor's structural power as well and gives labor an incentive to turn to the state for protection from the effects of industrializing so late.

The state, for its part, typically has an interest in responding to capital and labor's needs. Developmental logic leads many states to identify national prosperity with that of the private sector. The state is thus willing to come to capital's aid. At the same time, the inequities and turmoil associated with development make many states eager for a reliable popular ally. The state thus has an incentive to strike a corporatist bargain with organized labor. Collaboration rather than confrontation thus marks the relations among capital, labor, and the state in many LDCs, and this stands in marked contrast to class-state relations among the early industrializers. Given this collaborative relationship, both capital and labor have an interest in preserving the political status quo, even if the state is authoritarian.

The problem of generalized poverty also makes capital and labor wary about democratization and drives both social forces into the arms of the authoritarian state. For capital, generalized poverty heightens the fear that mass inclusion will undermine capital's property rights and privileges. Such inclusion would empower the propertyless, potentially giving them the means to overturn the social order or, at the very least, lead politics to be dominated by the logic of distribution. For organized labor, generalized poverty magnifies labor's aristocratic position and widens the divide between its own interests and that of other subordinate strata. Especially because labor's privilege is the consequence of a cozy alliance with the state, labor has less interest in building institutions that will make the state more accountable to the disenfranchised masses.

Since poverty was no less pervasive in eighteenth- or nineteenth-century Europe than it is in many contemporary late-developing countries, one might wonder why capital and labor would be more ambivalent about democracy today than during the first transition. The empowerment of the poor should have posed a commensurate threat to the interests of capital and should have made early capitalists equally leery of democracy. And the masses of poor people surely could have posed a fearsome challenge to any privilege that organized labor enjoyed.

But the difference in capital and labor's attitudes has less to do with the absolute number of poor people found in society across time and more to do with the changed political position of labor and the change in democratic discourse. Labor hardly enjoyed a privileged position in countries like Britain and France during the first century of the industrial revolution but rather suffered Dickensian conditions, and in none of these countries did organized labor benefit from a cozy political alliance with the state. If anything, labor suffered from repression at the state's hands, and so it had every reason to ally with other subordinate strata to campaign for democratization. As for democratic discourse, this has undergone profound change over the past two centuries. At the time of the first transition, the hegemonic discourse on democracy had a distinctly liberal rather than inclusionary cast. The embrace of democracy was understood to be entirely consistent with exclusion of the propertyless. Over the past century, however, democracy has come to stand for mass inclusion. In contemporary democratic discourse it is difficult to justify exclusion based on property, race, or gender. Today, with democratization spelling mass empowerment, the prospect of democratic reform appears much more threatening to the propertied classes and makes capitalists wary of democratization. In this way, the evolution in ideas and a change in labor's political position go far toward explaining capital and labor's divergent enthusiasm for democracy across time, even holding mass poverty constant.

The peculiar conditions of late development, the greater need for and availability of state sponsorship, the change in political discourse and its implications in the context of mass poverty, can thus disjoin the material interests of capital and labor from the cause of democratization and discourage these social forces from playing a leading role in the campaign for democracy. But in attending first and foremost to their material interests, these social forces are no different from their predecessors. Rather, like capital and labor in the first transition, capital and labor in late-developing countries are *contingent* democrats, for the very reason that they are *consistent* defenders of their material interests.[4] Like their predecessors, they champion democratic institutions when these institutions are perceived as advancing their material interests. But the pairing of material and democratic interest is contingent on specific historical circumstances that are not necessarily replicated in the context of late development, as we have seen.

Stalled Democracy

Capital and labor's disinterest in campaigning for democracy contributes to a larger phenomenon, "stalled democracy." Where democracy is stalled, the political system gets stunted halfway between autocracy and fully accountable government. Thanks to state sponsorship, a few privileged interests manage to make the state responsive to their interests. But the state falls far short of being accountable to society as a whole. Instead, the country gets stuck indefinitely in a messy intermediate category where the state is neither all-powerful nor open to nonprivileged strata.

Such has been the case in Tunisia. For decades, the country has been stuck in the mode of "benevolent" authoritarianism.[5] The regime is mildly responsive to the interests of a few privileged groups, as shown in its policy concessions to industrialists on trade protection and to labor on wages and labor law. But the regime has steadfastly opposed the enactment of political reforms that would institutionalize responsiveness to society as a whole. Although the regime embraces many of the formal trappings of democracy, such as regular elections and universal suffrage, it has refused to guarantee basic civil liberties to its citizens. By denying them freedom of speech, freedom of association, and freedom of the press, the regime has deprived them of the basic underpinnings of democracy and prevented the emergence of real political contestation and political accountability. Reneging on promises to guarantee civil liberties has been one of the major disappointments of Ben Ali's regime. It has allowed the regime to become increasingly autocratic over its near decade and a half of rule.

In Tunisia, as elsewhere, capital and labor have been complicitous in this political stasis. Neither has any wish to rock the authoritarian boat so long as the state is attentive to their interests and committed to underwriting their privilege. To the extent that a campaign for democracy has been mobilized, the initiative has come from other forces in society. Students, free professionals, and Islamists have been among the leaders of the democratization effort in Tunisia. They have organized demonstrations, written editorials, served in the human rights movement. They, rather than capital and labor, have led the fledgling drive for democracy.

Of course, capital and labor's alliance with authoritarianism is not cast in stone. One can imagine socioeconomic changes that would spell a disjuncture between the material interests of these classes and the persistence of the authoritarian state. Robust economic growth might absorb labor surplus and diminish labor's structural weakness and dependence on the state. The logic of international economic integration might compel the reduction of state sponsorship, leading capital to reconsider the advantage of coziness over formalized accountability as the surest route to profitability. Rapid growth combined with welfarist public policy might reduce mass poverty and diminish capital's sense of social threat. Under such conditions, capital and labor might reconsider the advantages offered by democratic reform. For labor, democracy holds out the promise of civil liberties, such as freedom of speech and association—the bedrock of collective action and collective power. For capital, democracy holds out the promise of institutionalized accountability and transparency— the means to more predictable policy influence for the well organized and the well-heeled. After weighing the costs and benefits, capital and labor might rethink their political disposition. Evidence from other late-developing countries suggests reason for optimism, for although state-sponsored development has contributed to stalled democracy, in many other LDCs, such comparison also suggests the positive conditions under which such political stasis may change.

CHAPTER 6

Stalled Democracy in
Comparative Perspective

State-sponsored development is more the rule than the exception among late-developing countries. Its prevalence calls into question the presumed relationship between industrialization and democratization in the context of late development. Classic works of political economy attribute the robust linkage between development and democracy to the emergence and empowerment of social classes that have a material interest in promoting democracy. At issue is whether capital and labor are likely to act as agents of democratization if they emerge in a context of state-sponsored growth. How generalizable is the *democratic paradox* found in the Tunisian case? Is Tunisia's experience, both the reluctance of sponsored classes to champion democracy as well as the causal mechanism suggested to explain this outcome, true for other late-comers as well? What implications might this pattern of stalled democracy have for the attenuation of authoritarianism in other cases of sponsored development?

A quick survey of late-developing countries suggests that class ambivalence about democracy is less rare than might be thought. In countries as diverse as Korea, Mexico, Egypt, Indonesia, and Brazil one finds class ambivalence about democracy. This common outcome, despite the cases' diversity in terms of economic condition, cultural heritage, and historical experience, suggests the animating power of one factor these cases do share, namely, extensive state sponsorship of the development process. The linkage between state sponsorship and class ambivalence gets its strongest confirmation from cases like Korea, Mexico, Brazil, and Egypt. These cases display internal variation in both variables, with the rise and fall in class support for democracy inversely mirroring the rise and fall in state sponsorship. Where capital and labor enjoy state sponsorship, class enthusiasm for democracy tends to be muted. Where state sponsorship is withdrawn, class enthusiasm for democracy flowers.

To support this hypothesis, chapter 6 begins with a brief investigation of eight cases. The chapter explores capital's attitude toward democracy in Indonesia, Korea, Mexico, and Brazil and labor's attitude in Mexico, Korea, Egypt, and Zambia. The goal of this analysis is to confirm the causal importance of state sponsorship in shaping class posture toward democracy as well as to reflect on the way sponsorship combines with other factors such as fear and aristocratic position to produce this outcome.

Next, the chapter reflects on the overall implications of state-sponsored development for the attenuation of authoritarianism among late developers. Comparison confirms the differential impact that state sponsorship has on class power and autonomy and the dual paradox this spells for the authoritarian state, both limiting the state's dictatorial power but also contributing to stalled democracy. Comparison also suggests the means by which democracy might be "unstalled" by identifying those conditions likely to mobilize capital and labor behind the cause of democracy.

While the logic of stalled democracy applies to late-developing countries in general, the chapter concludes by focusing on the lessons of this analysis for countries in one region, the Middle East and North Africa. Long a bastion of authoritarianism, the MENA region has also been the locus of many decades of state-sponsored industrialization. The Tunisian case gives reason to hope that sponsored development might foster a measure of political opening in this region as well. By drawing comparisons with Egypt, Turkey, and Syria, the chapter reflects on the transformative capacity of state-sponsored industrialization for state-society relations in the MENA region and its implications for the attenuation of authoritarianism there.

A word on case selection for testing our hypothesis on sponsorship: limited space prevents absolute parallelism in the cases investigated for capital and labor, just as it precludes recounting the experience of both capital and labor in every country mentioned. The original core cases were chosen for dramatic variation on the dependent variable: Indonesia and Korea for capital; Mexico and Korea for labor.[1] Additional cases were chosen for their utility in eliminating rival hypothesis; these are Brazil, Zambia, and Egypt.[2] Careful case selection cannot entirely eliminate the problem of indeterminacy and the possibility of biased results that comes with the investigation of a relatively small number of cases, largely selected on the dependent variable. As King, Keohane, and Verba (1994, 115–49) observe, only *random* selection of *many* cases can truly verify theory. Nevertheless, the evidence presented seems sufficient to suggest the plausibility, if not the incontrovertibility, of the hypothesis that variation in state sponsorship dramatically shapes class disposition toward democracy.

Political Posture of Sponsored Capitalists: Indonesia, Korea, Brazil, and Mexico

Evidence from Indonesia, Korea, Brazil, and Mexico makes clear the importance of state sponsorship in shaping the political leanings of private sector capital. *Parallelism across cases* supports this. In all four cases, state sponsorship has been central to the development of private sector capital, and in each case provision of such sponsorship has been associated with private sector ambivalence toward democratic reform. But *contrast within cases* provides even more robust validation of the causal relationship between state sponsorship and class ambivalence about democracy. Three of these cases (Korea, Brazil, and Mexico) exhibit internal variation in both variables over time, permitting more controlled comparison of the relationship between the two. All three cases of intertemporal variation confirm an inverse relationship between level of state sponsorship and class enthusiasm for democracy.

Indonesia: Patrimonial Capitalism and Democratically Diffident Capitalists

In Indonesia, state sponsorship has been a central force in the development of private sector capital since independence. A corresponding level of private sector disinterest in democratization has been the result.[3]

The Indonesian state nurtured private sector capital through a variety of means that included the provision of preferential access to government contracts, licenses, bank credit, and trade protection (Robison 1986; Robison 1990); the creation of an "entrepreneurial affirmative action program" designed to boost the number of indigenous (*pribumi*) entrepreneurs by legislative fiat (Robison 1986, 167); and the embrace of "bureaucratic capitalism," which permitted public officials to found private sector firms even while remaining in office (Hewison et al. 1993, 46).

State sponsorship of private sector development was patrimonial in nature, characterized by policies that blurred the boundary between public and private. Public officials distributed government support to private firms with an eye to securing personal profit and political clienteles. Officials doubling as entrepreneurs used their control over the allocation of licenses, concessions, and credit to promote their own companies. Nevertheless, Indonesia's "private" sector flourished under the state's loving care, growing dramatically during the first four decades of independence.

Throughout this time, private sector capital proved itself diffident toward democracy. For the better part of its first forty years Indonesia was ruled in authoritarian fashion by Sukarno and Suharto, two strongmen backed by the military, indifferent to the rule of law, and armed with corporatist-style parties and associations. The authoritarianism of the regime called forth popular protest on several key occasions, most notably from the organized left in the early 1960s and from intellectuals and free professionals in the late 1980s and 1990s. But the business community kept aloof from these protests. Among business elites (and the middle class in general) the prevailing political attitude was one of acquiescence. Most proved willing to go along with an illiberal regime in Indonesia rather than advocate political reform (Robison 1990; Hewison 1993).

The private sector's diffidence toward democratization is easily understood given the character of state sponsorship in Indonesia. Licenses, contracts, and credit were distributed on a discretionary basis, with access governed by political logic (or official gain) rather than by publicly formulated, economically rational criteria; hence prudent entrepreneurs were wise to nurture cozy relations with state elites rather than antagonize them with provocative campaigns for political reform. And because many officials doubled as entrepreneurs, the business community was reassured that state elites would anticipate private sector interests when formulating public policy. This obviated the need for more formal mechanisms of accountability, such as those associated with democracy. Finally, much of the business collaboration between state elites and private sector actors was quite shady in nature if not outrightly corrupt, and therefore political transparency, ordinarily a "good" associated with democracy, became less attractive. Private sector capitalists thus had reason to be unenthusiastic about democracy. So long as the state persisted in its delivery of economic prosperity, private sector capital had little incentive to push for political reform (Robison 1990, 5).

Of course, extensive state sponsorship was not the only factor encouraging the private sector to ally with authoritarianism. As in the Tunisian case, fear came into play as well. Pervasive poverty helped fuel the popularity of a strong Communist Party, and by 1965 the party had been implicated in a regime-threatening coup (Hill 1994, 57; May 1978, 117). The sense of revolutionary danger generated by this event turned the propertied classes against democratic experiments and pushed them into the arms of an authoritarian regime. In addition, ethnic cleavage divides much of the business community from the rest of Indonesian society. (The majority of domestic capitalists hail from the Chinese minority, whereas most Indonesians are Muslim Malay.) As a consequence, class discontent over inequity and exploitation has frequently been channeled along ethnic and religious lines, with violence directed against the Chinese community as a whole. This tension has contributed to a sense of social vulnerability within the capitalist class and has led many to prize political stability over freedom and a strong authoritarian state over popular empowerment (Mackie 1976; Hewison et al. 1993, 58–60; MacIntyre 1991).

Private sector capital thus proved unenthusiastic about democratization. Its dependence on state sponsorship as well as its fear of mass empowerment long allied it with the authoritarian order. Nor have recent events necessarily prodded the political conversion of the private sector. Catastrophic economic crisis in 1997–98 fueled regime change in Indonesia and a tentative transition toward democracy. But it also quadrupled mass poverty (eighty million were cast below the poverty line) and sparked interethnic strife (Schwartz and Paris 1999). Both fanned the business community's traditional fears about mass empowerment; these fears, together with concerns about the new regime's (IMF-supported) attacks on business-state cronyism, left business leaders skeptical about if not actually hostile to Indonesia's fragile new regime (EIU, *Country Report: Indonesia*, July–September 1998, 13).

South Korea: Variation Proves the Rule

Parallel experience in the South Korean case confirms the importance of state sponsorship in shaping the political disposition of private sector capital.[4] But the South Korean case is most compelling for the internal variation it exhibits over time. During the early decades of the postwar era, state sponsorship of the private sector was extensive and important. And throughout this period, the private sector proved diffident about democratization. From the mid-1980s, however, the state began to cut back on its sponsorship of private sector capital and the latter's need for state support also declined. Coincident with these changes, the private sector began to exhibit remarkable enthusiasm for political reform and democratization.

The decades of extensive state sponsorship divide into two periods: one in which the state's primary logic was patrimonial and one in which it was developmental.[5] During the patrimonial rule of Syngman Rhee, both the genesis and the success of private sector firms turned on political mediation and access to the state's discretionary favor. Cronyism governed the start of many private sector firms (Eckert 1990, 40; Ogle 1990, 42). And preferential access to government-controlled resources (such as tax breaks, trade monopolies, foreign aid disbursement, and low-interest loans) governed private sector growth (Fields 1995, 31–40; Kuk 1988, 110–17). But even when the state adopted a more "developmental" ethos under Park Chung Hee, the private sector's dependence on the state's discretionary favor persisted. The state retained control over access to credit, foreign currency, foreign loans and grants, tax breaks, and monopoly position in the local economy, and thus private sector success continued to be governed by political mediation and cultivation of the state's goodwill (Fields 1995, 95–96, 121).

The discretionary nature of state support spelled a culture of political compliance within the business community as well as wariness of political initiatives that might jeopardize the flow of state benefits. The shadiness of business-state relations, especially during the Syngman Rhee years, did not kindle a desire for transparency. And the state's identification with and anticipation of business interests during the Park Chung Hee years, and after, made more formal mechanisms of accountability unessential. For the better part of the postwar era, then, private sector capital was uninterested in democratization. Korean capitalists closed ranks behind the authoritarian state, eschewing the popular movements led by students, workers, and intellectuals that tried to push the regime toward political liberalization (Koo 1993, 31–35; Eckert et al. 1990, 347–88; Eckert 1990, 147). Members of the business community avoided any public role in politics, their silence signaling assent to authoritarian rule.

But all this began to change in the mid-1980s. The first glimmers of a shift in the political attitudes of capital came in 1986–87, when the leading business confederation, the Federation of Korean Industries (FKI), raised a new political agenda boldly independent of the ruling party.[6] More dramatically, in 1991 the founder and chair of one of Korea's largest *chaebol*,

Chung Ju Yung of the Hyundai Group, established a new political party designed to challenge the ruling Democratic Justice Party (DJP). The party succeeded in winning 17% of the popular vote in the general elections of 1992, and later that year Chung even made a bid for the presidency (Koo 1993, 47; Fields 1995, 60).

Such assertiveness marked an important departure for capital. How can this shift from complicity in authoritarian rule toward frank embrace of democratic contestation and pluralism be explained? Reduction in state sponsorship of the private sector, as well as a decline in the private sector's need for state support, account for much of it.

During the 1980s, worldwide recession engendered by the oil crisis of 1979 created serious economic difficulties for Korea and forced the Chun regime to adopt an ambitious program of structural reform that spelled decreased state support for the private sector. The regime reduced credit supplies, decreased protection of the domestic market, and enacted a new trade law that ended the long-standing monopoly positions enjoyed by many chaebol in the domestic market (Haggard and Moon 1993, 51–93). Political changes also cut into many of the private sector's privileges. In 1987, for reasons independent of the business community, the regime shifted toward the embrace of competitive electoral politics.[7] This shift created a new political imperative for the regime to woo popular support; as part of its campaign to build a popular base, the regime sought to distance itself from big business by attacking the chaebol for corruption, imposing stricter controls on bank credits, and raising inheritance taxes (Eckert et al. 1990, 377–79; Koo 1993, 48).

In short, structural adjustment and political opening meant that the state would no longer be reflexively solicitous of private sector interests. Many domestic capitalists began to view the state with increasing distrust, and some, like Chung of Hyundai, began to look for a new way to make the state more responsive to their concerns. This included the embrace of democratic reform.

The private sector's receptivity to democratization was also helped along by its declining *need* for state support. During the first postwar decades, Korea's late industrialization had spelled private sector dependence on the state for capital accumulation, entrepreneurial direction, and protection of the local market. By the mid-1980s, however, Korean industry was competitive enough to render state protection from foreign rivals nonessential, and it possessed a deep enough store of entrepreneurial experience to make state direction increasingly superfluous. In addition, many of the chaebol were sufficiently large to provide, on an in-house basis, many of the financial services that the state had previously supplied (Hamilton and Kim 1993, 116, 119; Koo 1993, 47). In short, because the private sector had overcome many of the dependencies associated with latecomer status, capital had new opportunities to break ranks with the regime and embrace political reform.[8]

Again, as in the case of Tunisia and Indonesia, capital's attitude toward democratization was also shaped by its level of fear. In the early postwar years pervasive poverty in South Korea,[9] as well as a popular, activist Communist Party,[10] meant that enfranchising the poor contained the potential to threaten the capitalist social order. Communism's victory in North Korea and the continuing state of war between North and South only heightened capital's sense of danger and dampened its enthusiasm for mass empowerment. But by the late 1980s, expanding prosperity had decreased the sense of a zero-sum conflict between capital and labor (Kong 1996, 241), and absolute poverty had largely been eliminated.[11] Moreover, the global decline of communism reduced the revolutionary implications of popular empowerment. Capital could be persuaded that mass exclusion was no longer essential to preserving the social order and that democratic reform might better serve its interests.

Declining state sponsorship and declining need for such sponsorship combined with reduced fear spelled increased enthusiasm for private sector capital in South Korea.

Corroboration from Brazil and Mexico

The logic governing capital's contingent commitment to democracy in Korea and Indonesia is corroborated by other cases as well. The Brazilian case, for example, replicates both the intertemporal variation found in Korea as well as its etiology.[12] Brazil's private sector was closely allied with the country's embrace of authoritarianism in 1964. But by the late 1980s, much of the private sector had come to endorse democratization. The reasoning behind this change of heart echoes that of the Korean case, with enthusiasm for democracy inversely correlated with the provision of sponsorship by the state and with capital's level of fear.

Briefly put, during the 1960s, the prosperity of Brazil's "infant industry" was highly dependent on state support in the form of subsidies, contracts, credit, and access to technology. Private sector capital was thus especially eager to support a state that would prioritize its interests (over, say, populist demands) and be committed to its growth. At the same time, the private sector was gripped by fear of revolutionary insurgence. Widespread poverty, a radical left eager to mobilize the economically disadvantaged, and a cold war context gave substance to the private sector's fear of social revolution. Both factors led the private sector to support the rise of an authoritarian regime, given its promise to sponsor the development of the private sector and contain the left.[13] But two decades later, conditions had changed to make the private sector reevaluate its support for authoritarianism. Already by the mid-1970s the authoritarian regime had proven less than fully responsive to capital's interests, privileging public enterprises over private, expanding the state's regulation of the economy at the expense of private sector interests, and failing to deliver important financial support to the capital goods sector (Cardoso 1986, 143–44). Furthermore, during the 1980s the private sector's fear of revolutionary insurgence dissipated with the deradicalization of the left after two decades of repression, the demise of the Soviet Union, and the end of the cold war. Both declining state support and declining fear persuaded the private sector to abandon the authoritarian regime and support democratic transition in Brazil.

Juxtaposition of the Brazilian and Korean case is especially useful because it helps eliminate rival hypotheses to our theory of capital's contingent commitment to democracy. Specifically, it helps defeat the claim that level of economic prosperity and/or cultural endowment determine class disposition toward democracy. Comparison of the two cases reveals significant similarity in private sector enthusiasm for democracy despite important variation in economic context. The private sector expressed enthusiasm for democracy in Brazil when that country was facing serious economic crisis, whereas in Korea private sector enthusiasm emerged while that country was experiencing rapid economic growth. Juxtaposition of these two cases suggests that level of economic prosperity alone cannot anticipate variation in class enthusiasm for democracy. Similarly, both cases show significant variation in the private sector's enthusiasm for democracy over time, despite constancy in each country's core cultural endowment. This evidence suggests that cultural heritage alone cannot account for variation in class enthusiasm for democracy.

Still outstanding for our hypothesis is the problem of collinearity between state sponsorship and fear found in all the cases presented thus far. But with some cases, the two variables do not covary. Preliminary evidence from these suggests that state sponsorship is a more powerful inhibitor of capital's enthusiasm for democracy than is fear. The Mexican case, for example, supports this impression.[14]

In Mexico, private sector capital chose to embrace democratization when the importance and level of state sponsorship declined, even as social fear persisted.[15] The private sector was long the dependent stepchild of the Mexican revolution. Excluded from any public role in politics, the private sector was generously nurtured by the state's "alliance for profits" strategy. As such, it acquiesced to the regime's authoritarianism. But beyond dependence on state support, the private sector's alliance with authoritarianism was also fueled by fear. Although the threat of an organized radical left had largely been shut out by the ruling "revolutionary" party, the mass poverty and income inequality found in Mexican society were grounds for concern among the propertied classes and reason to support an exclusionary, even repressive, state apparatus.

By the late 1970s and early 1980s, however, the rationale for capital's alliance with the authoritarian regime began to unravel. Not that massive poverty or income inequality, the grounds for private sector fear, had decreased. If anything, these scourges worsened as currency problems and fiscal deficits plunged Mexico into severe economic crisis during the 1980s (Edwards 1995; Middlebrook 1991). Rather, the private sector's economic dependence on the state, along with its confidence in state sponsorship, had begun to decline. A new group of private sector entrepreneurs emerged who were export-oriented and decreasingly reliant on state support and protected markets for their prosperity. They resented the state's corrupt intervention in the economy and were vexed by many of its policy decisions, notably the nationalization of banks during the currency crisis of 1982. Private sector entrepreneurs began to question the state's fidelity to the "alliance for profits," and under these conditions, an important segment of them "discovered democracy."[16] They began to push for the democratization of Mexico's political system and spearheaded political pluralization by bankrolling the political party PAN. In the Mexican case, invariable social threat as well as decreased provision and reliance on state sponsorship spelled private sector support for democratization.

Political Posture of Organized Labor: Mexico, Korea, Egypt, and Zambia

Evidence from Mexico, Korea, Egypt, and Zambia indicates the important role that state sponsorship plays in shaping the political disposition of *labor. Contrast across cases* supports this. The two core cases, Mexico and Korea, show dramatic variation in labor's support for democracy. That variation correlates inversely with the level of sponsorship labor received from the state. *Parallelism across cases* further supports this relationship. The Zambian case mirrors that of Korea in labor's enthusiasm for democracy; also, as in the Korean case, this enthusiasm emerged in a context where the state refrained from sponsorship of labor. Finally, *contrast within cases* provides additional validation of this relationship. Egypt, for example, shows intertemporal variation in labor's enthusiasm for democracy, and this variation correlates inversely with the level of sponsorship delivered by the state.

Mexico: State Sponsorship and Democratically Diffident Labor

The Mexican case provides compelling evidence of the *diffident* attitude organized labor may exhibit toward democratization when it is the beneficiary of extensive state sponsorship.[17]

The Mexican Confederation of Workers (CTM), one of the largest constitutive elements of organized labor in Mexico, long enjoyed an "authoritarian bargain" with the Mexican state. In exchange for the delivery of reliable political support and industrial peace, the CTM received a host of organizational and material benefits from the state. These included financial subsidies and legal concessions, such as exclusive domain and closed shop, which bolstered the movement organizationally, as well as profit-sharing schemes, privileged access to social welfare programs, and subsidized urban housing and credit, which advantaged CTM members materially (Collier 1992, 59, 83; Ponte 1991, 100; Whitehead 1991, 73). This bargain with labor was clearly lopsided, for the state's superior power, both coercive and administrative, enabled it to set the terms of the alliance with labor in self-serving fashion (Middlebrook 1991, 9; Whitehead 1991, 75). Still, the state delivered organizational and material benefits that *far exceeded what labor could have procured on its own.*

Many factors, among them high rates of unemployment, geographic dispersal of the labor force, small worker concentration per firm, and global pressures, undercut the structural position of organized labor in the Mexican economy (Middlebrook 1991, 9). State sponsorship was thus essential to compensate for labor's weakness and enable workers to achieve basic material and social rights (Murillo 1996; Middlebrook 1995, 288).

But the logic of state sponsorship hinged on the persistence of an *authoritarian* bargain in Mexico and, more specifically, on the leverage that labor enjoyed as a key guarantor of the regime's popular support.

Democratization, by contrast, presented the regime with new ways to forge political legitimacy and build a popular base. As such, it threatened to rob the labor confederation of its key political trump (and its certainty of political sponsorship).[18] Given the CTM's reliance on state sponsorship, its leaders proved less than enthusiastic about democratic reform.

The CTM's antipathy toward democratization was evident in many ways. The labor confederation remained steadfastly allied with the Mexican regime despite the latter's persistent repression of opposition forces, restrictions on civil liberties, and staging of noncompetitive elections. More surprisingly, when the regime itself began to move in a more democratic direction,[19] the CTM distinguished itself as one of the leading opponents of political reform. It denounced the legalization of leftist parties in 1977, called for the expulsion of Cárdenas's reformist movement from the ruling party in 1988, protested opposition successes in the general elections held that year, and refused support to opposition parties in the 1990s (Middlebrook 1991, 15; Ponte 1991, 94; 101–2; Rueschemeyer, Stephens, and Stephens 1992, 217–19; Middlebrook 1995, 292, 311). Ponte (1991, 102) observes that organized labor's greatest fear was the democratization of the political system. Labor's dependence on state sponsorship and the linkage of state sponsorship to an authoritarian system of rule make clear why.

Of course labor's diffidence about democratization was not solely the consequence of dependence on state sponsorship. As in the case of Tunisia, organized labor enjoyed an "aristocratic" position in society that disjoined labor's interests from those of other subordinate strata and diminished the allure of making the state accountable to mass interest. Unionized workers enjoyed a host of benefits such as privileged access to state-subsidized housing, health care, financial credit, and retirement funds, not to mention stable employment and social security benefits (Middlebrook 1995, 221).[20] These advantages distinguished unionized workers from the vast majority of their compatriots in a society where poverty remained rampant,[21] unemployment and underemployment remained high,[22] and the informal economy continued to claim a large proportion of the country's economic activity.[23] These advantages were to a large degree the consequence of political brokering (rather than market power), and labor therefore had an even greater incentive to preserve its special relationship with the state, even if that meant bolstering an authoritarian regime and forgoing democratic reform.

In short, diffidence about democracy long distinguished the leading Mexican trade unions, like the CTM. (After Vicente Fox's election deposed the PRI in 2000 and heralded Mexico's true transition to democracy, the CTM was forced to scramble to catch up. The union did not denounce the transition but rather tried to accommodate this fait accompli and, true to form, sought to curry favor with the new regime.) But the union's prolonged reluctance to break with authoritarianism prior to the 2000 election is best explained by its considerable dependence on state sponsorship as well as its aristocratic status in Mexican society.[24]

Korea: State Persecution, Economic Exclusion, and Democratically Committed Labor

In contrast to the Mexican case, organized labor in Korea has long been at the forefront of the struggle for democratization. But there the state eschewed the sponsorship of labor, opting instead for labor's repression and economic exclusion.[25]

The state's posture toward organized labor in Korea could not stand in starker contrast to the Mexican case. In Mexico, the regime's revolutionary origins gave it a populist bent and inclined it toward alliance with the working class. Moreover, its pursuit of an import-substituting strategy of industrialization until well into the 1970s protected the local market and workers from international competition and provided the regime with economic "space" to accommodate labor's demands. In Korea, however, the regime's emergence in a cold war context and its experience of civil war with the Communist-led North spelled hostility toward organized labor, which was perceived as a potential vehicle for communist insurgence. In addition, the regime's early embrace of an export-oriented strategy of industrialization put a premium on low-cost, quiescent labor, and this strategy set the regime at odds with the ambitions of organized labor.

Given these conditions, the ruthless repression of labor, not cozy corporatist alliance, emerged as the defining mark of the Korean regime. Every postwar government repressed labor, often brutally: Syngman Rhee crushed the independent trade union movement and replaced it with a state-controlled structure; Park Chung Hee ordered mass arrests of union militants; and Chun Doo Hwan espoused torture and "purification camps" (Ogle 1990, x-xiv, 6–9, 48–55; Koo 1993, 131–39, 150; Deyo 1989, 120; Lee 1988, 135–40). Such relentless persecution gave labor little incentive to side with the authoritarian regime and every reason to push for reform that would make the state more responsive to mass interest.

Lack of state sponsorship gave labor both the independence and the interest to embrace the cause of democratization. But labor's independence was also fostered by its market position, which ultimately made it less needy of state sponsorship. In contrast to the Mexican case, where high levels of unemployment, low levels of industrialization, and low skill levels spelled a structurally weak position for labor and hence dependence on state propping, labor in Korea enjoyed an increasingly strong structural position. The country's rapid growth rate and dramatic expansion of industry led to an increasingly tight labor market, which strengthened labor's negotiating muscle (Koo 1984, 1030; Deyo 1989, 24). In addition, the regime's shift into heavy industry reinforced labor's position by creating gargantuan industrial sites that concentrated workers and facilitated trade union organizing (Deyo 1989, 34–42; Ogle 1990, 109). Finally, the regime's shift into heavy industry and consequent reliance on skilled labor insulated Korean workers from competition with the poorest of the unskilled poor in the global proletariat (Deyo 1989, 25).[26] In short, Korea's development path favored labor with independent structural power. Labor did not have to rely on state propping to advance its interests, and this freed labor to embrace political causes not favored by state elites.

Thus, in contrast to Mexico's CTM, organized labor in Korea allied itself with the cause of democratic reform. Twice in Korea's postwar history authoritarian rule was interrupted, and on both occasions organized labor played an active role in the popular movements agitating for reform (Eckert et al. 1990, 352–56; Hamilton and Kim 1993, 118–21). In 1960, workers followed student-initiated protest, organizing scores of strikes and demonstrations that called for an end to corrupt government (Ogle 1990, 13–16). Similarly, during the 1980s, workers joined forces with students, intellectuals, and church activists to pressure the regime to reform (Eckert et al. 1990, 380; Lee 1988, 149; Koo 1993, 39; Ogle 1990, 116).

Again, as in the Tunisian and Mexican cases, labor's level of aristocratic privilege also shaped its disposition toward democratic reform. But in contrast to these other cases, labor in Korea scored low in terms of aristocracy. For all its growing structural strength, labor did not enjoy a privileged economic position in Korean society. Wages remained deplorably low, lagging far behind productivity gains, and substantially trailing wages in many service sectors.[27] Working conditions were appalling.[28] And working hours were interminable.[29] This hardship was especially difficult for workers to bear, given the material progress made by so many other sectors in society (Kong 1996, 226–37). Workers "came to see themselves as the principal victims of economic development" (Lee 1988, 144), not as the beneficiaries of aristocratic privilege. Worse still, the harsh treatment of workers was the deliberate intent of the regime, which saw the extreme exploitation of labor as the cornerstone of its development strategy. In contrast to the situation in Mexico and Tunisia, organized labor in Korea had no special, politically mediated privilege to conserve and every reason to support democratization of the political system.

In the Korean case, low scores on state sponsorship and aristocratic position help explain organized labor's interest in and capacity for embracing democratization.

Corroboration from Zambia and Egypt

The importance of state sponsorship and aristocratic position for shaping labor's commitment to democracy is further corroborated by evidence from Zambia and Egypt. The Zambian case parallels that of Korea and confirms that low scores on both these variables incline labor toward championing democratization.[30]

The Zambian trade union movement (ZCTU), long one of the strongest in sub-Saharan Africa, was based primarily in copper mining. This sector provided the lion's share of the country's foreign exchange and government revenues. During the 1980s, however, a steep decline in international copper prices plunged the country into economic crisis. Workers experienced a huge erosion in wages, eliminating any vestige of aristocratic privilege.[31] The state, moreover, did nothing to insulate labor from the crisis but rather embarked on an energetic campaign of labor repression (Mihyo 1995, 208).

In this context of low aristocracy and negative state sponsorship, Zambia's labor movement emerged as one of the most enthusiastic campaigners for democratization. The ZCTU swung its support behind the Movement for Multiparty Democracy. It organized strikes, mobilized an extensive network of trade union committees, and provided key leadership for the cause (Mihyo 1995, 201; Rakner 1992). Like Korea, Zambia provides an example of a trade-union movement cut loose from the moorings of state support and exposed to harsh economic conditions that, in turn, emerges as a major champion of democratic reform.

Besides such parallelism, the Zambian case is also useful because its comparison with the Korean case helps eliminate a rival hypothesis that links level of enthusiasm for democracy with level of economic growth and prosperity. In Zambia, labor's activism on behalf of democratization came precisely at a time of great economic crisis. By contrast, in Korea labor's agitation for democratization developed in a context of economic prosperity.

Our final case, Egypt, is most useful for its intertemporal variation that both confirms an inverse relationship between sponsorship and democratic advocacy and helps eliminate a rival hypothesis that links class enthusiasm for democracy to cultural endowment.[32] In Egypt, the labor movement has long been party to a corporatist bargain with the Egyptian state. In exchange for the delivery of worker restraint and political support, the union received essential material and organizational benefits from the state. These included financial subsidies to the union, prestigious political positions for union leaders, and important nonwage benefits for workers, such as job security, social security benefits, and generous leave policy (e.g., maternity leave). Access to such politically mediated privilege spelled aristocracy for organized labor. It also wedded the trade union movement to the authoritarian status quo, making it unreceptive to democratic reform. Thus, when Sadat began to move Egypt toward a multiparty system in the early 1970s, trade union leaders vigorously condemned the plan because it threatened to reduce the influence they had enjoyed under the country's single-party system (Bianchi 1986, 438; Bianchi 1989, 138).

By the mid-1990s, however, international pressure to undertake structural adjustment forced the regime to retreat from its historic bargain with labor and cut back on its sponsorship of the movement. Specifically, the regime committed itself to reforming the labor code with the intention of axing organized labor's most treasured advantage—job security. The regime also endorsed privatization schemes that would contract the sphere of labor's political protection (Posusney 1997). With the essence of labor's aristocratic privilege now under attack, trade union leaders began to express support for democratization.[33] Persistent dependence on state support made the labor movement hesitant about dramatically endorsing political reform (e.g., it did not form an independent labor party to contest the ruling party), but declining sponsorship, declining aristocracy, and hence the declining value of the authoritarian bargain made labor receptive to political reform, so long as it came at someone else's initiative.

All told, organized labor in Egypt shifted from candid negativism to an ambivalent attitude toward democratization. The decline in state sponsorship and aristocratic privilege best explain this change of heart.[34] The intertemporal variation found in this case also suggests that cultural heritage alone cannot account for variation in class enthusiasm for democracy. Organized labor revised its political stance in Egypt without any revolution in the country's core cultural endowment.

Sponsored Development and the Erosion of Authoritarianism

The variety of these cases suggests a number of general lessons about the attenuation of authoritarianism in the context of late development.

First, state sponsorship hinders the development of class enthusiasm for democracy. Case after case reflects the fact that when state sponsorship is high, capital and labor are unlikely to champion democratic reform. With state sponsorship a standard strategy among developing countries today, this finding suggests a much more ambiguous relationship between industrialization and democratization in the context of late development than that suggested by the classic works of political economy.

Second, analysis of these cases clarifies the causal mechanism behind class ambivalence toward democracy in the context of late development. Capital and labor are everywhere and always contingent democrats. They support democracy when it is in their material interest to do so. What distinguishes late developers is the pervasiveness of state sponsorship that allies the material interests of capital and labor with the state, even if that state is authoritarian. The sponsoring state anticipates their interests, bolsters their position, protects their privileges. The appeal of democracy is diminished when the state is responsive even in the absence of institutionalized guarantees, when transparency threatens to undermine cozy links with state elites, and when state-sponsored privilege disjoins class interest from mass concerns. The pervasive poverty found in many late-developing countries only further fuels capital and labor's alliance with authoritarianism, planting fear of mass empowerment in capital and heightening the divide between organized labor and other subordinate groups in society. Capital and labor thus have compelling material reasons to stand by authoritarian regimes in the context of late development.

Third, the cases suggest that many countries get stuck halfway between authoritarianism and democracy because of the differential impact that state sponsorship has on the development of class power and autonomy. State-sponsored industrialization clearly fosters the empowerment of capital and labor. Industrialists in Korea and Indonesia have grown in number, size, contribution to GNP, and employment creation, amassing significant structural power in the process, thanks to state sponsorship. Labor in Mexico and Egypt has grown in size, concentration, and generational depth, reinforcing workers' capacity for collective action and political influence, thanks to the state's policy of sponsored industrialization. The power developed by these classes has enabled capital and labor to command policy responsiveness from the powers that be. Organized labor has been able to slow the process of privatization in Egypt (Posusney 1997). Private sector capital has been able to extract government bailouts for faltering firms in Korea (Koo 1993). These states can no longer set the course of public policy unilaterally but rather have been forced to take into account the interests of class forces in society.

In this way, state-sponsored industrialization pluralizes power in society and chisels away at the peremptory rule dominion of authoritarian states. The state does "sow the seeds of its own demise," or at least the demise of its own unilateral power, by nurturing social groups that can nibble away at the state's autonomy. Thus, while state-led development may in many ways lead to the mutual empowerment of state and society,[35] it yields a zero-sum game in terms of their respective autonomy. State-sponsored industrialization empowers society at the expense of the state's own autonomy. This is the essence of the developmental paradox discerned first in the Tunisian case and replicated in many other cases of late-developing authoritarian states. But at the same time, state-sponsored industrialization also compromises the autonomy of the very classes it empowers. When both capital and labor become beholden to the goodwill of the state for their well-being, they are discouraged from championing the cause of democratic reform. Sponsored classes don't want to rock the boat of state patronage, they are less than enamored of democracy's transparency, they don't need institutionalized mechanisms to secure state responsiveness, and their relative privilege cools their enthusiasm for populist governance. Their reluctance to embrace democracy yields the democratic paradox of state-sponsored development. In Tunisia, as in our other cases, the very factor that enables these social forces to elicit a measure of responsiveness from the state is the same factor that discourages them from campaigning for guaranteed responsiveness in the form of democratic institutions.

The consequence of these dual paradoxes is stalled democracy. As in the Tunisian case, many developmentally minded authoritarian states get stuck in an intermediate zone between authoritarianism and democracy where the state is responsive to a few privileged interests but not to society as a whole. This was true for South Korea through the mid-1980s and for Mexico through the mid-1990s. It is still true for Egypt today. To the extent that these countries have moved toward democracy, political change has come at the initiative of other forces in society—reform-minded party elites in Mexico; church activists, students, and free intellectuals in Korea, assisted by labor, which did not enjoy state-sponsorship. The lesson of the Tunisian case is, Don't look to capital and labor to lead the charge. Contrary to the lore of the first transition, the protagonists of industrialization are not likely to be heroes of democratization in the context of late development. If anything, these cases suggest that capital and labor often have good reason to stall democracy.

But comparative analysis also suggests some of the conditions that might "unstall" democracy and mobilize capital and labor behind the cause of reform. Integration into the international economy may force late-developing states to embrace market logic and reduce sponsorship of social forces (Korea, Egypt). Robust growth may improve the structural position of either capital or labor, decreasing their dependence on state sponsorship (Mexico, Korea). Robust growth that is widely shared may eliminate mass poverty, diminishing capital's fear of mass empowerment and closing the gap of privilege that divides organized labor from other subordinate strata in society (Korea). Under these conditions, capital or labor may perceive democratization in a new light and choose to embrace it. The intertemporal variation found in cases like those of Korea, Mexico, and Egypt makes this possibility clear.

Lessons for the Middle East and North Africa

The Middle East and North Africa is a region renowned for entrenched authoritarianism. Many factors—culture, history, economic endowment—are said to contribute to this outcome.[36] But the MENA region, like other parts of the late-developing world, has also been the site of experiments in state-sponsored industrialization. Turkey, Egypt, Tunisia, Morocco, and to a lesser extent, Syria, Jordan, and Saudi Arabia, have all embraced this strategy for a decade or two, if not more.[37] What implications does this developmental strategy have for the attenuation of authoritarianism there? Has state-sponsored industrialization reconfigured the power relations between state and society in these countries, eroding the state's capacity for peremptory rule? Has state sponsorship exercised the same paradoxical influence here, as elsewhere, stalling the emergence of democracy? By focusing on three cases—Egypt, Syria, and Turkey[38]—the remainder of this chapter considers the lessons of stalled democracy for many countries in the MENA region, exploring both the limits and possibilities of authoritarianism's erosion that have been set in motion by the embrace of state-sponsored industrialization.[39]

Pluralization of Power: Capital

Perhaps the most encouraging news is that Egypt, Syria, and Turkey, like other late-developing countries that have followed a path of state-sponsored industrialization, have seen a pluralization of power that is eroding the state's capacity to rule peremptorily. The pluralization of power is most evident with regard to private sector capital. In these countries, as in many others across the region, conscious state policy has encouraged the growth of the private sector, enabling it to play an ever-larger role in capital formation, employment creation, and the production of value added.[40] In Turkey, for example, the private sector accounted for 68% of fixed capital investment, 67% of wages paid in manufacturing industry, and 60% of value added by the mid-1980s (Bugra 1994, 66). In Egypt, the private sector accounted for 49% of the country's industrial investment and 58% of industrial output by 1992–93, and it significantly outpaced the public sector in employment creation (Giugale and Mobarak 1996, 32, 142).[41] And in Syria, the private sector accounted for 55% of the country's gross domestic product, 45% of employment in manufacturing industry, and 37% of value added in "converting industries" by the early 1990s (Perthes 1995, 59, 119).[42]

The expanded contribution of the private sector to the economy has spelled significant structural power for this class. At the same time, the change in the private sector's structural position has led to the rehabilitation of its public image. Where the private sector was once derided by many states in the region as selfish, short-sighted, and parasitic, now it is publicly embraced as the leader of national development (Hinnebusch 1993, 166; Perthes 1995, 236). This rehabilitation, in turn, has opened the way for private sector participation in electoral politics, often for the first time. As early as 1987, Egypt counted eighty business executives among its 450 members of parliament (Hinnebusch 1993, 166)—an unprecedented percentage for a country that had long been famous for its commitment to "Arab socialism" and whose ruling party still technically reserves 50% of all parliamentary seats for peasants and workers. In

Syria, by May 1990, three members of the Damascus and Aleppo chambers of commerce were elected to parliament—"the first clearly defined 'representatives of business' to serve in parliament since 1963" (Perthes, cited in Heydemann 1993, 93).

Recognition of the private sector's contribution to the economy has also translated into increased access to the executive and inclusion in state policy making. In Egypt, all the major business associations—the Egyptian Businessman's Association, the Federation of Egyptian Industry, the Alexandria Business Association—enjoy institutionalized representation on the major government committees that shape economic law and chart the country's economic course (Brouwer 1995, 86, 91, 98). As such, they engage in "national dialogues," participate in restructuring the economy, and oversee the implementation of policy. In addition, private sector leaders are also granted access to the executive on an individual basis, as the president and leading ministers frequently hold meetings with leading Egyptian businessmen (Kandil 1989, 9). In Syria as well, there is evidence of an increasingly large consultative role played by the private sector in the state's economic decision making. The Damascus Chamber of Commerce is frequently invited to sit on key economic policy-making committees (the Guidance Committee, the Committee for the Guidance of Imports and Exports), and the chambers are increasingly recognized as useful sources of economic information and advice by the executive and by parliamentary committees (Heydemann 1993, 92; Perthes 1995, 211, 216, 223). This recognition marks a dramatic departure from the days when the private sector was ignored, if not hounded, by the state in so many MENA countries.

The private sector's expanded structural power together with its inclusion in the political process has given it new influence over policy outcomes. In Egypt, this is evident in the proliferation of tax exemptions won by the private sector, despite the complaints of the Ministry of Finance; the rollback of agrarian tenancy laws, despite the opposition of farm workers and peasants; the low capital gains tax Egypt maintains; the reversal of customs duties increases; and the repeal of government decrees to regulate the foreign currency market (Hinnebusch 1993, 165–66; Kandil 1987, 9). In Syria, it is evident in the content of export/import laws and the terms of currency exchange (Perthes 1995). Private sector power has thus eroded the state's capacity to set policy unilaterally.

Of course, the private sector's power should not be overstated. Significant obstacles still prevent the private sector from "capturing the state" or dictating policy,[43] and here the lessons of the Tunisian case are instructive. First, as in Tunisia, the small size of the vast majority of private sector enterprises handicaps their ability to exercise the full clout merited by their aggregate structural position.[44] In addition, the high level of indebtedness that characterizes the lion's share of these firms, their tenuous (global) competitiveness, combined with the persistence of a sizeable public sector, also clips the private sector's structural power (World Bank 1996; Gobe 1997, 59). Second, the institutional legacy of many MENA states, in particular the lack of competitive multiparty politics,[45] the failure of the ruling party to develop institutional distance and financial autonomy from the state, and the absence of guaranteed civil liberties, undermines the capacity of private sector capital to translate structural power into instrumental and hegemonic power. Specifically, it hinders the private sector's ability to exercise the power of the purse in politics,[46] organize effective lobbies to defend their interests,[47] or establish cultural leadership through control of the media.[48] Third, the limited historical and generational depth of the industrializing experience in the region prevents many private sector business people from developing the self-image necessary to lead a hegemonic project culturally or intellectually. Few as yet have opted to build media empires or endow universities. Finally, field size undermines the development of collective clout by the private sector. The small size of the elite in most of these countries encourages the personalization of problem solving and undermines the mobilization of collective power on the part of private sector leaders (Baroudi 1997; Perthes 1995).

Despite these obstacles, the private sector stands out as the most dynamic sector in the economy of almost every MENA country, offering the greatest promise for capital procurement, employment creation, and productivity. As such, it possesses undeniable structural power. Given the realities of declining rents and international pressures faced by most MENA states, reliance on the private sector is bound to rise further. The private sector's capacity to influence the state and shape public policy is likely to rise commensurately.

Pluralization of Power: Labor

By contrast, the picture looks decidedly less bright for labor. State sponsorship of labor has been a more checkered affair, and the state's developmental project has had mixed impact on the evolution of labor's power. Historically, the early embrace of etatism by countries like Syria, Turkey, and Egypt multiplied the number of industrial workers and concentrated them in large state enterprises. This boosted the structural conditions for militance and collective action for a significant number of workers and endowed them with influence over such policy issues as wage and working conditions (Longuenesse 1985; Hinnebusch 1990; Posusney 1997). In addition, the state's populist bent, especially in countries that embraced "Arab socialism" (like Syria and Egypt), and its need for political allies led to the negotiation of an "authoritarian bargain" with labor. In exchange for labor's delivery of reliable political support and workplace restraint, the state provided essential support to organized labor, including financial subsidies, privileged political access, and above-market wages. Thus, in the early decades of independent statehood, these states did sponsor the development of organized labor and endow it with a measure of policy influence.[49]

In more recent years, however, the state's developmental strategy has undermined the structural position of labor and compromised the basis of its power. In the wake of state fiscal crisis and the forced embrace of economic liberalization, the state's encouragement of private rather than public sector growth and the espousal of privatization, even in fledgling fashion, has fostered the dispersion of the workforce to smaller private enterprises where collective action is harder to organize.[50] The shift toward international economic integration (courting international investment, attempting to conquer export markets) has exposed MENA workers to significant wage pressure from the global proletariat, further discouraging worker militance.[51] Moreover, the state's development efforts have not been robust enough to overcome some of the classic corrosives to labor's power. Unemployment rates in the MENA region rank among the highest in the world (World Bank 1995a, 28).[52] Poverty rates remain high and have only worsened in recent years.[53] And the informal sector has grown dramatically across the region (Moghadam 1996, 91–100; Goldberg 1996a, 181; U.S. Dept. of Labor, *Foreign Labor Trends Report: Turkey*, 1992–93, 3; Farsoun 1995, 275). All these factors exert extreme wage pressure on workers, heighten their sense of economic precariousness, and undermine their capacity for militance. Add to this the decline of ideologies like Arab socialism that constituted the conceptual underpinning of the state's populist alliance with labor, and labor's increasingly vulnerable position becomes clear.

Despite these challenges, however, organized labor still manages to exercise some influence over policy, and this influence is in large part a consequence of the state's own making. As in Tunisia, labor's ultimate trump lies in its potential value as a political ally and its capacity to deliver an organized base of mass support to the regime in power. Across the region, regimes have long turned to organized labor to bolster their political position, from Nasser's reliance on labor to fend off democratic challenges to his regime in 1954 and again in 1968 (Beinin and Lockman 1987),[54] to Assad's dependence on labor to generate support for his regime whenever he faced "critical" challenges (as in the wake of the regime's unpopular intervention in Lebanon 1976 and during the Hama uprising in 1982) (Perthes 1995, 176). In recent years, labor's value as a political ally has only increased as slowed growth and economic austerity have undermined the popularity of so many MENA regimes. Popular opposition movements have grown in Syria, Egypt, and beyond, and these movements have frequently taken an Islamist cast. In this context, the trade-union movement stands out as one of the few mass organizations that has resisted Islamization (Stork 1995, 29). As such, it is in a unique position to mobilize mass support for beleaguered regimes and serve as a counterweight to a vigorous Islamist opposition (Lawson 1992, 132). Regimes under Islamist attack thus have an interest in sustaining the trade-union movement and including it in the political game.

Thanks to its political value, as well as surviving pockets of structural power centered in public sector enterprises that hail from the etatist era, organized labor continues to exercise some influence over the policy-making process in countries like Egypt and Syria. In Egypt, union influence is evident in the slowed pace of privatization pursued by the state under Mubarak (Posusney 1997). In Syria, it is evident in the "selective liberalization" undertaken by Assad's regime, a consequence of the government's desire to keep the labor constituency on board (Heydemann 1992). In this way organized labor does prove capable of exercising limited veto power over policy formation (Bianchi 1986), and its persistent influence is a consequence of the state's own logic and sponsorship.

Thus, in these MENA countries, as in their fellow late developers from other regions, the authoritarian state has found itself caught in a developmental paradox. By its own logic the state has nurtured the power of social forces that can now limit its capacity to rule in peremptory fashion. And even if the state's developmental logic spells a less triumphal trajectory for labor's power than for that of capital,[55] still, the policy influence exercised by both marks an important erosion in the state's unilateral power—a significant step in the attenuation of authoritarianism.

The Democratic Paradox

But if state-sponsored development has led to the erosion of authoritarianism in these MENA states, it has also handicapped the process of democratization. This is primarily the consequence of its differential impact on class power and autonomy. For while state sponsorship has augmented the power of capital and labor in many MENA countries, it has also consigned these classes to a position of dependence vis-à-vis the state. The well-being of both capital and labor continues to be beholden to the state's discretionary goodwill, thus diminishing class interest in provocative political causes such as democratization that are likely to jeopardize the flow of state benefits.

Dependence on the state's discretionary goodwill is heightened in the MENA region by several factors. For labor, the key obstacle to independence is a persistently weak market position. In a context of high unemployment, widespread poverty, and low skill levels, organized labor is highly susceptible to the temptation of falling back on political remedy to secure adequate wages and working conditions for its base. In Egypt, Turkey, Syria, and beyond, a weak market position has historically led trade unions to acquiesce in their own clientalization, conceding the loss of basic organizing rights (e.g., the right to strike) as well as trade-union autonomy in exchange for contextually high wages, job security, and other benefits (Bianchi 1984; Bianchi 1986; Beinin and Lockman 1987; Cizre-Sakallioglu 1992; Berik and Bilginsoy 1996). Liazu captures this in harsh terms, arguing that labor's complicity in clientalization has turned unionized workers in the region into rentiers, a privileged sector who derive special profit from their close relation to the state but who pay for this privilege "in the coin of political independence" (1996, 218). Such dependence binds labor to an authoritarian bargain with the state and spells disinterest in political reform so long as the state continues to deliver patronage benefits.

For capital, as well, dependence on the state's discretionary goodwill is augmented by the sector's weak market position. Many private sector firms are globally uncompetitive and could not survive the discipline of open market competition. They have grown up in the lap of state support and prospered thanks to substantial rents harvested from preferential policies negotiated from the state (e.g., see Sadowski 1991; Bugra 1994; Perthes 1995; Gobe 1997).[56] Their failure to be competitive means they are often unenthusiastic about replacing political mediation with market principle as the arbiter of economic allocation. It locks them into clientalistic relations with the state.

Capital's dependence on state discretion is also augmented by a policy failure in much of the region, specifically, the problem of incomplete liberalization. For all the economic reform undertaken, most states in the region continue to play a major role in the local economy, serving as principal contractors, buyers, credit suppliers, and regulators (Bugra 1994, 65; Giugale and Mobarak 1996, 150–54; Gobe 1997, 50). Moreover, the state's distribution of credits, contracts, and other supports is far too often driven less by economic rationality than by reigning officials' desire to build political clienteles and/or line their pockets (Hinnebusch 1994, 102; Bugra 1994, 154; Perthes 1995, 111; Murphy 1995, 19, 21).[57] Add to this the fact that the state's regulatory regime is often complex, ambitious, internally inconsistent, and ever-changing,[58] and it is clear that a fair measure of arbitrariness rules the fortunes of the private sector. Cozy clientalistic relations with state insiders are often essential to business success.

Finally, the problem of incomplete institutionalization also augments the play of state discretion in ruling private sector fortunes. To this day, most MENA countries have failed to develop the institutions necessary for reliable rule setting, rule enforcement, and rights protection (e.g., uncorrupted courts, police, and legislatures). This "institution deficit" is highly problematic for the private sector. It raises transaction costs and forestalls the predictable and contestable business environment that the private sector requires to thrive (Giugale and Mobarak 1996, 35).[59] In this context business people are forced to cultivate personal relations with state elites to help control for the uncertainty they face. In a context of unreliable institutions, the discretionary power of state elites over business fortunes is magnified.

These assaults to the autonomy of capital and labor only compound the classic reasons for disinterest in democracy found among state-sponsored classes. As elsewhere, capital and labor in the Middle East and North Africa are less than enthusiastic about democratization when the authoritarian state anticipates their interests, when transparency threatens to undermine patronage links with the state, and when relative privilege in a context of mass poverty divorces them from mass interest. And so, as in other late-developing regions, neither class has been at the forefront of the cause of democratization. Rather, in the MENA region, the private sector has been, first and foremost, concerned with order, rule of law, secure property rights, and special access to policy makers (Giguale and Mobarak 1996, 31). And organized labor, though often rhetorically committed to the goal of democratization, has in practice done little to promote the cause. In some cases, it has even actively resisted it (Berik and Bilginsoy 1996, 37–41; Bianchi 1986, 438).[60]

Of course, none of this is irremediable. In the MENA region as elsewhere, private sector capital and organized labor are *contingent* democrats. Should contextual conditions change to align the material and political interests of capital and labor in new directions, then the political agenda of these social forces might change as well. For example, should integration into the international economy and marketization of the domestic economy progress, state sponsorship of capital and labor would likely decrease. Should institution building advance, clientalism would decline as the axiom of private sector success. Should mass poverty be eliminated (through robust growth and poverty-reducing policies), capital's fear and labor's disinterest in mass empowerment would be reduced. Under such conditions, capital and labor would likely prove more enthusiastic for democratization than they are today.

This possibility is already suggested by one MENA country—Turkey. There, private sector capital and organized labor have been at the forefront of the campaign for democratization—or, at the very least, significant segments of both have been. In March 1997 the leading Turkish business federation, TUSIAD, published an elaborate report urging faster progress toward full democracy in Turkey and specifying the reforms necessary to achieve this goal (*New York Times*, 23 March 1997, 4). And, since 1993, the three leading labor confederations in Turkey have worked together under the umbrella of the "Democracy Platform" to promote increased democratization that includes freedom of speech and freedom of association (U.S. Dept. of Labor, *Foreign Labor Trends: Turkey*, 1993–94, 12).

The enthusiasm shown by both TUSIAD and the leading labor confederations for democratization confirms the important role that reduced dependence on state sponsorship may play in converting capital and labor to the cause of democratization. In Turkey, it is TUSIAD, the association that represents the larger, more globally competitive, more export-oriented firms that has publicly promoted democratization. This segment of the private sector sees its profits linked less to state sponsorship and more to conquering export markets in Europe.[61] As such, they are freer to recognize the benefits of democratization. Similarly, it is labor unions that have been cut off from state sponsorship in recent years which have embraced the cause of democratization. Where leading unions took a passive stance toward high politics in Turkey during the 1950s, 1960s, and even 1970s (Berik and Bilginsoy 1996, 37–41), today, in the wake of the regime's more repressive stance toward labor, Turkey's leading unions have been converted to the democratic cause. And if reduced clientalism has had this effect, there is every reason to believe that progress on other fronts—reduction of mass poverty, successful institution-building, and increased marketization of the economy—will advance this trend as well.

But all this will take time. In the interim, other forces in society—students, free professionals, intellectuals, and perhaps even Islamists—may lead the campaign for democracy in the MENA region, although exceptional conditions may impede their progress.[62] No matter their efforts, however, it is clear that lasting democratization in the Middle East and North Africa ultimately hinges on important changes in state-society relations and the gradual pluralization of power in MENA societies. The region has already seen some progress along these lines, as state-sponsored industrialization has reconfigured social forces and the distribution of power in many MENA countries. This process has led to some attenuation of authoritarianism through the erosion of the state's peremptory power. Still, the gap between such attenuated authoritarianism and full-fledged democracy remains wide. Its closure is challenging. But not impossible.

Appendix 1

Comparative Wage Rates in Forty-one Countries, 1990

Country	Wage	Rank
Switzerland	19.23	1
Sweden	18.70	2
Denmark	18.35	3
Belgium	17.85	4
Netherlands	17.84	5
West Germany	16.46	6
Norway	16.37	7
Italy	16.13	8
Australia	15.70	9
Finland	14.44	10
Japan	13.96	11
Canada	12.83	12
France	12.74	13
Austria	10.34	14
Great Britain	10.20	15
United States	10.02	16
Ireland	9.15	17
East Germany	8.28	18
Spain	7.69	19
Israel	7.09	20
Greece	5.85	21
Taiwan	4.56	22
South Korea	3.22	23
Hong Kong	3.05	24
Singapore	3.83	25
Tunisia	*2.82*	*26*
Portugal	2.75	27
Mexico	2.21	28
Brazil	1.97	29
Uruguay	1.86	30
Turkey	1.82	31

Country	Wage	Rank
Morocco	1.28	32
Hungary	1.24	33
Thailand	0.92	34
India	0.72	35
Philippines	0.67	36
Egypt	0.45	37
Pakistan	0.39	38
China	0.37	39
Indonesia	0.25	40
Sri Lanka	0.24	41

Source: Werner International, cited in *Courrier de l'industrie*, no. 58 (May 1991).

Note: Wage rates are expressed in dollars, with social costs included.

Appendix 2

Number of Strikes in Tunisia, 1970–1994

Year	Strikes	% Legal
1970	25	
1971	32	
1972	150	
1973	409	
1974	131	
1975	363	
1976	372	
1977	452	
1978	178	
1979	240	
1980	346	5
1981	575	9
1982	530	11
1983	570	15
1984	545	26
1985	391	12
1986	170	0
1987	241	6
1988	385	n.a.
1989	430	6
1990	564	21
1991	466	n.a.
1992	496	11
1993	513	13
1994	425	18

Sources: Strike levels—reported by Ministry of Social Affairs, reprinted in *ILO Yearbooks*, 1980–94; percentage legal—reported by Ministry of Social Affairs, available through Ministry of Social Affairs (internal documents) and (for 1990s) U.S. Department of Labor, *Foreign Labor Trends: Tunisia*, 1990–94.

Appendix 3

Organizational Structure of the Union Générale de Travailleurs Tunisiens

Executive Bureau	13 members elected by National Assembly
Administrative Commission	80 members
	13 from the Executive Bureau
	23 secretaries general of regional syndicates
	44 secretaries general of federations and national syndicates
Federations/national syndicates	44*
Regional syndicates	23**
Union locals	Approximately 7,000
Rank and file	Approximately 300,000

*Federations and national syndicates are structurally identical. Federations encompass all the union locals belonging to a single sector (e.g., textiles). National syndicates encompass all the public sector unions that fall under the auspices of a single ministry.

**Regional syndicates group together all union locals located within a single governorate (e.g., the unions of Sfax). The regional syndicates tend to focus on regional issues (e.g., regional unemployment levels) and can organize strikes on a region-wide basis.

Appendix 4

Membership Numbers in the Union Générale de Travailleurs Tunisiens

In the late 1980s, the total number of UGTT members was generally estimated to be around 300,000 (although this seems exaggerated, given the estimates of constituent federations given below).

Estimates of membership in the largest federations were as follows:

Agricultural Syndicates Federation	30,000
Civil Service Federation	27,500
Public health workers	10,000
Primary school teachers	12,000
Secondary school teachers	4,000
University-level teachers	1,500
Metallurgy Federation	15,000
Mining Federation	15,000
Tourism and Alimentation Federation	16,000
Petroleum and Chemicals Federation	12,000
Construction Federation	12,000
Transport Federation	12,000
Textile Federation	11,000
Bank Federation	7,000
PTT Syndicate	3–5,000

Sources: All figures are estimates gleaned from interviews with numerous union activists. They should be trusted to indicate orders of magnitude only.

Notes

Introduction

1. Those, like Barrington Moore, Charles Moraze, Eric Hobsbawm, and James Kurth, who identify the capitalist class as the historical agent of democracy, generally trace this enthusiasm for democracy to capital's collision with the absolutist state over the feudal barriers posed by the state to their advance. Motivated by this material interest, capitalists mobilized their economic power to create parliamentary institutions and thus restrain the ambitions of the absolutist state. By contrast, those, like T. H. Marshall, E. P. Thompson, Goran Therborn, Dietrich Rueschemeyer, Evelyne Stephens, and John D. Stephens, who identify the working class as the historical agent of democracy, argue that capitalists were primarily interested in establishing liberal forms of rule, not democracy. Thus, while capitalists supported the introduction of representative government and the protection of civil liberties, they opposed the extension of political rights to the lower classes. Instead it was the working class, organizationally empowered by capitalist development and materially motivated by the desire to see political redress for economic subordination, that fought for universal suffrage, the "true" mark of democracy.

2. This research also argues for a zero-sum relationship between the autonomy of the state and the autonomy of society. Dependence on state sponsorship (i.e., compromised autonomy) on the part of social forces spells increased autonomy for the state, since dependence limits the degree to which social forces will campaign for institutionalized restraints on the state, that is, democratic institutions.

3. For example, access to externally derived rents endows many regimes with substantial fiscal autonomy, subsidizing their unaccountability; the institutional legacies of traditional Middle Eastern states (not to mention those of colonial rule) reinforce tendencies toward authoritarianism; religious and ethnic fragmentation undermines horizontally based solidarity in many Middle Eastern societies, handicapping their ability to discipline the state. For a superb overview of the debate on the sources of Middle Eastern authoritarianism, see Brynen, Korany, and Noble 1995.

Chapter 1. Genesis of the Private Sector in Tunisia

1. Tunisia was seen as a fount of agricultural products like grain, olive oil, dates, and wool and as a potential market for European manufactured goods.

2. These mineral deposits included lead, zinc, iron, copper, and most important, phosphates.

3. Turner offers both a summary and a critique of Weber's work on the Islamic world. Others who expound Islam's "retarding" influence (though they tend to stress Islamic "fatal-

ism" rather than Islam's failure to imbue capitalist rationality) include Charles (1958) and Renan (1883). A convincing critique of this approach is provided by Rodinson (1978) and Stone (1974). The latter offers an interesting account of the development of a capitalist spirit (akin to Weber's Protestant work ethic) among Tunisian merchants originating from the island of Djerba.

4. Tunisian-made chechias were especially prized and traded throughout the region. Valensi (1969) argues that in addition to the chechia industry, much of the textile and leather industries were also organized along capitalistic lines. For more, see also Stambouli and Van Sivers n.d., 12.

5. This borrows from Rogers Brubaker's definition of Weber's capitalist rationality cited in Callaghy 1988, 70.

6. Tunisian Jews were quicker to embrace industrial ventures than many of their Muslim counterparts because their history as commercial intermediaries between Europe and Tunisia encouraged them to learn French, adopt French manners, and gain familiarity with European business practices. Acculturated in this way, many also took advantage of France's offer to become naturalized French citizens. Citizenship afforded them access to credit from the European-controlled banks in Tunisia, and this eased the way to mounting industrial ventures (Sebag 1951, 130–32).

7. Tunisia eschewed the path of defiant, unilateral nationalization of European-held enterprises, a tactic common among newly independent nations, such as Egypt and Iran, that were eager to challenge colonial domination (recall Nasser and the Suez Canal Crisis; Mossadegh and his challenge to the Anglo-Iranian Oil Company). Instead, Tunisia took control of strategic European enterprises by following a prudent path of negotiation and sequenced buy-out (Guen n.d.; Signoles 1987, 744). For example, the state acquired control of the Sfax-Gafsa Phosphate Company (one of the country's major phosphate concerns) by negotiating with its European owners to expand the company's capital by 100%, thereby acquiring a 50% share of the company's control. The state's goal was to maintain friendly relations with foreign interests and Western governments, that is, sources of potential foreign direct investment and foreign aid (Bedaoui 1987, 59–60).

8. Actually, the rise of the dirigiste wing of the elite can be traced two years earlier to 1960, the year Ahmed Ben Salah was appointed secretary of state for planning. The meteoric rise and fall of Ben Salah's career personified the fate of dirigisme in Tunisia throughout the 1960s (Signoles 1987, 747).

9. This nationalization followed a clash with France over continued French control of an army base in Bizerte (northern Tunisia). No doubt, Tunisian elites were also influenced by the recent Algerian example of expropriation of French-owned land. Even in this case, however, Tunisia did not follow a course of brutal expropriation, offering financial compensation for the confiscated property. Interestingly, when local capital proved too deficient to cover the cost, France stepped in with a loan of $13.2 million to the Tunisian government to help compensate the departing colons (Gouia 1976, 233).

10. Initially, this was not reflected in the plans' investment targets. Under the First Plan, industry came in third, after agriculture and infrastructure, in share of public investment. In the Second Plan (1965–68), industry was put on par with agriculture. By the Third Plan (1969–72), industry finally took first place, with 31.7% of planned investment compared to only 14.8% for agriculture (Gouia 1976, 273, 281, 286).

11. The term *industrializing industries* is that of G. Destanne de Bernis, a French economist influential in North Africa at this time (Philipeaux 1973, 357).

12. The petroleum industry was the exception, the only nonmanufacturing industry with sizeable private sector involvement. Gouia (1976) estimates that 46% of capital formation in the petroleum sector came from (largely foreign) private sector sources during the decade 1962–71.

13. Even the earliest plan asserted that the state would act largely as "associated partner" to private capital, providing the capital and cadres necessary for private sector promotion (*Plan triennal*, 1962–64, 141).

14. Most of these sweeteners were limited to investment projects that met specific regime goals, such as the location of industry in the underdeveloped South and job creation.

15. By 1969, the manufacturing industry contributed 9.9% of Tunisia's GDP, up from 7.7% in 1961 (Romdhane and Signoles 1982, 63).

16. Tunisia's limited local market was the product of the country's small and relatively impoverished population. Tunisian citizens numbered under six million in the early 1960s. Wages were low, unemployment was high, taxes were rising. Dimassi shows that the average consumer in 1965 devoted half his salary to food (Ghabi 1978, 34–40; Dimassi 1983, vii–x).

17. A limited market meant industry could not produce at full capacity, nor could the economy often support multiple firms in the same sector (especially in the more capital intensive industries), resulting in limited competition.

18. Ben Salah himself sought to increase industry's export orientation and encourage more private sector investment in industry by enacting a new investment law in 1969 and brokering a new trade arrangement with the EC to permit entry of European inputs.

19. Successive years of drought, the lack of competent cadres, insufficient capitalization, corruption, stifling bureaucratization, and peasant resistance to the cooperatives led to dramatic declines in agricultural productivity during the Ben Salah years (Dimassi 1983, 330–79; Bennour 1977).

20. Of course, Ben Salah's dismissal and the termination of the etatist/cooperative experiment was not driven by the logic of the state's developmentalist ethos alone. Clearly, "interest" supplemented developmentalist logic as well. Over the course of a decade, Ben Salah had generated many enemies: peasants pauperized by the cooperative experiment, merchants driven out of business by commercial reform, and large-scale landowners whose privileges and property were threatened for the first time in 1969, with radicalization of the cooperative law that year. All these social forces lobbied for Ben Salah's removal. But the state only proved receptive to these complaints once the developmental failings of etatist ISI strategy had become clear.

21. Actually, by the late 1960s, Ben Salah's regime had already begun to realize the importance of orienting the economy outward; for example, it established the National Council of Foreign Commerce in 1967 to encourage development of exports in Tunisia (Dimassi 1983, 631). But the primary thrust of Ben Salah's industrialization strategy throughout most of the 1960s was aimed at import substitution.

Interestingly, the triumph of an elite committed to a more liberal, extroverted development strategy coincided with a change in the conventional wisdom held by the international development establishment. In 1972 the World Bank published a report suddenly disavowing ISI and embracing export-oriented development as the best way for LDCs to assure growth and overcome balance of payment difficulties (Dimassi 1983, 648; Signoles 1984, 781; Gouia 1987, 320). As ever, Tunisia proved to be an astute student of the international community's conventional wisdom on development.

22. The state, however, retained control of land that had either been abandoned by colons or historically had been in the state's domain. These constituted the basis of state farms, which persisted especially in the North (Dimassi 1983, 666–71).

23. The government did, however, retain close control over a few commodities that constituted the country's major export earners (e.g., olive oil, phosphates, and petroleum).

24. Specifically, the regime eased the importation of primary materials and spare parts not produced in Tunisia but essential to Tunisian industrialists. Otherwise, import trade remained highly controlled, subject to a system of state licensing and high tariff barriers, all designed to protect the development of local industry.

25. API facilitated realization by guiding entrepreneurs through the bureaucracy and helping them procure licenses and loans.

26. The CNEI (Centre national des études industrielles) was also created in 1974 to conduct industrial research and help identify potentially profitable directions for the development of industry in Tunisia. The CNEI was ultimately absorbed by API in the late 1980s.

27. For example, the Fond national de garantie, established in 1981.

28. For example, the FOPRODI fund, created in 1973, was designed to provide easy credit to new entrepreneurs short on capital but rich in technical skills.

29. In the early 1980s API was renamed the Agency for the Promotion of Industry. The duties of the institution, which kept the same acronym, remained largely unchanged.

30. The public sector, however, seemed to play a much smaller role in supplying managers for small- and medium-sized enterprises (Petites et moyennes entreprises, PMEs) than for large enterprises. For smaller firms, commerce appeared to be the most important fount of entrepreneurs (Gouia 1987, 438).

31. An exact count of private manufacturing enterprises in 1970 and 1980 was not available from the INS. Numbers were calculated by taking the INS count of all manufacturing enterprises in 1970 and 1980 and subtracting the number of public enterprises extant in each sector during these two periods. The number of public enterprises for 1970 was taken from the Sixth Plan. The number of public enterprises in 1980 was taken from *Preparation for the Seventh Plan*, published in 1981. Note that the INS count of private enterprises in 1983, for some inexplicable reason, does not include a count of shoe manufacturing firms, hence it undercounts the number of firms in textiles/leather for that year.

32. For the vast majority of Tunisian firms, small size was a consequence of limited investment capital on the part of private sector industrial entrepreneurs as well as their limited vision and experience in industry (see Tables 1.9 and 1.10 for the professional origins of these entrepreneurs). Nevertheless, in some cases small firm size was *an act of strategic choice* on the part of Tunisian entrepreneurs. Small size was seen as conferring greater flexibility to the firm; it also helped the entrepreneur contain the influence of organized labor and avoid state scrutiny. More than one industrialist admitted to opening several small firms (under fifty employees each) to produce the same product (e.g., different brands of baby clothes, ladies' lingerie) rather than start one large firm to produce these goods. The underlying logic was that smaller firms were easier to open and close in response to changes in demand. (Neither the state nor the national labor federation would take much notice of a small firm, whereas a large firm would certainly attract their attention.) Moreover, it was easier to maintain a "family feeling" in a small firm and thus thwart the penetration of the labor movement (interview, 21 July 1988).

33. The public sector was virtually absent from the shoe industry and its contribution to textile exports was overwhelmingly dwarfed by that of the private sector. Public sector textile firms focus largely on the production of goods destined for the local market (such intermediate inputs as thread and fabric) rather than on finished garments, which compose the bulk of Tunisia's textile exports.

34. The ensuing drop in revenues was equivalent to 10% of GDP in 1986 (World Bank 1994, 5).

35. The Tunisian government was forced to appeal to the IMF for help as early as 1982, when the combination of drought and plunging world phosphate prices pitched the country into economic crisis. The IMF counseled a number of reforms, including the retraction of subsidies for basic consumer goods. These measures sparked the infamous bread riots of 1984, which forced the government to reinstate the subsidies. Tunisia was left to muddle through, caught between the rock of fiscal crisis and the hard place of economic reform's destabilizing potential.

36. Primary materials and semifinished goods imported for local use were largely freed from tariff barriers.

37. The World Bank's 1995 report on developing countries also "singled out Tunisia among the states of North Africa and the Middle East as the one making most progress in structural adjustment" (EIU *Country Report: Tunisia*, October–December 1995, 17). However, the World Bank's 1996 report, *Tunisia's Global Integration and Sustainable Development*, was more critical, chastising Tunisia for the slow pace of reform (especially with regard in trade liberalization) and warning Tunisia that it was falling behind comparable developing countries in terms of growth and competitiveness.

38. These figures understate the number of firms that actually failed because they include only those firms that requested permission to lay off workers from the Ministry of Social Affairs' Commission de controle de licenciement. (They do not count firms that avoided the ministry's intervention and simply closed up shop.) Official bankruptcy statistics are not published in Tunisia. But even if they were, they would far understate the number of firm failures in the country. Bankruptcy laws are highly punitive in Tunisia (entrepreneurs who declare bankruptcy, for example, lose some of their civil rights, such as the right to vote); hence, many failing businessmen avoid official bankruptcy. Instead, they let their firms go under, arranging debt repayment as best they can on an individual basis, out of court.

39. Again, the assumption here is that the vast majority of firms in the manufacturing sector are private sector firms. This identification of the manufacturing sector with the private sector has generally become the norm in Tunisia since the early 1990s. As the authors of the Eighth Plan (1992–96) wrote, from the period of the Seventh Plan (1988–92) on, "the quasi-totality of manufacturing activity is dependent on private initiative" (Ministry of Plan, *Huitième plan de développement*, vol. 2, 55).

40. The INS census counted 2,320,610 people actively employed in Tunisia in 1994. Of these, 500,989 (22%) worked in the agricultural sector; 455,716 (20%) worked in the manufacturing sector; 36,764 (1.6%) in the mining and energy sector; 305,761 (13%) in construction and public works; 600,515 (26%) in services; 382,244 (16%) in education, health, and government administration; and 38,621 (2%) in miscellaneous other areas.

41. It is difficult to state precisely the private sector's share of value added in manufacturing, but it was clearly preponderant. A study cited by the World Bank put the private sector's contribution to value added in manufacturing at 62% in 1988. However, as the World Bank pointed out, this figure "probably understates the shares of the private sector because it was based on a sample that is biased towards larger firms and hence gives too much weight to public enterprises." Moreover, the World Bank added, "Since 1988 the private sector's predominance has increased" (World Bank 1994, 9).

42. As observed by the World Bank, the families and small groups who control most private enterprise in Tunisia resisted delegating management to professional managers; moreover, they preferred not to raise capital through public stock offerings in order to retain close control of their firms and to avoid the public disclosures required for issuing stock (World Bank 1994, iv, 13).

43. Note how the Eighth Plan (1992–96), published in July 1992, endorsed the role of the private sector: the regime praised the private sector for its potential efficiency and capacity for rapid intervention and response; asserted that it sought to harness the private sector "to realize certain *public* missions"; and stated that its vision of the private sector "opens the way to new relations between sectors (i.e., public and private), which surpass simple coexistence in order to realize the notion of complementarity and to assure the satisfaction of the needs of the collectivity" (*Huitième plan*, vol. 1, 56).

44. For example, the government's economic budget for 1996 described the Mise à niveau program as a five-year program running from 1996 to 2000, which sought to reform four thousand enterprises and make them ready for integration into the new free trade zone in Europe. The program offered technical consulting to help these firms improve their

competitiveness and was partly financed by the European Community (*Economic Budget*, 1996, 74–75).

Chapter 2. *The Developmental Paradox*

1. Miliband (1969) stresses that extensive recruitment of state elites from the "capitalist class" goes a long way toward explaining the state's tendency to favor capitalist interests. C. Wright Mills (1956) argues that the development of a "power elite," a single interlocking elite that shuttles back and forth between the public and private sector, fosters the emergence of a common world view and a common interest in defending the interest of industry even when industrialists do not personally occupy state office.

2. Of course, economic autonomy is *not always* a prerequisite of political influence or independence, as the American auto industry makes clear. See more on this later in the chapter.

3. In the early 1970s, Prime Minister Hedi Nouira cited a rate of 50% as the financially orthodox minimum—a minimum he ultimately decided to flout in the hopes of stimulating rapid growth in Tunisia (Signoles 1985, 795).

4. During the first ten years of the program's existence, only 823 FOPRODI projects were realized, accounting for 136 million dinars worth of investment (API, internal document, 1988).

5. This 10% minimum applies only to projects worth less than 250,000 dinars. For those projects worth more, the minimum jumps to higher than 17% (API, n.d.).

6. A return trip to Tunisia in 1996 turned up somewhat less favorable figures for the contribution of personal funds to industrial investment in the early 1990s. In its 1996 *Rapport économique*, 48, the Institut arabe des chefs d'entreprises published the following table estimating personal fund contributions to be between 19 and 36% in industry:

Structure of Enterprise Financing in the Industrial Sector, Average for 1990–1993 (in %)

	Personal Funds	Long-term Debt	Short-term Debt	Total
Agro-alimentary	36	14.75	49.25	100
Construction materials, ceramics, glass	31.25	27.50	41.25	100
Electrical appliances, machinery	19.75	29.50	50.75	100
Chemicals	28.25	13.75	58	100
Textiles, leather	30.5	16.5	53	100
Diverse	33.75	10.5	55.75	100

Source: Institut d'études quantitatives.

7. The reasoning behind this calculation is as follows: in 1986, API reported that large industrial projects worth more than 500,000 dinars accounted for 60% of total industrial investment registered in the country. Assuming that the investors backing these mammoth projects put up the minimum personal contribution that is legal (30%), the percentage of personal funds invested by smaller firms might be calculated in the following way:

Global rate of self-finance in Tunisia = (Big projects' share of global investment) (Big projects' rate of self-finance) + (Small projects' share of global investment) (Small projects' rate of self-finance).
That is; 42.5% = (60%) (30%) + (40%) (x).
Therefore, x = 61.25%.

8. For example, Tunisia boasts seven daily newspapers. Two are published by the government (*La presse*, *Al-Ṣiḥāfa*), and one by the ruling RCD Party (*Le renouveau*), two are privately owned independent papers (*Le temps*, *Al-Ṣabāḥ*), and two are privately owned tabloid-style papers (*Al-Shurūq*, *Al-Ray' al-ʿām*). According to the editor of the leading independent paper, none of these papers is aligned in any way with the business community (interview, 10 December 1996).

9. The importance of state subsidies to the survival of the independent press cannot be underestimated. The Communist Party made this clear in its regular complaints during the winter of 1987–88 that the state was strangling the party's newspaper, *Al-Ṭarīq al-jadīd*, by refusing to deliver its regular supply of (subsidized) newsprint.

10. Despite its failure to control the media, the private sector has managed to get a fair bit of "good press" in recent years for its contribution to national development. But this probusiness slant is less an indicator of the private sector's capacity to wield the media as a tool for ideological domination than a consequence of the global shift in conventional wisdom about development due to the persuasive powers of the IMF, World Bank, and other such external forces and examples.

11. These small parties included the Communist Party, legalized in 1981, and the Social Democratic Party (MDS) and the Popular Unity Party (PUP), both legalized in 1983.

12. Opposition parties were routinely denied permission to organize public rallies, and they were not given television time to campaign. Moreover, elections were subject to widespread fraud aimed at guaranteeing near-unanimous victories for the Destour Party.

13. One such dinner held in late 1988 brought in one million dinars' worth of pledges. The sum swelled to six million during the next few weeks as additional businessmen joined the fund-raising bandwagon (interview, 14 December 1988).

14. Note President Ben Ali's 7 November 1995 promise to subsidize the four opposition parties that had been elected to the Chamber of Deputies (EIU, *Country Report: Tunisia*, January–March 1996, 9).

15. This might be different if the private sector jobs taken by former government officials upon retirement constituted "compensation" for years of faithful service to the private sector while in public office. In many countries, the provision of such post-retirement sinecures for "friendly" civil servants is common practice. (In Japan, the practice of accepting such a post after retirement from the civil service is tellingly called "the descent from heaven.") This arrangement clearly works to ally the interests of civil servants and private sector entrepreneurs even in cases of unidirectional pantouflage. In Tunisia, however, state elites who leave government employment for the private sector rarely settle into cushy jobs offered to them by established firms. Rather, they tend to start *new* ventures, often with their own funds, exchanging secure government employment for the risks of self-propelled entrepreneurial capitalism. The jump to the private sector thus marks a clear break between industrialist and state elite that in turn undermines the notion of a "power elite" in Tunisia.

16. The debates over the party's economic platform are impressive for their democratic and spirited character. In the committee sessions I observed during the summer of 1988, businessmen from all points on the economic and political spectrum expressed their views freely and forcefully.

17. Besides six industrialists (Hedi Jelani, Hamadi Trabelsi, Bechir Ben Amor, Abdesselem Ben Ayed, Hamadi Bousbia, and Fouad Lakhoua), there were also two bankers (Ezzeddine Chelbi, Habib Belhaj Said), one leader in the assurance business (Afif Chiboub), and one major merchant/exporter (Tahar Rejeb).

18. Besides the UTICA, the IACE, and the Chamber of Commerce, other associations in Tunisia service the business community, though none of them see "defending business's collective interests to the state" as their primary mission. These include the Jaycees (Junior Chamber of Commerce), the Lions, the Kiwanis, and the Rotarians, as well as several foreign chambers of commerce (e.g., German and British).

19. As the organization's name implies, the UTICA represents all of Tunisia's *patronat* (i.e., proprietors), not just Tunisian industrialists. However, until the early 1980s, the UTICA was the only association legally permitted to organize and represent business interests in Tunisia, hence any discussion of collective lobbying on the part of Tunisian industrialists must begin with this organization. Much of the following history of the UTICA draws on interviews held during 1988 and 1989 with Ferjani Bel Haj Ammar (one of the founders of the UTICA and its long-time secretary general). For more, see Bellin 1993 and Chekir 1974.

20. These four were the UTICA, the businessmen's association; the UNAT, the peasants' union; the UGTT, the trade union federation; and the UNFT, the women's union.

21. Those familiar with the organization's history will note that, for simplicity's sake, I use the name UTICA throughout this book in reference to Tunisia's premier businessmen's association. The organization has undergone several name changes over the years, but nonetheless has shown remarkable continuity in leadership, membership, and mission. For more detail, see Bellin 1993, 199–203.

22. Ben Salah's commercial reform aimed at putting most of Tunisia's import-export trade under state control; establishing a state-run network of wholesalers, designed to replace private wholesalers in Tunisia; and forcing the closure of many retail outlets deemed redundant by the state.

23. As Ferjani saw it, "They couldn't stand up to Bourguiba, with all his historic legitimacy as a leader" (interview, 16 January 1989). But interestingly, Ferjani himself also deferred to Bourguiba. After his dismissal from the UTICA, Ferjani was approached by a group of disgruntled merchants who did not want to take Ben Salah's reforms "lying down" and appealed to Ferjani to lead their opposition. By his own report, Ferjani responded, "I am still a Bourguibist . . . we cannot fight this. Continue to work with Ezzedine Ben Achour because the future is with Bourguiba" (interview, 16 January 1989). Needless to say, in addition to being dismissed from the UTICA, Ferjani was also expelled from the Destour Party's executive committee (bureau politique). Bourguiba, however, permitted Ferjani to remain a member of the party's central committee. This gesture showed Bourguiba's typical shrewdness with regard to political opponents: disgrace them but never court their undying enmity by excluding them entirely from the political game. Waterbury (1970) identified a similar strategy in the workings of Moroccan politics.

24. For the most part, this meant they chose to deal directly with the state rather than work through UTICA's mediation (Chekir 1974, 86).

25. Nouira's decision to resurrect UTICA was not simply the product of his commitment to the private sector. Rather, the new minister also needed an institutional counterweight to negotiate with the increasingly troublesome national labor federation (the UGTT). Nouira needed credible representatives of both business and labor to participate in his plan for corporatist-style negotiation of wage and working conditions.

26. Those publications were *Flash UTICA*, a weekly French bulletin; *Al-Bayān*, a monthly Arabic magazine; *Le mensuel de l'exportation*, a monthly bulletin published for exporters; *Al-Risāla*, a sporadically published bulletin in Arabic aimed at small traders and artisans; and *Annuaire économique*, a biannual, trilingual publication containing all the commercial accords signed between Tunisia and other countries, import/export and trade laws, as well as a list of merchants and industrialists in Tunisia.

27. The National Federation for Textiles (FENATEX), the Hotel Federation, and the Federation for Exports (FEDEX) were cited by many interviewees as especially effective organizations.

28. The UTICA's autonomy was also compromised by the sizeable number of UTICA activists who became involved in the organization, not so much to defend the interests of business as to promote their own political careers. Said one industrialist in the construction

materials sector: "UTICA is a political stepping stone. People play an active role in it because they see it as a stepping stone to membership in the Social and Economic Council or election as a deputy in parliament or appointment to a ministerial post. Defending the economic interests of business is completely secondary" (interview, 14 June 1988).

29. Actually, UTICA's finances turned out to be a rather murky affair. In 1974, Hefida Chekir reported that UTICA was financed by an annual membership fee of 2.4 dinars. This fee was augmented by various outside *subsides*, the largest of which came from the Destour Party (at the rate of 20,000 dinars per year) (Chaker 1974). By 1988, UTICA's president, Hedi Jelani, affirmed that the UTICA was primarily funded through the *chiffre d'affaires* tax. However, subsidies from other sources, such as Germany's Konrad Adenauer Foundation, continued to supplement the UTICA's income.

30. This insistence on a nonconfrontational relationship between business association and state is not unique to the UTICA; see Camp 1989, Kochanek 1974, and Kaplan 1972 for similar tendencies among business associations in Mexico, India, and Japan.

31. Actually, lack of vision is not unique to UTICA. Ehrmann (1957) writes that a "defensive, short-run horizons character . . . is typical of all business associations and most interest groups." For similar accounts in Britain, France, and India, see Hayward 1975 and Kochanek 1974.

32. Other factors mentioned by interviewees that have undermined the UTICA's effectiveness as an advocate for the business community include (a) the heterogenous nature of the UTICA's constituency (artisans, merchants, and industrialists are all housed under one organizational roof despite their conflicting interests and perspectives), which has led to immobilism and vagueness in UTICA's policy initiatives; (b) the UTICA's poor research facilities, which make it impossible for the union to collect the data necessary to defend its positions; (c) the UTICA's financial autonomy from its members (thanks to state support), which renders it less accountable to its base. Many of these problems might be solved if the UTICA were to sever its linkage with the party-state.

33. This disinclination to collective action is further compounded by the fact that many of the terms of business (e.g., prices and import licenses) were the product of individual bargains struck by particular firms with the state. They were not determined on a sector-wide basis.

34. Peter Evans (1992) also emphasizes the importance of field size in determining the character of relations between state and society, though he is less concerned with its impact on the organization of collective action than on its potential for corrupting the developmental state. In his work on embedded autonomy and the predatory state, Evans argues that the fewer the number of firms interacting with the state, the more personalistic relations between these firms and the state become. Such states risk degenerating into "particularistic predation" (e.g., "insider trading" or unproductive rent-seeking) that undermines the state's capacity to lead the development effort.

35. Information on the Tunisian Chamber of Commerce was drawn from various sources, including the texts of relevant laws and decrees published in the *Journal officiel de la République Tunisienne*, interviews with the president, vice president, and long-time director general of the chamber, as well as two articles appearing in *Conjoncture*: "La réactivation des chambres de commerce est à l'ordre de jour," no. 59 (July–August 1981): 58–59, and "Chambres de commerce: Vers la dynamisation," no. 125 (June 1988): 14–16.

36. According to one chamber official, during the spring of 1988, President Ben Ali expressed dissatisfaction with the UTICA's performance as the regime's organizational link to the business community. Reform of the UTICA, however, appeared difficult given the union's entrenched leadership and heavily bureaucratized structure. Instead, Ben Ali chose to revive the chamber of commerce (interview, 10 August 1989). Ultimately, however, UTICA's leadership *was* changed, and its relations with Ben Ali's regime improved. State interest in the revival of the chamber consequently diminished.

37. Information on the IACE was collected from interviews with IACE members as well as from the IACE's annual reports and other publications (especially *Actes des journées de l'entreprise*).

38. The IACE's founders included Mansour Moalla, former minister of finance; Mondheur Gargouri and M. Triki, both university professors; and Moncef Cheikhroukhou, an executive officer of Best Bank.

39. Though, of course, the IACE, like all associations in Tunisia, had to receive authorization from the Ministry of Interior before it could begin operation.

40. These were set at 1,100 dinars for the first year and 600 dinars every year thereafter—a considerable sum of money in a country where per capita GNP is under 1,800 dinars. Clearly, only the most successful entrepreneurs were able to afford membership in the IACE.

41. For example, the IACE's kitchen and computer facilities were donated by various member companies.

42. The IACE annual report for 1988 counted 247 full-fledged members, up from 93 in 1986.

43. Industrialists and bankers made up nearly two-thirds of the membership. Overall, members were a select group. One IACE official estimated that 90–95% of all members had a university degree, and this resulted in a high level of debate at IACE meetings.

44. Leaders in the IACE acknowledged "failure" in only one of their goals—the development of the institute's "clubby" side." According to the IACE's annual reports, the institute's facilities were underutilized by its members. As one official explained: "It's not in our culture to meet, say, for drinks in a public place. Instead, we go to each other's homes. But we do hold lunches here, so there is some social aspect to the institute" (interview, 25 May 1988).

45. Moalla had indeed been a dynamic figure in Tunisia. His career spanned both the public and private sector. He had served as a high-level cadre in Tunisia's Central Bank; had been one of the founders of the country's prestigious École nationale d'administration (which he directed for four years); had helped found BIAT, one of Tunisia's largest private sector banks; and had served as Tunisia's minister of finance during the early 1980s. His illustrious career helped attract many members to the IACE. One member explained this by pointing out, "Moalla had contacts everywhere," and people were eager to cultivate him because "he might well be appointed to a high government post again" (interview, 25 May 1988).

46. Interestingly, the legitimacy of business lobbies and the practice of collective consultation with the business community has gotten a boost recently, thanks to endorsement by the World Bank. In a 1994 report, the World Bank advised Tunisia to imitate the example of many successful East Asian economies and create "deliberative councils" that would bring state and private sector actors together for regular consultation and collaboration in the development of the economy (World Bank 1994, ii–iii). To further reinforce the point, in 1996 the president of the World Bank visited Tunisia and arranged for a roundtable meeting with President Ben Ali and the UTICA to discuss ways to promote the private sector and foreign investment (EIU, *Country Report: Tunisia*, July–September 1996, 17–18).

47. These are chosen by the president of Tunisia from a list suggested by the Central Bank. The appointment is for three years and is renewable (interview, governor of the Central Bank, 16 August 1988).

48. As explained in chapter 1, n. 38, more precise statistics on the number of bankruptcies and failing firms in Tunisia are impossible to obtain. The Ministry of Social Affairs most likely undercounts failing firms in Tunisia. Nevertheless, the overall explosion in the number of private sector firms during this period attests that the state's embrace of more liberal economic reforms did not eviscerate private sector industry.

49. One story told by a textile exporter gave an indication of how bad for business these controls could be:

I got a call from my partner in France telling me he liked my work and asking me to send another thousand pieces [of baby clothes] pronto in order to make the spring season. He knew I didn't have the equipment to turn out that much product in so short a time so he offered to send me some machinery at his own expense. The prospect was exciting but of course I had to turn him down. I knew the machinery would get bogged down at customs and by the time I managed to get all the dossiers together to get it out, the season would be over. This happens at a time when the state wants to encourage exports and when the country is crying out for more jobs! (Interview, 21 July 1988)

50. During the period of the loan, the civil servant is paid by his outside sponsor but retains civil service rank and accrues civil service seniority.

51. Note that even after ten years of structural adjustment reform, Tunisians were still complaining about the complexity, changeability, and burdensomeness of the legal framework governing the establishment and operation of economic enterprises in their country (Baccouche and Ben Hamdane 1996, 77–91). Consequently, personal contacts within the administration continued to be important to business success in Tunisia.

52. In fact, this flight to business by former political activists was actually encouraged by the political leadership, since it provided the politicians with an easy way to rid themselves of political troublemakers. One textile industrialist spoke with pride of his early years as a labor organizer loyal to the socialist wing of the national labor federation (UGTT). After Ben Salah's fall from grace in 1969, the man was driven out of both the party and the union. To earn a living he decided to start a textile venture. Hearing of the plan, President Bourguiba invited the man in for a personal interview. After some discussion, Bourguiba made a call to the Central Bank and arranged to have a small loan approved for the man's project. The loan enabled him to open a small textile workshop employing four workers. (N.B.: Eighteen years later this man, who had once worked to depose Bourguiba, had parlayed the small workshop into a textile firm worth 4 million dinars that employed sixty-five workers [interview, 15 August 1988].)

53. This is not to say that the Tunisian state is free from corruption. Toward the end of the Bourguiba era especially, certain ministers were notorious for their corrupt behavior (see, e.g., "Les points noirs de l'ancien régime," Réalités, 4 November 1988). Nonetheless, as one businessman put it, "The state as an institution is not corrupt. Rather, individuals are occasionally bought" (interview, 8 July 1988).

54. No doubt, one would expect some response bias when asking businessmen whether shady connections with the state were essential to business success. Nonetheless, nearly every businessman I interviewed rejected the importance of such relations (even while admitting the prevalence of petty corruption), and independent academics corroborated this view; hence, a relatively convincing case can be made that corrupt relations with the state were not the typical route to making an industrial fortune in Tunisia. To substantiate this view, one Tunisian banker pointed to a French study on comparative corruption in the southern Mediterranean that asked French enterprises to report the bribes they paid to get contracts in the region. The French firms apparently reported that they had to pay 45% of the value of the sales to close their deals in Libya and 35% in Morocco, but only 12% in Tunisia (interview, 15 December 1993).

55. Of course, the autonomy of the private sector is still compromised by one persistent form of economic "wrongdoing" that is widespread in the Tunisian business community, namely, tax fraud. Tax fraud is standard operating procedure for Tunisian entrepreneurs (so much so that when Monceur Moalla was minister of plan, he appeared on television saying that Tunisia's tax rates were so high that no businessman could possibly pay all the taxes legally due and still expect to stay in business). Unfortunately, pervasive tax fraud does compromise the political autonomy of the private sector. Tax fraud becomes the sword of Damocles that hangs over the head of nearly every businessman in Tunisia. And like state-

sanctioned corruption elsewhere (Waterbury 1976), it serves as a control mechanism that muzzles the political assertiveness of the offenders. More than one well-placed businessman confessed that he had blunted his criticism of the state for fear of retribution from some vengeful bureaucrat armed with a well-documented dossier on his business affairs. The good news is that recent reforms to lighten tax burdens for business may work to diminish tax fraud in Tunisia and so remove this obstacle to private sector autonomy.

56. For example, Henry Ehrman prefaced his book on organized business in France with a simple forthright disclaimer: "we have no exact way of measuring political power" (1957, xi).

57. The hope was that a dynamic industrial bourgeoisie would help fuel the growth process as well as help shoulder the burden of the employment creation.

58. Similarly, the most recent round of liberalization measures (which serve the interests of at least certain segments of the industrial bourgeoisie) should not be taken as a measure of that class's clout. Rather, a foreign exchange crisis and the IMF's insistence on a structural adjustment program forced progressive liberalization of prices, imports, and interest rates in Tunisia. The decisive shove that overcame the state's inertia to liberalizing reform came not from potent domestic constituencies but rather from external forces (like the IMF) and the logic of integration into the world economy. (I thank Mondheur Gargouri for the comparison of probusiness legislation to the legislation of personal status law.)

Chapter 3. A Checkered Alliance

1. This counterposing of the logic of accumulation and the logic of distribution borrows from Callaghy 1994.

2. French and Communist syndicalists supported the admission of native Tunisians in the hopes of drowning out the influence of their Italian and Socialist rivals (Dellagi 1980, 9).

3. The challenge was led by Salah Ben Youssef. For more on the Youseffist conflict, see Hermassi 1972, 153–56, and Moore 1965, 61–69.

4. The economic and social program proposed by the UGTT, under Ben Salah's leadership in 1956, called for the nationalization of Tunisian industry as well as extensive land reform.

5. The vast majority of the UGTT's elite and rank and file were card-carrying Destourians. Consequently, Bourguiba could control UGTT politics from within by passing directives to his followers within the movement.

6. Ben Salah made clear his renunciation of a class-specific approach to economic change by condemning strike activity at the UGTT's Sixth Congress (Belquith 1987, 56). Years later, in an interview with Marc Nerfin, Ben Salah said: "I believe that the syndical movement was never exclusively a workers' movement. It was a popular movement, . . . a movement of the poor." For this reason, he argued, the union's mandate was not limited to seeking higher wages for workers but rather had grander dimensions: "to transform the whole of society," "to rid it of exploitation" (Nerfin 19/1, 34–36).

7. Tlili's credentials as a labor activist were also impressive. He had led many strikes during the 1940s and 1950s and had served time in prison for his labor activism.

8. Specifically, he foreswore strikes and accepted a virtual freeze on workers' wages.

9. Bourguiba used an unfortunate ferry-boat accident in Kerkenna as a pretext to jail Achour. Achour was the director-general of the society that managed the ferry boat and thus was held responsible for the accident.

10. In August 1965, one month *after* Achour's removal from office, Bourguiba announced a 10% wage increase to be effective from January 1966 (Sassois 1971, 84–86). This measure was apparently designed to compensate workers for the additional 5% rise in the cost of living that Tunisia had registered between 1960 and 1964 as well as to help compensate for the inflation that was anticipated to follow the IMF-inspired devaluation of the dinar.

11. These strike statistics need to be viewed with caution, for there is no consistently reliable source of strike statistics in Tunisia. All but the most major strikes go unreported in the mainstream press, and the Ministry of Social Affairs and the UGTT press, when it is permitted to publish, both have incentives to inflate or deflate statistics, as political conditions require. Consequently, students of Tunisian labor history often come up with wildly varying strike statistics depending on the sources they use (e.g., cf. Romdhane 1981, 430, and Belhassen 1977, 22). The strike statistics presented in this chapter are those reported by the Ministry of Social Affairs to the ILO. They are best used to get a sense of the general order of magnitude of strikes as well as for tracking general trends, rather than as a precise enumeration of strikes. No matter the source consulted, however, all find a lull in strike activity during the 1960s and a significant increase in strike activity during the 1970s.

12. Notice that Achour was *designated* secretary general by President Bourguiba rather than *elected* by the union's administrative commission. This move reflected the regime's continued willingness to flout union rules (and self-determination), even as it strove to make the UGTT a more credible representative of the working class (Azaiez n.d., vol. 2, 11–12).

13. This right was stipulated by the 1973 Collective Convention. Previously, only working conditions, not wages, could be the subject of collective bargaining.

14. The right to strike had been guaranteed by the labor code of 1966, although workers had to obtain prior approval from the trade union central for a strike to be considered legal. In 1976 the state added an additional constraint specifying that workers also had to give ten days' advance warning of a strike for it to be legal. Although this added constraint retarded the strike process, the new labor code actually served to affirm workers' legal right to strike in Tunisia.

15. As often as not, top union officials greeted rank-and-file militance with ambivalence, if not outright hostility, denouncing the strikes as the work of elements foreign to the UGTT, expelling strike leaders from the trade union, and/or declaring the strike illegal. The UGTT central gave prior approval of only a minuscule percentage of strikes actually carried out (Dimassi 1983, 935–39).

16. Bedaoui finds that during the 1960s, the real value of the minimum wage in Tunisia declined at an average rate of 0.6% per year, while the real value of the average salary in Tunisia grew at only 2.6% per year—well below real GNP growth rates (Bedaoui 1996, 141).

17. The exact terms for calculating this index, however, remained vague, meaning that salary levels continued to be a test of power between labor and business rather than the automatic product of a precisely defined formula.

18. Their integration was symbolized by the appointment of Taieb Baccouche, a young, left-leaning activist from the syndicate of higher education, to the trade union's executive bureau at the union's Fourteenth Congress, held in March 1977.

19. It is a matter of dispute whether this disturbance was instigated by agents provocateurs planted by the state (the UGTT's story) or incited by irresponsible trade union leaders (the state's story). No doubt, the rioting was amplified by hordes of unemployed youths unaffiliated with the trade union who seized the opportunity to protest their frustration.

20. According to one trade union activist, the government skewed election results by resorting to a variety of tactics, including notifying only part of the electorate as to when and where elections would be held (interview, 16 December 1988).

21. Exact figures are hard to find given the political sensitivity of the issue. One former secretary general of the banking sector syndicate reported that membership in his syndicate dropped from more than 1,500 in 1977 to fewer than 400 in 1978–79.

22. His name was Taieb Baccouche, a linguistics professor long identified with the independent left wing of the union and active in the higher education syndicate since 1973 (*Jeune Afrique*, 13 May 1981). Note that immediately following this resurrection of the UGTT, the ruling party sought to bolster the popular base of the regime by asking the trade union to join with it to create a "National Front" in the upcoming legislative elections. After acrimonious debate within the UGTT over whether this would signal a return to past

infeudation of party and union, the Administrative Commission decided to join the Front, albeit with some face-saving conditions. The creation of this Front constituted the high point of reconciliation between the party and the union.

23. This council (composed of representatives from various national organizations as well as government officials, academics, and technocrats all appointed by the government) is designed to serve as an advisory board to the government and makes nonbinding recommendations regarding the regime's social and economic policies.

24. The exclusion of these seven was clearly the product of clan politics and competition over turf (rather than ideological cleavage). Having eliminated the syndical right, Achour later moved to remove the syndical left in 1984. Achour's main ambition was to eliminate any challenge to his absolute dominion rather than orient the union in any particular ideological direction (*Jeune Afrique*, 12 March 1984; *Réalités*, 23 March 1984).

25. The excluded UGTT leaders balked at their summary dismissal from the UGTT's helm. These men were not "trade union puppets"; their trade union credentials were long and legitimate. Denouncing Achour for his antidemocratic tactics (as well as for poor management of the union central), the Frontists left the UGTT and, on 19 February 1984, announced the creation of their own trade union, the UNTT.

26. The offensive editorial was apparently written by Taieb Baccouche. It denounced the government's project to raise bread prices by 10% (Raulier 1985).

27. Traditionally, 1% of public sector workers' salaries had been automatically deducted by the government and turned over to the trade union, amounting to approximately 2 million dinars each year (*Annuaire de l'Afrique du Nord* [*AAN*] 1985, 713).

28. These detaches numbered as many as four hundred and constituted the lion's share of the permanent staff at UGTT headquarters (*Libération* [France], 16 January 1986).

29. Achour's imprisonment was clearly a product of his political rivalry with Mzali and the latter's sense of threat. Mzali told reporters at the time: "We believed it would be better for a short period of time to deprive [Achour] of freedom in order to preserve public order. . . . He was determined to insult us *and demand my head*. . . . I assure you, this is a problem of Achour" (*Le quotidien de Paris*, 14 November 1985).

30. For example, delegates to the extraordinary congress held in April 1986 were appointed by the ruling party. The secretary general ultimately elected by this congress (Ismail Lajri) was actually the managing director of a metallurgic enterprise, United Foundries, and not even a worker (ILO, report 246, 103). The heavy hand of the state was also apparent during the second extraordinary congress held in January 1987. In that case, the union's new Executive Bureau was chosen at party headquarters in consultation with party leader Hedi Baccouche (*Dialogue*, 29 December 1986), and the congress itself was presided over by President Bourguiba (*La presse*, 20 January 1987).

31. For the details of their reinstatement, both in terms and numbers of people affected, see *La presse*, 14 May 1988, 16 June 1988, 24 June 1988, 9 November 1988.

32. For details, see *La presse*, 23 March 1988, 2 April 1988, 5 April 1988, 3 May 1988, 21 May 1988. To prevent old rivalries from overwhelming the reconciliation process, Ben Ali persuaded both UNTT president Bouraoui as well as Achour to renounce all further syndical activity and let the elections proceed without their participation. Bouraoui called it "a sacrifice for the well-being of the country" (*La presse*, 7 April 1988).

33. Ismail Sahbani was elected the new secretary general of the UGTT. He had once been secretary general of the Metallurgic Union, hailed from the légitime wing of the trade union movement, and had suffered long-term imprisonment and torture for his past trade union activities.

34. For example, one leading UGTT figure, Ali Romdhane, was known to play on Islamist themes with some success in the late 1980s, and 15% of the delegates in the 1989 UGTT convention identified themselves as Islamists (Zeghidi 1990). State labor official A. Yombai put the number of Islamists elected in 1989 at 20–25% (interview, August 1993).

35. During the local UGTT elections held in 1992, the Islamist candidates were largely swept out of power, thanks to a combination of popular disaffection with Islamists in the wake of the Algerian civil war, deliberate manipulation of the elections by UGTT leaders to undermine Islamist candidates, and repression of Islamist activists by the state (U.S. Dept. of Labor, *Foreign Labor Trends: Tunisia* 1992, 4; 1993, 4).

36. The state took quite purposive steps to limit "infiltration" of the trade union by Islamists. For example, it arrested UGTT activists reputed to be Islamist sympathizers for the duration of the local elections in 1993 in order to make them "unavailable" for office (interview, 11 December 1993). Another beneficiary of the regime's strategy to cultivate popular allies to countervail the Islamists was the Union des femmes démocrates (UFD). The regime granted the organization a visa in 1989, despite the competition the UFD posed to the women's organization sponsored by the regime itself, the UNFT, because the UFD had the potential to mobilize a significant force of feminists behind the regime's campaign to battle the Islamists (interview, 9 December 1993).

37. Membership levels fell to a reputed low of 100,000 (8–9% of the active population) by the mid-1990s, according to many UGTT critics (interviews, labor activists, 16 December 1996, 17 December 1996). Explanations for this decline vary. Some observers pointed to the difficult economic conditions that prevailed in Tunisia and that discouraged trade union activism on the part of many workers. Others pointed to the perception common to UGTT critics that the trade union was "in the pocket of the state" and hence not of much use to many workers.

38. For example, the regime did not intervene when Ismail Sahbani orchestrated the expulsion of two democratically elected and independent-minded members of the Executive Bureau, Ahmed Ben Remila and Abdelmajid Sahraoui, from their trade union functions. Sahbani claimed that the two had "defamed" his character (*Jeune Afrique*, 2–8 October 1996).

39. For example, after his expulsion from the UGTT's Executive Bureau, Abdelmajid Sahraoui set about creating an independent trade union movement in his home base of Sousse. He was quickly hauled in by the Ministry of Interior and warned against any further organizing work, on the grounds that his activities were harming syndical unity. Needless to say, nothing in the law forbids syndical pluralism in Tunisia. To the contrary, the state itself endorsed this principle in the mid-1950s and again in the mid-1980s, when it served state purposes (interview, labor activist, 18 December 1996).

Chapter 4. Influence under Constraint

1. Kerr writes that higher skill levels also empower workers because skilled workers "are given responsibility for more expensive equipment and more essential processes. Their consent becomes more important. The need for their consent gives them influence" (Kerr et al. 1960, 285).

2. Piore's "birds of passage" refers to the Italian workers who migrated to the United States on a temporary basis to work in American factories, save their wages, and return to Italy as quickly as possible (cited in Katznelson 1985, 449). Gate's term "part-time proletariat" refers to the women recruited to work in light, export-oriented industries in many parts of the Third World and who tend to see their employment in these factories as "a temporary interlude between childhood and marriage" (cited in Deyo 1984, 288).

3. The commitment of "part-time" workers to working class institutions like unions is further reduced by the lack of "generational depth" to their working class experience. Historically, second-generation workers have tended to be more militant and more receptive to union organizing than first-generation workers, since their identities are more intensely and securely rooted in the working class (Arrighi and Silver 1984, 196; Mericle 1977).

4. For more extensive discussion of the implications of ISI, EOI, and the NIDL (New International Division of Labor) for labor strength, see Bellin 1993.

5. Of course, this isn't always the case. In Korea the embrace of a market-driven strategy ultimately led to growth in heavy industry, where workers were concentrated, skilled, and committed. But for many late-developing countries, adopting this strategy means a concentration of growth in small, low-tech, consumer goods industries, where workers' structural position is weak.

6. The figure for the early 1960s is a very rough guess. Romdhane (1981, 75) counts somewhere between 150,000 and 200,000 salaried workers in Tunisia at independence, but his number includes all salaried workers (including service sector and civil service employees) and doesn't specify the number of industrial workers. Given the relatively small number of industrial enterprises extant in Tunisia in 1961 (the National Institute of Statistics counted a total of 955 in its 1961 *recensement industrielle*), and given the likelihood that few enterprises employed more than 20 workers, it seems reasonable to argue that the number of industrial workers in Tunisia fell well under 100,000 at this time.

7. The degree to which structural conditions favored labor's militance and solidarity should not be exaggerated. Persistently high rates of unemployment and underemployment in Tunisia, combined with the persistently small size of the vast majority of industrial enterprises (62% of all firms in the industrial sector still employed fewer than ten workers in the mid-1970s), meant that labor's dispersal and relative abundance continued to curb working class power. Still, the general thrust of the state's development strategy worked to create structural conditions that fostered militance and solidarity among an important segment of Tunisian workers.

8. See chapter 1, n. 42, for elaboration of this point.

9. This should not be overstated. The National Institute of Statistics (1989, 119) found that as of 1989, 81% of manufacturing industry was still located in urban areas.

10. For example, the CEO of Bacosport, a leading textile manufacturer, located a factory in his home town expressly aimed at employing local women. Few of these women had ever worked out of their homes. To convince the townsmen to let their wives and daughters work in the factory, the CEO promised each employee her very own bicycle.

11. An INS survey conducted in 1989 found that women made up 43% of all employees in manufacturing industry; 60% of these women worked fewer than six months each year (National Institute of Statistics 1989, 119). Preliminary findings of the INS population survey conducted in 1994 show similar results.

12. Progressive integration into the world economy exerts downward wage pressure because wage levels in Tunisia are relatively high when compared to those in similarly developed countries (e.g., Turkey, Morocco, and Hungary) and much higher than those in poorer countries like Egypt, Pakistan, or Sri Lanka. See appendix 1 for Tunisia's world rank in terms of wage rates.

13. Official unemployment rates have ranged around 15–16% in Tunisia during the 1990s (Central Bank, *Annual Report*, 1995, 799–81). Underemployment is estimated at around 24% (U.S. Dept. of Labor, *Foreign Labor Trends: Tunisia*, 1991).

14. The structural position of organized labor in Tunisia is also being undermined by the state's decision to downsize the state bureaucracy (to close the fiscal deficit) and to convert state farms into private holdings. Both measures threaten to shrink the UGTT's most populous unions by eliminating many civil service jobs and by turning agricultural proletarians into peasants.

15. This section draws heavily on Tarchouna 1984, Mzid 1986, and Jaziri 1980–81, as well as on the original texts of Tunisia's labor code (1966, 1973, 1976) published in the ILO's legislative series.

16. Prior to independence, the strike had been regularly used as a tool in the anticolonial struggle. But once independence was achieved, the strike came to be seen by the Tunisian political elite as a subversive, antinational act. In January 1958, the constituent assembly considered guaranteeing the right to strike in the text of the constitution but ulti-

mately voted to adopt only the vague phrase "syndical rights are guaranteed" (Dellagi 1980, 13–14).

17. This proscription, originating in a 1949 colonial law and reaffirmed by the 1966 labor code, effectively emptied syndical activism of its most important content for many years (Sfar 1985).

18. Unlike other associations, trade unions were not required to obtain a visa from the Ministry of Interior to secure legal existence. To get started, they were required simply to declare their existence and submit a list of their union's leaders and rules to the local governorate.

19. The 1966 code declared that strikes would be lawful only if grievances were first submitted to a conciliation board (article 376) and if the trade union central had given its approval to the strike action (article 387).

20. The 1966 code set these penalties at 1–3 months' imprisonment and 5–240 dinars in fines. The 1973 Labor Code amendment increased these penalties to 3–8 months' imprisonment and 100–500 dinars in fines.

21. Clearly, the more impressive size and reach of Tunisia's trade union movement is also a consequence of the boost it got from the experience of settler colonialism (described in chapter 3) as well as the popular legitimacy it accrued through its central contribution to the independence struggle. Still, there is no question that the state's tolerance of trade union organizing played a key role in enabling the UGTT to sustain its initially strong position and build on it further during the next forty years.

22. See appendix 2 for a comprehensive chart listing strike rates in Tunisia between 1970 and 1994.

23. In contrast to workers in much of the Arab heartland (Bill and Leiden 1984; Starr 1977; Zakarya 1977), the Tunisian working class is not divided by a profusion of subnational identities based on religion, ethnicity, and tribe. Although some vertical distinctions do persist (based primarily on region and "clan"), these distinctions are not so significant as to undermine a sense of common fate and purpose among workers—the essential ingredients for the development of class-based identification and solidarity.

24. Seidman (1994), Beinin and Lockman (1987), and others argue that collective conscience and solidarity among workers develops *through* the experience of collective action, rather than prior to it. If this is the case, Tunisian workers have had ample opportunity to develop such collective conscience and solidarity, as described in chapter 3.

25. For example, when the authentic UGTT was repressed in 1978 and 1985, labor activists organized independent collections to finance strike funds. In the mid-1980s they continued to meet in secret and maintain "shadow unions" that management relied on to help settle conflict when the official government-imposed unions proved ineffective.

26. For example, all strikes must be approved by the union central.

27. Prior to 1985, the major share of UGTT financing came via a system of automatic check-off instituted in the public sector. These funds were turned over by the state to the UGTT central, which was responsible for their distribution. Since 1985, the UGTT has survived financially in large part thanks to subsidies from the state. These funds are also handled by the UGTT central. This centralized sourcing of the UGTT deprives the base of its capacity to exercise fiscal discipline over the leadership. Instead, local unions are forced to solicit funds from the center to cover their expenses.

Most trade union activists argued that the disbursement of funds in the UGTT was generally fair. Locals were compensated in proportion to their activism and no single sector was systematically mistreated (save perhaps the teachers' syndicate, which was routinely at loggerheads with Secretary General Achour) (interviews, November 1988). But political favoritism or disfavor did at times come into play. A union car might not be available for use by out-of-favor activists, and disbursement might be slow in coming to troublesome locals (interview, 19 December 1988). By contrast, a well-connected local might be showered with funding whenever monies were requested (interviews, 3 November 1988, 21 November 1988).

There is no question that the system of UGTT finances suffered from a lack of institutionalization. As one leading UGTT activist said: "Everything budgetary is badly organized [in the UGTT]" (interview, 8 November 1988). An attempt to correct this was made in 1981, with the creation of an elected finance commission to oversee the executive bureau's financial decisions. But its limitation to a consultative role meant it lacked the real teeth necessary to discipline forceful trade union leaders (interview, 8 December 1988).

28. See appendix 3 for the pyramidal structure of trade union federation. Rank-and-file members of the UGTT elect their own leadership at the enterprise-based local. These leaders in turn elect leadership at regional, national, and federation levels. The secretaries general of these mid-level unions oversee the work of the UGTT's ruling board, the Executive Bureau. The latter is chosen by the union's National Assembly, a body of several hundred delegates elected by the base on a strictly proportional basis (e.g., 1 for every 350 trade union members). Secret ballots are used at every level of election.

Despite the democratic appearance of trade union structure and electoral procedures, democratic practice is flouted with some regularity within the UGTT. The trade union leadership might hand down lists of appropriate candidates to trade union locals or send a supervisor to oversee the election process and lobby for their favorite candidate. During the long reign of Habib Achour, it was not unusual for local elections to be unilaterally voided when the secretary general was disappointed with the election results, especially in the more politically active and left-leaning unions, such as the PTT syndicate and the teachers' syndicate (interviews, 26 November 1988, 19 December 1988). The persistent pull of clan politics and the domination of the trade union executive with towering figures from the independence movement often overwhelmed the UGTT's young institutions.

29. Of course, not all sectors of the working class exhibit such weakness. Workers in nontradeable sectors (e.g., transportation and banking) as well as in sectors where workers remain highly skilled and concentrated (e.g., petrochemicals and metallurgy) still retain the structural conditions for combativeness and are less likely to look to the state to intervene on their behalf. In fact, in recent years the workers in the petrochemicals and banking sectors have actually threatened strikes to keep the government *out* of their contract negotiations (Alexander 1996, 315 n. 8).

30. As described in chapter 3, the principle of automatic check-off for UGTT dues was partly restored in the early 1990s but the amount permitted fell far short of previous levels. This spelled persistent financial dependence on state subsidies for the union.

31. Berg (1969, 602, 612), demonstrates the role of such variables effectively in the case of Nigerian workers, arguing that the rise in wages enjoyed by labor during the late 1930s and 1940s should not be seen as an indicator of trade union power but rather the ideological predisposition of the elites sitting on the wage commission, specifically, their philosophical commitment to social justice.

32. For example, Tunisian labor law requires that all employee dismissals be cleared with the state labor inspector; dismissed workers are then entitled to severance pay equal to a significant portion of their salary, making dismissal an extremely costly prospect.

33. Instead, the state accommodated private sector interests by turning a blind eye to the sector's increasing reliance on "temporary workers," whose contracts put them outside the protective purview of Tunisia's labor law (interview, U.S. Dept. of Labor attaché, August 1993).

Chapter 5. Capital and Labor

1. The Destourian Party was renamed the Rassemblement Constitutionel Démocratique after Ben Ali took over the presidency in 1987.

2. On an individual basis, however, activists associated with the trade union movement *have* participated in the political process. Several were elected to parliament in 1994 on both ruling party and opposition party lists (U.S. Dept. of State, *Labor Report*, 1994, 5).

3. Revisionist historians have taken issue with any simple mythology that ascribes the rise of Western European democracy to the work of a single, self-conscious social class, whether capitalists or workers (Callinicos 1989). Classes were internally divided, individual classes were often forced to work in coalition with others to achieve political success, and other factors (institutional or international) also shaped regime change. The best works of political economy recognize the complexity of this process. In fact, a careful reading of Rueschemeyer, Stephens, and Stephens reveals a nuanced argument along just these lines (see Ertmann 1998).

4. Guillermo O'Donnell (1992) first used the term *contingent democrats* to describe the Latin American bourgeoisie.

5. Tunisian authoritarianism is called "benevolent" because it is committed to national development and, in contrast to other authoritarian regimes in the region, like Syria and Iraq, has largely eschewed the systematic use of terror and torture to sustain its rule.

Chapter 6. Stalled Democracy in Comparative Perspective

1. Capital has exhibited enthusiasm for democratization in Korea (post-1987) but wariness toward it in Indonesia. Labor has exhibited enthusiasm for democratization in Korea but hostility toward it in Mexico.

2. Rival hypotheses include the claims that cultural heritage and/or level of economic growth/prosperity play the major role in determining social forces' disposition toward democracy. To disprove the hypothesis that cultural heritage is decisive, comparison is drawn between cases showing overall similarity in cultural endowment (Brazil before and after the 1980s for capital; Egypt before and after the 1990s for labor) but that nevertheless display a crucial difference in outcome. To disprove the hypothesis that economic growth and prosperity are decisive, comparison is drawn between cases showing overall difference in level of economic growth and prosperity (Zambia and Korea for labor; Brazil and Korea for capital) but that nevertheless display a striking similarity in outcome.

3. The analysis of Indonesia draws extensively on Robison 1986, Robison 1990, MacIntyre 1991, and Hewison et al. 1993.

4. The analysis of South Korea draws extensively on Eckert et al. 1990, Eckert 1990, Koo 1993, Fields 1995, Hamilton and Kim 1993, and Ogle 1990.

5. The term *developmental state* was coined by Chalmers Johnson (1982).

6. The chairman of the federation and head of the leading chaebol, Lucky-Goldstar, announced the FKI's plans to solicit political funds openly from the business community and then distribute those funds solely to those parties deemed committed to protecting the interests of the business community. This constituted a rebuke and a challenge to the ruling DJP (Eckert 1990, 129).

7. The regime introduced competitive elections in response to widespread popular demonstrations for democracy in 1986–87. The effectiveness of this popular protest was heightened by the pending summer Olympic Games, scheduled to be held in Korea in 1988, which subjected the regime to greater international scrutiny. The business community was not at the vanguard of this popular movement; see Hamilton and Kim 1993, 119–20.

8. The private sector's independence was also helped along by the liberalization of the banking sector in 1980, the creation of nonstate financial institutions, and the internationalization of financial markets, all of which meant that the business community had access to independent sources of corporate financing beyond the state's control (Koo 1993, 88).

9. In 1953 Korea was ranked as one of the poorest countries in the world, with a GNP per capita of $67 (in 1996 dollars) (Song 1994, 60). An estimated ten million people were

without homes, adequate food, or medical care in the war-ravaged economy (Hasan 1976, 26).

10. Actual membership in the Korean Communist Party remained small (not more than 40–60,000 members), but the party's extraordinary capacity to organize citizens in a network of youth, labor, and peasant organizations meant it could mobilize hundreds of thousands, if not millions, for Communist purposes (Scalapino and Lee 1972, 268).

11. Although income inequality remained significant, absolute poverty had declined to 12% by 1978, down from 41% in 1965 (Koo 1984, 1030–31). By the late 1980s, less than 10% of the population lived below the poverty line (Savada and Shaw 1992, 177).

12. This analysis draws extensively on Payne 1994, Cardoso 1986, Payne and Bartell 1995, and O'Donnell 1992.

13. The Goulart regime that existed prior to the 1964 coup was perceived to be unpredictable, incompetent, and inattentive to private sector interests (Payne 1994, 13).

14. The case of Saudi Arabia also supports this view; see Bellin 2000.

15. This analysis draws extensively on Purcell 1981, Camp 1989, and Maxfield and Montoya 1987.

16. The phrase is borrowed from Cardoso 1986, 143.

17. This analysis draws extensively on Middlebrook 1991, Middlebrook 1995, Morris 1995, Collier 1992, and Rueschemeyer, Stephens, and Stephens 1992.

18. Nor was this fear unfounded. By the late 1980s and early 1990s, political reform within the ruling party (the PRI) that aimed to dismantle the party's corporatist structure *had* resulted in a drop in labor candidates/deputies on the PRI slate and a decline in the political influence of the CTM (Murillo 1996, 10).

19. For explanations of the regime's decision to embrace democratic reform, see Morris 1995, 7–31.

20. Wage concessions won by the CTM generally translated into higher minimum wages that benefited all workers, not just union members; see also Van Ginneken 1980, 68–69.

21. In 1989, 23% of Mexicans still lived below the poverty line, and 7.3% lived in "extreme poverty" (Edwards 1995).

22. In 1995, urban underemployment reached 25.9% and official unemployment figures for urban areas clocked in at 6%; see EIU, *Country Profile: Mexico*, 1996–97, 48.

23. In 1996, the informal sector was the source of jobs for 20–30% of the Mexican labor force (EIU, *Country Profile: Mexico*, 1996–97, 10; EIU, *Country Report: Mexico*, January–March 1997, 21).

24. A counterhypothesis suggested by an anonymous reader argues that internal trade union democracy, more than dependence on state sponsorship or aristocratic position, might be the better predictor of organized labor's support for democracy. But the fact that even democratically inclined trade unions have made pacts with authoritarianism when they were handicapped by structural weakness (and hence dependent on state sponsorship) makes me skeptical (Ponte 1991, 87, 100; de la Garza Toledo 1991, 159, 174). Additional research is necessary to test this counterhypothesis.

25. This analysis draws extensively on Eckert 1990, Ogle 1990, Koo 1984, and Deyo 1989.

26. Wage comparison was made with workers in Europe and the United States, not Bangladesh.

27. Throughout the 1970s, only 10% of workers in manufacturing and mining earned incomes equal to the minimum living standard set by the government. Only 50% made even half of that standard (Ogle 1990, 76; Kong 1996, 240). For figures on wage failure to keep pace with productivity gains, see Sohn 1989, 234 n. 81. For wage differentials between industrial workers and workers in the service sector and agriculture, see Park 1979, 102 and Park 1993, 59.

28. Manufacturers routinely ignored even the most basic health and safety regulations (Ogle 1990, 77).

29. Manufacturing workers averaged the longest work week in the world, officially clocking in at fifty-four hours per week (though some argue that sixty hours per week was a more common average) (Ogle 1990, 77; Deyo 1989, 98).

30. This analysis draws extensively on Mihyo 1995, 201–14.

31. Low- and middle-income workers saw their wages decline by an average of 55% during the 1980s (Mihyo 1995, 203).

32. This analysis draws extensively on Posusney 1997, Beinin and Lockman 1987, Bianchi 1986, Bianchi 1989, and Goldberg 1992.

33. Bianchi (1986, 443) anticipated this development as early as the mid-1980s.

34. The collinearity found between sponsorship and aristocracy in our cases on labor is less problematic for our hypothesis than the collinearity found between sponsorship and fear in our inquiry into capital. That is because state sponsorship and labor's aristocratic privilege might, to some extent, be collapsed into one variable. (In the cases analyzed, labor's aristocratic privilege was generally a consequence of state sponsorship, since labor was structurally weak and lacked the market power to command these privileges on its own.) Such collinearity does not undermine the importance of state sponsorship in shaping class disposition on democracy. By contrast, collinearity is more of a problem in our inquiry into capital because fear cannot be collapsed into sponsorship. Additional evidence is required to show the preeminence of sponsorship over fear in shaping class disposition. Presentation of the Mexican case is an attempt to satisfy this concern.

35. The term *mutual empowerment* was suggested by Joel Migdal, personal communication, May 2000. For more on this, see Kohli, Migdal, and Shue 1994; Bratton 1989.

36. See the introduction, n. 3, for more on this.

37. I am excluding from this club countries like Iraq and Algeria, where the state has led the country's industrialization effort to the near exclusion of participation from the private sector. These cases of state-*led* industrialization, where public sector enterprises predominate, should be contrasted with cases of state-*sponsored* industrialization (such as that of Tunisia and Turkey), where development of the private sector is an integral part of the state's developmental vision. Countries like Syria and Saudi Arabia fall somewhere between the two categories, though the commitment of both countries to the development of private sector industry in the past decade would argue for placing them in the state-sponsored category.

38. The choice of cases was governed by the availability of secondary sources. Egypt, Syria, and Turkey each boast a relative abundance of good, up-to-date, easily accessible secondary sources analyzing their respective political economies.

39. Of course, the Middle East and North Africa is a very large region, diverse in terms of country size, social composition, and resource endowment. It is hazardous to generalize about the entire region as though it were an undifferentiated whole. Nor do the three cases discussed in this chapter embrace all the diversity of the region. Nevertheless, comparative analysis of the cases yields general lessons about obstacles and opportunities shaping the prospects for democratization in those MENA countries that are committed to state-sponsored industrialization even though they are relatively rent-poor.

40. This enthusiasm for the private sector developed after declining rents (due to declining petroleum prices, diminished petroleum reserves, or reduced geostrategic aid in the post–cold war era) combined with the self-limiting logic of an ISI development strategy to yield fiscal crisis in state after state in the region. Under prodding from international lenders (Tunisia, Egypt, Jordan) or at the initiative of their own state technocrats (Syria, Algeria), a major share of MENA states embraced liberalization of their economies and came to prize the potential contribution the private sector might make to the economy (Harik 1992; Sullivan 1992; Hinnebusch 1993; Hidouchi 1994; Brand 1992; Satloff 1992; Pfeifer 1992; Vandewalle 1992; Heydemann 1992; Polling 1994; Tangeaoui 1993; Bugra 1994;

Perthes 1995, 51–56; Hinnebusch 1996, 156–66; Murphy 1995, 19; Guigale and Mobarak 1996, 125; Waterbury 1997).

41. There is some debate on the figures for the private sector's role in Egyptian industry. In contrast to the figures cited above (reported by the Central Bank of Egypt), the Egyptian Federation of Industries claims that parastatals still dominate Egyptian industry, accounting for two-thirds of the value of manufacturing production (Giugale and Mobarak 1996, 141). But even this more pessimistic account argues that the private sector's share of production and employment in manufacturing is increasing.

42. The latter led one veteran scholar of Syrian affairs to declare that the private sector in Syria "is now regarded not as a mere auxiliary of a 'leading' public sector but as an engine of economic development, at least the equal of the public sector" (Hinnebusch 1994, 106).

43. To the contrary, Hinnebusch makes clear that in Egypt, the *state* continues to act unilaterally, often at the expense of the private sector, even in this context of increased private sector inclusion and consultation. He points to the investment law of 1989 as evidence of this. The law was drafted with little consultation with the private sector and contained provisions that would be objectionable to the private sector, such as workers' profit sharing (Hinnebusch 1993, 165). Similarly, in Syria, Perthes tells the tale of business inclusion in parliamentary debate on a law to lower taxes on business profits. The businessmen carried the day, and parliament voted to amend the law in the private sector's favor. But the decision was subsequently overturned by an executive-led intervention that manipulated the parliamentary quorum and coerced a second, contrary vote (Perthes 1995, 223).

44. In Syria, Egypt, Turkey, and elsewhere, the typical private sector manufacturing enterprise is a small, family-run firm that employs fewer than ten workers and remains quasi-artisanal in its production methods (Perthes 1994, 250; Perthes 1995, 60; Giugale and Mobarak 1996, 8; Bugra 1994, 62; Tangeaoui 1993; Goldberg 1996a). In Syria, Perthes reports, fewer than 1,800 industrial establishments (out of the 85,000 officially registered) employ a workforce of ten or more (1994, 250). In 1992, the average workforce in the private manufacturing sector still clocked in at fewer than three workers per firm (Perthes 1995, 60). In Egypt, Giugale and Mobarak report, small and microenterprises constitute 98% of private economic units, account for 75% of private sector jobs, and provide 80% of the country's value added (the Egyptian figures include nonmanufacturing enterprises in the private sector) (1996, 8). In Turkey, Bugra reports, 95% of all manufacturing enterprises employ a workforce of twenty-five or less (1994, 62). Thus, although these enterprises exercise significant economic clout *in aggregate*, on an individual basis few are "heavy hitters" in terms of employment creation, capital procurement, or production of value added. Problems of collective action impede their translation of aggregate structural power into policy influence.

45. As in Tunisia, most MENA countries do not uphold truly competitive political systems. Multiparty systems may exist in name, but the state's overwhelming financial and political support to the designated "ruling" party (as well as its hounding and handicapping of the opposition) reduces multipartyism to little more than a façade (Springborg 1998; Goodson and Radwan 1997; Hinnebusch 1985; Hinnebusch 1990; Perthes 1995).

46. By contrast, in Turkey, where the institutional context is quite different (the political system *is* truly competitive, and the leading parties *are* dependent on self-generated financing), the private sector *has* demonstrated its capacity to exercise such leverage over the political system (Patton 1992, 118; Barkey 1989, 309–10).

47. In country after country, the state has routinely intervened to disorganize and/or contain private sector associations, resorting to such tactics as the periodic reshuffling of association law to reconstitute membership in a "favorable direction" (Egypt, Turkey), direct interference in association elections (Egypt, Syria), and retention of the right to appoint a substantial portion of association leadership (Syria, Egypt) (Brouwer 1995, 86; Giugale and Mobarak 1996, 41; Bugra 1994, 237; Pethes 1995, 172–73).

48. The editor of the leading Arabic newspaper *Al-Ḥayat* bemoaned the lack of interest on the part of private sector forces to run ads in, let alone directly finance, the press in the Arab world (*Al-Ḥayāt* editor Jihad Khazen, personal communication, April 1997).

49. Of course, not all MENA states have chosen the route of an authoritarian bargain with labor. Some, like Saudi Arabia, have banned trade unions altogether; others, like Iraq, have utterly extinguished them.

50. This trend only reinforces the dispersion and fragmentation of the workforce long fostered by the fact that small, family-run firms are the norm in industry across the region (Goldberg 1996a, 4; Longuenesse 1996, 116–20; Perthes 1995, 96–97).

51. See appendix 1 for the wage ranking of MENA countries in comparison to other late-developing countries.

52. Unemployment rates for 1990–95 average around 13% in the MENA region. By contrast, the OECD countries clock in at around 7.5%, Eastern Europe and Central Asia at 7.5%, sub-Saharan Africa at around 5%, Latin America and the Caribbean at just under 5%, and East Asia and the Pacific at around 2.5% (World Bank 1995a, 28).

53. The absolute number of people surviving on less than $1 a day reached 11 million in the MENA region in 1990, an increase of 700,000 between 1985 and 1990 (World Bank 1995a, 28–29). This has largely been a consequence of slow growth (combined with rapid population growth) in the region. On a more positive note, poverty levels in the MENA region are relatively low compared to those in other regions in the world. In 1990, only 5.6% of people in the MENA region lived on less than $1 a day, compared with 14.7% in East Asia and 28% in Latin America. Income distribution is also somewhat less skewed in the MENA region than in other parts of the late-developing world, thanks to rapid growth in the 1970s and early 1980s and generous government programs that effectively reduced poverty and transferred income to the poorest (World Bank 1995a, 34).

54. Similarly, Nasser's successor, Anwar Sadat, also courted the support of organized labor, in this case to offset the president's lack of popular legitimacy (Bianchi 1986, 437–38).

55. The essence of private sector power lies in its capacity to deliver investment capital, jobs, and productivity—in short, national prosperity. With other financial resources scarce, and unlikely to increase in the near term, private sector power is bound to rise. By contrast, labor's primary power lies in its capacity to deliver political support to beleaguered regimes. Since regimes may find other means to build popularity (say, through economic growth), the power position of labor is more tenuous, as these other means diminish labor's long-range political value.

56. These policies include access to subsidized inputs, guaranteed state contracts, and monopoly position in the domestic market.

57. The ability of so many MENA states to resist submitting to the discipline of economic rationality and embracing developmentalism as their top governing priority does set them apart from many other late-developing states (e.g., in Asia, Southeast Asia, and Latin America). Two interesting explanations have been put forward to explain this "exceptionalism." First, the region's abundant supply of external rents (petroleum and geostrategic) have long subsidized the failure to be developmentally rational (Richards 1984; Richards and Waterbury 1990). Second, the region's unique security context (long at the center of a bitter regional conflict) has provided many regimes with a route to legitimation separate from economic success, and this has enabled many of them to dodge developmental discipline when it threatened to come at high political cost (Waterbury 1994).

58. The World Bank reports that regulatory compliance remains a major challenge for businessmen in the MENA region; for example, it estimates that the average entrepreneur in Egypt devotes 30% of his time to resolving regulatory problems. Businessmen in Jordan and Lebanon voice similar complaints of administrative obstacles (Saba 1995, cited in World Bank 1995a, 25).

59. In Syria, this institution deficit is evident in the private sector's pervasive fear that property rights are revocable. It is also evident in the proliferation of small-sized firms—a strategic decision made by many businesspeople in the hopes of avoiding the attention of an unpredictable state (Perthes 1995, 102). In Turkey, the institution deficit is evident in the private sector's reliance on family-based management, a reflection of the importance placed on personal trust in an environment where the legal basis of business activity is ambiguous (Bugra 1994, 169).

60. For example, in the case of Turkey, Berik and Bilginsoy (1996, 37–41) argue that the Turkish labor movement did not play an active role in the country's turn toward democratization in the mid-1950s and again in 1961. Rather, due to the movement's structural weakness and dependence on state favor, labor restricted itself to a largely passive role in Turkish politics. In the case of Egypt, as described in the text, the labor movement was extremely unenthusiastic about Sadat's introduction of democratizing reforms, specifically, his plan to move Egypt to a multiparty system in the 1970s. Union leaders saw this reform as a means to dilute the influence that the labor movement had long enjoyed under the country's corporatist single-party system (Bianchi 1986, 438; Bianchi 1989, 138).

61. The conquest of these markets turns in part on political deals that ride on Turkey's progress on democratization. Thus, these businessmen have a doubly strong incentive to campaign for democratization.

62. As in other late-developing countries (Indonesia is a recent example), democracy's best chance probably lies, unfortunately, with economic crisis—crisis that would cripple the reigning authoritarian regimes, divide them internally, and open them to the prospect of political reform. But a mix of special conditions makes the prospect of political disorder in the region especially intolerable to outside powers. These include Western concern for secure delivery of petroleum resources and U.S. commitments to geostrategic alliances in the region. Consequently, it is unclear whether authoritarian crises in this region would be left as free to take a "natural" course as, say, would be the case in much of Latin America, sub-Saharan Africa, or Southeast Asia.

References

Agence de Promotion de l'Industrie (API). N.d. "Al-Mu'assasāt al-ṣināʿiyya al-ṣaghīra wa al-mutawassita wa al-lāmarkaziyya" (Small and medium industrial enterprises and decentralization). Internal document.

Ahmed, Eqbal. 1966. "Trade Unionism." In *State and Society in Independent North Africa*, edited by Leon Carl Brown. Washington, D.C.: Middle East Institute.

Ahmed, Eqbal. 1967. "Politics and Labor in Tunisia." Ph.D. dissertation, Princeton University.

Al-'Akrami, Sami. 1988. "Al-Lajna al-niqābiyya al-waṭaniyya al-mahamma al-ṣaʿba" (The National Union Commission: The difficult mission). *Al-Maghreb*, no. 107 (July).

Alexander, Christopher. 1996. "State, Labor, and the New Global Economy in Tunisia." In *North Africa: Development and Reform in a Changing Global Economy*, edited by Dirk Vandewalle. New York: St. Martin's.

Amin, Samir. 1970. *Le Maghreb moderne*. Paris: Minuit.

Anderson, Lisa. 1986. *The State and Social Transformation in Tunisia and Libya, 1830–1980*. Princeton: Princeton University Press.

Anderson, Perry. 1979. *Lineages of the Absolutist State*. London: Verso.

Anon. "Al-Maṭlūb: Rabṭ al-'ujūr bi al-asʿār" (Wanted: Linkage of wages with prices). *Al-Ṭarīq al-jadīd*, 13 October 1988.

Anon. "Hal satataḥassan al-maqdara al-sharʿiyya?" (Will the legislative capacity improve?). *Al-Ṭarīq al-jadīd*, 13 October 1988.

Anon. "Kayfa nuʿālij al-yawm al-qaḍāyā al-niqābiyya?" (How shall we handle the trade union matters today?). *Al-Baṭl* 1 December 1988.

Arrighi, Giovanni, and Beverly Silver. 1984. "Labor Movements and Capital Migration: The United States and Western Europe in World Historical Perspective." In *Labor in the Capitalist World Economy*, edited by Charles Bergquist. Beverly Hills, Calif.: Sage.

Ashraf, Ahmad. 1969. "Historical Obstacles to the Development of a Bourgeoisie in Iran." *Iranian Studies* 2, no. 2–3: 54–79.

Ayadi, M. 1969. "Les entreprises publiques en Tunisie." Ph.D dissertation, Tunis, ENAT.

Azaiez, Boubaker Letaief. N.d. *Tels syndicalistes, tels syndicats, ou Les péripéties du Mouvement syndical tunisien*. 2 vols. Tunis: Imprimerie Tunis (STEAG).

Baccouche, Neji, and Imed Ben Hamdane. 1996. "L'investissement: Cadre juridique et tutelle administrative en question." In *L'ouverture, la croissance, l'investissement, et l'emploi*," edited by IACE. Tunis: IACE.

Barkey, Henri. 1989. "State Autonomy and the Crisis of Import Substitution." *Comparative Political Studies* 22, no. 3 (October): 291–314.

Baroudi, Sami. 1997. "Business Groups and the Representation of Business Interests in Postwar Lebanon." Paper presented at Middle East Studies Association, November 1997.

Bates, Robert. 1971. *Unions, Parties, and Political Development: A Study of Mineworkers in Zambia.* New Haven: Yale University Press.

Bedaoui, Abdeljelil. 1996. "La question des salaires et de la repartition: Aperçu historique et dynamique de transition." In *L'ouverture, la croissance, l'investissement, et l'emploi,* edited by IACE, 133–62. Tunis: IACE.

Bedaoui, Abdeljelil, and Khalid Manoubi. 1987. *Économie tunisienne, état, et capital mondial.* Tunis: Cahiers du CERES, Série économique 5.

Bedaoui, Abdeljelil, et al. 1986. "Al-Mu'assasāt al-niqābiyya al-ʿummāliyya fī Tūniṣ khuṣuṣiyyatuhā wa dawruhā wa azmatuhā" (The labor union organization in Tunis: Its specificity, role, and crisis). *Utrūḥat,* no. 10.

Beinin, Joel, and Zachary Lockman. 1987. *Workers on the Nile.* Princeton: Princeton University Press.

Belhassen, Souhayr. 1977. "Syndicalisme et politique: L'expérience tunisienne." *Jeune Afrique,* no. 856.

Beling, Willard. 1965. *Modernization and African Labor: A Tunisian Case Study.* New York: Praeger.

Bellin, Eva. 1993. "Civil Society Emergent? State and Social Classes in Tunisia." Ph.D. dissertation, Princeton University.

Bellin, Eva. 1994. "The Politics of Profit in Tunisia: Utility of the Rentier Paradigm?" *World Development* 22, no. 3: 427–36.

Bellin, Eva. 1995. "Civil Society in Formation: Tunisia." In *Civil Society in the Middle East,* edited by A. R. Norton. Leiden: E. J. Brill.

Bellin, Eva. 2000. "Contingent Democrats: Industrialists, Labor, and Democratization in Late-Developing Countries." *World Politics* 52, no. 2 (January): 175–205.

Bellon, Bertrand. 1986. *L'interventionnisme liberal: La politique industrielle de l'état fédéral américain.* Paris: Economica.

Belquith, Sami. 1987. "Syndicalisme et pouvoir en Tunisie: L'intégration et l'opposition." Master's thesis, Institut National du Travail, Tunis.

Bendix, Reinhard. 1964. *Nation-Building and Citizenship.* Berkeley: University of California Press.

Ben Hammed, Hammadi. 1980. "UGTT telle que Bourguiba et Hached l'ont voulue." *Dialogue,* no. 319 (13 October): 20–26.

Bennour, Yassine. 1977. "L'expérience tunisienne en matière d'industrialisation: De l'industrie de substitution aux importations aux entreprises exportatrices." Master's thesis, University of Tunis.

Berg, Eliot. 1969. "Urban Real Wages and the Nigerian Trade Union Movement, 1936–60: Comment." *Economic Development and Cultural Change* 17, no. 4 (July): 604–17.

Berger, Suzanne, ed. 1981. *Organizing Interests in Western Europe: Pluralism, Corporatism, and the Transformation of Politics.* Cambridge: Cambridge University Press.

Bergquist, Charles. 1986. *Labor in Latin America.* Stanford, Calif.: Stanford University Press.

Berik, Gunseli, and Cihan Bilginsoy. 1996. "The Labor Movement in Turkey: Labor Pains, Maturity, Metamorphisis." In *The Social History of Labor in the Middle East,* edited by Ellis Goldberg. Boulder, Colo.: Westview.

Bermeo, Nancy. 1990. "The Politics of Public Enterprises in Portugal, Spain, and Greece." In *The Political Economy of Public Sector Reform and Privatization*, edited by Ezra Suleiman and John Waterbury. Boulder, Colo.: Westview.

Bertrand, Jacques. 1997. "Business as Usual in Suharto's Indonesia." *Asian Survey* 37, no. 5 (May).

Bianchi, Robert. 1984. *Interest Groups and Political Development in Turkey*. Princeton: Princeton University Press.

Bianchi, Robert. 1986. "The Corporatization of the Egyptian Labor Movement." *Middle East Journal* 40, no. 3 (Summer): 429–42.

Bianchi, Robert. 1989. *Unruly Corporatism: Associational Life in Twentieth-Century Egypt*. New York: Oxford University Press.

Bill, James. 1972. "Class Analysis and the Dialectics of Modernization in the Middle East." *International Journal of Middle Eastern Studies* 4, no. 4: 417–34.

Bill, James, and Carl Leiden. 1984. *Politics in the Middle East*. Boston: Little, Brown.

Birks, J. S., and C. A. Sinclair. 1980. *Arab Manpower*. New York: St. Martin's.

Boone, Catherine. 1990. "The Making of a Rentier Class: Wealth Accumulation and Political Control in Senegal." *Journal of Development Studies* 26 (April): 425–49.

Bowles, Samuel, and Herbert Gintes. 1976. *Schooling in Capitalist America*. New York: Basic Books.

Brand, Laurie. 1992. "Economic and Political Liberalization in a Rentier Economy: The Case of the Hashemite Kingdom of Jordan." In *Privatization and Liberalization in the Middle East*, edited by Iliya Harik and Denis Sullivan. Bloomington: Indiana University Press.

Bratton, Michael. 1989. "Beyond the State: Civil Society and Associational Life in Africa." *World Politics* 41, no. 3: 407–30.

Bromley, Simon. 1994. *Rethinking Middle East Politics*. Austin: University of Texas Press.

Brouwer, Imco. 1995. "Les élites économiques et les groupes de pression égyptiens." *Égypte/Monde arabe* 21 (January): 73–114.

Brown, L. Carl. 1974. *The Tunisia of Ahmed Bey: 1837–1855*. Princeton: Princeton University Press.

Brumberg, Daniel. 1995. "Authoritarian Legacies and Reform Strategies in the Arab World." In *Political Liberalization and Democratization in the Arab World*, vol. 1, edited by Rex Brynen et al. Boulder, Colo.: Lynne Rienner.

Brynen, Rex, Baghat Korany, and Paul Noble, eds. 1995. *Political Liberalization and Democratization in the Arab World*. Boulder, Colo.: Lynne Rienner.

Bugra, Ayse. 1994. *State and Business in Modern Turkey*. Albany, N.Y.: State University of New York Press.

Burawoy, Michael, and Theda Skocpol, eds. 1982. *Marxist Inquiries: Studies of Labor, Class, and States*. Supplement to *American Journal of Sociology*, vol. 88. Chicago: University of Chicago Press.

Burgat, François. 1988. *L'islamisme au Maghreb: La voix du sud*. Paris: Karthala.

Callaghy, Thomas. 1984. "External Actors and the Relative Autonomy of the Political Aristocracy in Zaire." In *State and Class in Africa*, edited by Nelson Kasfir. London: Frank Cass.

Callaghy, Thomas. 1988. "The State and the Development of Capitalism in Africa: Theoretical, Historical, and Comparative Reflections." In *The Precarious Balance: State and Society in Africa*, edited by Donald Rothchild and Naomi Chazan. Boulder, Colo.: Westview.

Callaghy, Thomas. 1989. "Toward State Capability and Embedded Liberalism in the Third World: Lessons for Adjustment." In *Fragile Coalitions: The Politics of Economic Adjustment*, edited by Joan Nelson. Washington, D.C.: Overseas Development Council.

Callaghy, Thomas. 1994. "Civil Society, Democracy, and Economic Change in Africa: A Dissenting Opinion about Resurgent Societies. In *Civil Society and the State in Africa*, edited by John Harbeson, Donald Rothchild, and Naomi Chazan. Boulder, Colo.: Lynn Rienner.

Callinicos, Alex. 1989. "Bourgeois Revolutions and Historical Materialism." *International Socialism* 43 (June): 113–71.

Camau, Michel. 1978. *La structure hiérarchique des rénumérations au sein de la fonction publique tunisienne*. Tunis: ENA.

Camau, Michel. 1984. "L'état tunisien: De la tutelle au désengagement." *Maghreb-Machrek* 103 (January–March): 8–38.

Camp, Roderic. 1989. *Entrepreneurs and Politics in Twentieth-Century Mexico*. New York: Oxford University Press.

Cardoso, Fernando. 1986. "Entrepreneurs and the Transition Process: The Brazilian Case." In *Transitions from Authoritarian Rule: Comparative Perspectives*, edited by Guillermo O'Donnell et al. Baltimore: Johns Hopkins University Press.

Charles, R. 1958. *L'âme musulmane*. Paris: Flammarion.

Chekir, Hafida. 1974. "L'UTICA." Master's thesis, University of Tunis.

Cheng, Jun-Jen. 1990. "Is the Dog Barking? The Middle Classes and Democracy Movements in the East Asian NICs." *International Studies Notes* 15, no. 1: 10–16.

Cheng, Jun-Jen, and Eun Mee Kim. 1994. "Making Democracy: Generalizing the South Korean Case." In *The Politics of Democratization: Generalizing East Asian Experiences*, edited by Edward Friedman. Boulder, Colo.: Westview.

Cizre-Sakallioglu, Umit. 1992. "Labour and State in Turkey, 1960–80." *Middle Eastern Studies* 28, no. 4 (October): 712–28.

Cohen, Youssef. 1989. *The Manipulation of Consent: The State and Working Class Consciousness in Brazil*. Pittsburgh: University of Pittsburgh Press.

Collier, Ruth Berins. 1992. *The Contradictory Alliance: State-Labor Relations and Regime Change in Mexico*. International and Area Studies Research Series, no. 83. Berkeley: University of California Press.

Collier, Ruth Berins, and David Collier. 1979. "Inducements versus Constraints: Disaggregating Corporatism." *American Political Science Review* 73, no. 4 (December): 967–87.

Collier, Ruth Berins, and David Collier. 1991. *Shaping the Political Arena: Critical Junctures, the Labor Movement, and Regime Dynamics in Latin America*. Princeton: Princeton University Press.

Conaghan, Catherine. 1988. *Restructuring Domination: Industrialists and the State in Equador*. Pittsburgh: University of Pittsburgh Press.

De la Garza Toledo, Enrique. 1991. "Independent Trade Unionism in Mexico." In *Unions, Workers, and the State in Mexico*, edited by Kevin Middlebrook. San Diego: University of California, San Diego.

Dellagi, Moncef. 1980. "Syndicalisme et politique." *Democratie* (December): 9–15.

Deyo, Frederic. 1984. "Export Manufacturing and Labor: The Asian Case." In *Labor in the Capitalist World Economy*, edited by Charles Bergquist. Beverly Hills, Calif.: Sage.

Deyo, Frederic, ed. 1987. *The Political Economy of the New Asian Industrialism*. Ithaca: Cornell University Press.

Deyo, Frederic. 1989. *Beneath the Miracle: Labor Subordination in the New Asian Industrialism.* Berkeley: University of California Press.

Diamond, Larry. 1993. *Political Culture and Democracy in Developing Countries.* Boulder, Colo.: Lynne Rienner.

Dimassi, Hassine. 1983. "Accumulation du capital et répartition des revenues. Essai sur la reproduction de la formation sociale tunisienne post-coloniale. Fin des années 50–fin des années 70." Ph.D. dissertation, University of Tunis.

Dimassi, Hassine. 1984. "La crise économique en Tunisie: Une crise de régulation." *Maghreb-Mashrek* 103 (January–March): 57–69.

Dumas, Lucy. 1976. "Points de repère pour une histoire du mouvement ouvrier tunisien." *Revue d'histoire maghrebine* no. 5–6: 208–19.

Duvignaud, Jean. 1965. "Classe et conscience de classe dans un pays du Maghreb: La Tunisie." *Cahiers internationaux de sociologie* 38: 185–200.

Eckert, Carter. 1990. "The South Korean Bourgeoisie: A Class in Search of Hegemony." *Journal of Korean Studies* 7 (Fall).

Eckert, Carter, Ki-baik Lee, Young Ick Lee, Michael Robinson, and Edward Wagner. 1990. *Korea Old and New: A History.* Korea Institute, Harvard University. Cambridge: Harvard University Press.

Edwards, Sebastian. 1995. *Crisis and Reform in Latin America: From Despair to Hope.* New York: Oxford University Press.

Ehrmann, Henry. 1957. *Organized Business in France.* Princeton: Princeton University Press.

Elmanoubi, Khaled. 1993. *Industrialisation et compétitivité de la Tunisie.* Tunis: l'Or du Temps.

Ertman, Thomas. 1998. "Democracy and Dictatorship in Interwar Europe Revisited." *World Politics* 50, no. 3 (April): 475–505.

Evans, Peter. 1992. "The State as Problem and Solution: Predation, Embedded Autonomy, and Structural Change." In *The Politics of Economic Adjustment: International Constraints, Distributive Conflicts, and the State*, edited by Stephen Haggard and Robert R. Kaufman. Princeton: Princeton University Press.

Evans, Peter, and James Rauch. 1999. "Bureaucracy and Growth: A Cross-National Analysis of the Effects of 'Weberian' State Structures on Economic Growth." *American Sociological Review* 64, no. 5 (October).

Evans, Peter, Dietrich Rueschemeyer, and Theda Skocpol, eds. 1985. *Bringing the State Back In.* Cambridge: Cambridge University Press.

Evans, Peter, and John D. Stevens. 1988. "Studying Development since the Sixties: The Emergence of a New Political Economy." *Theory and Society* 17, no. 4: 713–45.

Fakhfakh, Mohamed. 1975. "Sfax et sa région." Ph.D. dissertation, University of Paris VII.

Farsoun, Samikh. 1988. "Class Structure and Social Change in the Arab World: 1995." In *The Next Arab Decade: Alternative Futures*, edited by Hisham Sharabi. Boulder, Colo.: Westview.

Farsoun, Samikh, and Christina Zacharia. 1995. "Class, Economic Change, and Political Liberalization in the Arab World." In *Political Liberalization and Democratization in the Arab World*, edited by Rex Brynen, Bahgat Korany, and Paul Noble. Boulder, Colo.: Westview.

Feridhanusetyawan, Tubagus. 1997. "Survey of Recent Developments." *Bulletin of Indonesian Economic Studies* 33, no. 2 (August).

Field, Michael. 1984. *The Merchants: The Big Business Families of Saudi Arabia and the Gulf States.* New York: Overlook Press.

Fields, Karl. 1995. *Enterprise and the State in Korea and Taiwan*. Ithaca: Cornell University Press.

Finer, S. E. 1956. "The Political Power of Private Capital," parts 1 and 2. *Sociological Review* 3 (December 1955): 279–94; 4 (July 1956): 5–30.

Finer, S. E. 1973. "The Political Power of Organized Labour." *Government and Opposition* 8, no. 4 (Autumn).

Fröbel, Folker, Jürgen Heinrichs, and Otto Kreye. 1980. *The New International Division of Labour*. New York: Cambridge University Press.

Gasiorowski, Mark. 1992. "The Failure of Reform in Tunisia." *Journal of Democracy* 3, no. 4: 759–77.

Gates, H. 1979. "Dependency and the Part-Time Proletariat in Taiwan." *Modern China* 5.

Ghabi, Salem. 1978. "L'industrie de substitution aux importations—problèmes et conséquences: Application au cas de la Tunisie durant la décennie 1960–1970." Master's thesis, University of Tunis.

Giugale, Marcelo, and Hamed Mobarak, eds. 1996. *Private Sector Development in Egypt*. Cairo: American University in Cairo.

Gobe, Eric. 1997. "Égypte: Les hommes d'affaires et l'état dans le capitalisme de l'infitah, 1974–1994." *Monde Arabe: Maghreb Machrek*, no. 156 (April–June): 49–59.

Gold, David, Clarence Lo, and Erik Olin Wright. 1975. "Recent Developments in Marxist Theories of the Capitalist State." *Monthly Review* 27 (October–November).

Goldberg, Ellis. 1992. "The Foundations of State-Labor Relations in Contemporary Egypt." *Comparative Politics* 24, no. 2 (January).

Goldberg, Ellis, ed. 1996a. *The Social History of Labor in the Middle East*. Boulder, Colo.: Westview.

Goldberg, Ellis, ed. 1996b. "Reading from Left to Right: The Social History of Egyptian Labor." In *The Social History of Labor in the Middle East*, edited by Ellis Goldberg. Boulder, Colo.: Westview.

Goodson, Larry, and Soha Radwan. 1997. "Democratization in Egypt in the 1990s: Stagnant or Merely Stalled?" *Arab Studies Quarterly* 19, no. 1 (Winter): 1–21.

Gouia, Ridha. 1976. "Les investissements en Tunisie et leurs effets sur la croissance économique de 1881 à nos jours." Ph.D. dissertation, University of Paris X.

Gouia, Ridha. 1987. "Régime d'accumulation et modes de dépendance: Le cas de la Tunisie." Ph.D. dissertation, University of Tunis.

Guen, Moncef. N.d. *La Tunisie indépendante face à son économie*. Tunis: Publication du Cercle d'études économiques.

Hached, Noureddine. 1989. "Aux origines de l'UGTT." *La presse*, 20–21 January, 2.

Haggard, Stephan, and Robert Kaufman. 1995. *The Political Economy of Democratic Transition*. Princeton: Princeton University Press.

Haggard, Stephan, and Chung-in Moon. 1993. "The State, Politics, and Economic Development in Postwar South Korea." In *State and Society in Contemporary Korea*, edited by Hagen Koo. Ithaca: Cornell University Press.

Hamilton, Nora, and Eun Mee Kim. 1993. "Economic and Political Liberalization in South Korea and Mexico." *Third World Quarterly* 14, no. 1.

Hamzaoui, Salah. 1970. "Conditions et genèse de la conscience ouvrière en milieu rural: Cas des mineurs du sud de la Tunisie." Thèse du troisième cycle, University of Paris VI.

Harik, Iliya. 1992. "Privatization and Development in Tunisia." In *Privatization and Liberalization in the Middle East*, edited by Iliya Harik and Denis Sullivan. Bloomington: Indiana University Press.

Harik, Iliya. 1994. "Rethinking Civil Society: Pluralism in the Arab World." *Journal of Democracy* 5, no. 3: 43–56.

Harris, Nigel. 1988. "New Bourgeoisies?" *Journal of Development Studies* 24, no. 2 (January): 237–49.

Hasan, Parvez. 1976. *Korea.* Baltimore: Johns Hopkins University Press.

Hayward, Jack. 1975. "Employer Associations and the State in France and Britain." In *Industrial Policies in Western Europe*, edited by Steven Warnecke and Ezra Suleiman. New York: Praeger.

Henry, Clement M. 1997. "Crises of Money and Power: Transitions to Democracy?" In *Islam, Democracy and State in North Africa*, edited by John Entelis. Bloomington: Indiana University Press.

Hermassi, Abdelbaki. 1966. "Mouvement ouvrier en société coloniale: La Tunisie entre les deux guerres." Thèse du doctorat de troisième cycle, École pratiques des hautes études.

Hermassi, Abdelbaki. 1972. *Leadership and National Development in North Africa: A Comparative Study.* Berkeley: University of California Press.

Hermassi, Abdelbaki. 1984. "La société tunisienne au miroir islamiste." *Maghreb-Machrek* 103: 39–56.

Hermassi, Abdelbaki. 1989. "L'état tunisien et le mouvement islamiste." *Annuaire de l'Afrique du Nord* 28: 297–308.

Hermassi, Abdelbaki. N.d. "State, Development Policies, and Social Classes in Tunisia." Unpublished manuscript.

Hewison, Kevin, Richard Robison, and Garry Rodan, eds. 1993. *Southeast Asia in the 1990s: Authoritarianism, Democracy, and Capitalism.* St. Leonards, Australia: Allen and Unwin.

Heydemann, Steven. 1992. "The Political Logic of Economic Rationality: Selective Stabilization in Syria." In *The Politics of Economic Reform in the Middle East*, edited by Henri Barkey. New York: St. Martin's.

Heydemann, Steven. 1993. "Taxation without Representation: Authoritarianism and Economic Liberalization in Syria." In *Rules and Rights in the Middle East: Democracy, Law, and Society*, edited by Ellis Goldberg, Resat Kasab, and Joel Migdal. Seattle: University of Washington Press.

Hidouci, Mohamed Nazim. 1994. "Égypte: Une économie à la croise des chemins." *Arabies* no. 89 (May): 20–21.

Hill, Hal, ed. 1994. *Indonesia's New Order.* Honolulu: University of Hawai'i Press.

Hinnebusch, Raymond. 1985. *Egyptian Politics under Sadat.* New York: Cambridge University Press.

Hinnebusch, Raymond. 1990. *Authoritarian Power and State Formation in Ba'thist Syria.* Boulder, Colo.: Westview.

Hinnebusch, Raymond. 1993. "The Politics of Economic Reform in Egypt." *Third World Quarterly* 14, no. 1: 159–71.

Hinnebusch, Raymond. 1994. "Liberalization in Syria: The Struggle of Economic and Political Rationality." In *Contemporary Syria: Liberalization between Cold War and Cold Peace*, edited by Eberhard Kienle. London: British Academic Press.

Hinnebusch, Raymond. 1996. "Democratization in the Middle East: The Evidence from the Syrian Case." In *Political and Economic Liberalization*, edited by Gerf Nonneman. Boulder, Colo.: Lynne Rienner.

Hobsbawm, Eric. 1969. *Industry and Empire.* Harmondsworth, U.K.: Penguin.

Huppert, Remi. 1971. "Origines et attitudes de chefs d'entreprise industrielle dans un pays de sous développement—la Tunisie." Doctorat de Troisième Cycle, University of Paris.

International Labor Office. 1960. *Labor Survey of North Africa*. Studies and Reports, N.S., no. 60. Geneva: ILO.

International Labor Office. 1956–91. *Yearbook of Labor Statistics*. Geneva: ILO.

International Labor Office. 1962–91. *Legislative Series*. Geneva: ILO.

International Labor Office. 1974–91. *Social and Labor Bulletin*. Geneva: ILO.

Ismail, Yasri Khaddar, and Ridha al-Zribi. 1971. "Taqrīr ʿan tanẓīm wa idārat al-muʾassasāt al-ʿāmma fī al-jumhūriyya al-tūnisiyya" (Report on the organization and administration of public enterprises in the Tunisian Republic). Mimeograph. Rabat: First Arab Convention on the Organization and Administration of Public Enterprises.

Jaziri, Hedi. 1980–81. "La politique des salaires en Tunisie." Master's thesis, University of Tunis.

Johnson, Chalmers. 1982. *MITI and the Japanese Miracle*. Stanford: Stanford University Press.

Jones, Leroy, and Il Sakong. 1980. *Government, Business, and Entrepreneurship in Economic Development: The Korean Case*. Cambridge: Harvard University Press.

Kandil, Amany. 1989. "Labour and Business Interest Representation in Egypt." Unpublished paper.

Kaplan, Eugene. 1972. *Japan: The Government-Business Relationship*. Washington, D.C.: U.S. Government Printing Office.

Karoui, Hachemi, and Mahdi Messaoudi. 1982. "Le discours syndical en Tunisie: À la veille du 26 janvier 1978: L'élan suspendu." *Annuaire de l'Afrique du Nord* 21: 285–304.

Kasfir, Nelson. 1984a. "Relating Class to State in Africa." In *State and Class in Africa*, edited by Nelson Kasfir. London: Frank Cass.

Kasfir, Nelson. 1984b. "State, Magendo, and Class Formation in Uganda." In *State and Class in Africa*, edited by Nelson Kasfir. London: Frank Cass.

Katznelson, Ira. 1985. "Working Class Formation and the State: Nineteenth-Century England in American Perspective." In *Bringing the State Back In*, edited by Peter Evans, Dietrich Rueschemeyer, and Theda Skocpol. Cambridge: Cambridge University Press.

Kerr, Clark, John T. Dunlop, Frederick H. Harbison, and Charles Myers. 1960. *Industrialism and Industrial Man: The Problems of Labor and Management in Economic Growth*. Cambridge: Harvard University Press.

King, Gary, Robert O. Keohane, and Sidney Verba. 1994. *Designing Social Inquiry: Scientific Inference in Qualitative Research*. Princeton: Princeton University Press.

Kochanek, Stanley. 1974. *Business and Politics in India*. Berkeley: University of California Press.

Kohli, Atul, ed. 1986. *The State and Development in the Third World*. Princeton: Princeton University Press.

Kong, Tat-Yan. 1996. "Origins of Economic Liberalization and Democratization in South Korea." In *Political and Economic Liberalization*, edited by Gerd Nonneman. Boulder, Colo.: Lynne Rienner.

Koo, Hagen. 1984. "The Political Economy of Income Distribution in South Korea." *World Development* 12, no. 10: 1029–35.

Koo, Hagen, ed. 1993. *State and Society in Contemporary Korea*. Ithaca: Cornell University Press.

Kraiem, Mustapha. 1975. "La question du droit syndical en Tunisie, 1881–1932." *Revue d'histoire maghrebine*, no. 3–4: 27–44.

Kraiem, Mustapha. 1980a. *La classe ouvrière tunisienne et la lutte de libération nationale, 1939–52.* Tunis: UGTT Press.

Kraiem, Mustapha. 1980b. "Syndicalisme et pouvoir." *Démocratie* (February): 10–13.

Kraus, Jon. 1976. "African Trade Unions: Progress or Poverty?" *African Studies Review* 19, no. 3 (December).

Kuk, Minho. 1988. "The Governmental Role in the Making of Chaebol in the Industrial Development of South Korea." *Asian Perspective* 12, no. 1 (Spring): 107–34.

Kurth, James R. 1979. "Industrial Change and Political Change: A European Perspective." In *The New Authoritarianism in Latin America*, edited by David Collier. Princeton: Princeton University Press.

Larif-Beatrix, Asma. 1988. *Édification étatique et environnement culturel: le personnel politico-administratif dans la Tunisie contemporaine.* Paris: Publisud.

Lawson, Fred. 1992. "Divergent Modes of Economic Liberalization in Syria and Iraq." In *Privatization and Liberalization in the Middle East*, edited by Iliya Harik and Denis Sullivan. Bloomington: Indiana University Press.

Leca, Jean. 1988. "Social Structure and Political Stability: Comparative Evidence from the Algerian, Syrian, and Iraqi Cases." In *Beyond Coercion: The Durability of the Arab State*, edited by Adeed Dawisha and William Zartman. London: Croom Helm.

LeDuc, Gaston, ed. 1952. *Industrialisation de l'Afrique du Nord.* Paris: Armand Colin.

Lee, Jeong Taik. 1988. "Dynamics of Labor Control and Labor Protest in the Process of EOI in South Korea." *Asian Perspective* 12, no. 1 (Spring): 135–57.

Lepidi, M. Jules. 1955. *L'économie tunisienne depuis la fin de la guerre.* Tunis: Imprimerie officielle de la Tunisie.

Liazu, Claude. 1978. *Salariat et mouvement ouvrier en Tunisie: Crises et mutations, 1931–39.* Paris: Centre national de la recherche scientifique, les cahiers du CRESM, Éditions du CNRS.

Liazu, Claude. 1979. *Militants, grévistes, et syndicats: Études du mouvement ouvrier maghrebine.* Nice: CMMC (Cahiers de la Méditerranée).

Liazu, Claude. 1996. "The History of Labor and the Workers' Movement in North Africa." In *The Social History of Labor in the Middle East*, edited by Ellis Goldberg. Boulder, Colo.: Westview.

Liddle, R. William, and Rizal Mallarageng. 1997. "Indonesia in 1996." *Asian Survey* 37, no. 2 (February).

Lindblom, Charles. 1977. *Politics and Markets.* New York: Basic Books.

Lipset, Seymour Martin, Martin Trow, and James Coleman, eds. 1956. *Union Democracy: The Internal Politics of the International Typographical Union.* Glencoe, Ill.: Free Press.

Lockman, Zachary. 1991. "The Uses of 'Class' in Middle Eastern Labor History: The Case of Egypt." Unpublished manuscript.

Longuenesse, Elisabeth. 1985. "The Syrian Working Class Today." *Middle East Report* 15, no. 4 (July–August): 17–24.

Longuenesse, Elisabeth. 1996. "Labor in Syria: The Emergence of New Identities." In *The Social History of Labor in the Middle East*, edited by Ellis Goldberg. Boulder, Colo.: Westview.

Luebbert, Gregory. 1991. *Liberalism, Fascism, or Social Democracy: Social Classes and the Political Origins of Regimes in Interwar Europe.* New York: Oxford.

MacIntyre, Andrew. 1991. *Business and Politics in Indonesia.* Kensington, Australia: Allen and Unwin.

Mackie, J. A. C. 1976. *The Chinese in Indonesia.* Sydney: Australia Institute of International Affairs.

Mahjoub, Azzam. 1978. "Industrie et accumulation du capital en Tunisie depuis la fin du XVIIIème siècle jusqu'à nos jours." Ph.D. dissertation, University of Grenoble II.

Mann, Michael. 1984. "The Autonomous Power of the State: Its Origins, Mechanisms, and Results." *Archives européennes de sociologie* 25: 185–213.

Manoubi, Khaled. 1984. "État infra-rentier, endettement extérieur, et mouvements populaires urbains en Tunisie." *Annuaire de l'Afrique du Nord* 23: 587–600.

Marshall, T. H. 1950. *Citizenship and Social Class.* Cambridge: Cambridge University Press.

Maxfield, Sylvia, and Ricardo Anzaldua Montoya, eds. 1987. *Government and Private Sector in Contemporary Mexico.* Monograph Series 20. San Diego: University of California, San Diego.

May, Brian. 1978. *The Indonesian Tragedy.* Boston: Routledge and Kegan Paul.

Mericle, Kenneth. 1977. "Corporatist Control of the Working Class: Authoritarian Brazil since 1964." In *Authoritarianism and Corporatism in Latin America,* edited by James Malloy. Pittsburgh: University of Pittsburgh Press.

Michels, Robert. 1962. *Political Parties.* New York: Free Press.

Middlebrook, Kevin, ed. 1991. *Unions, Workers, and the State in Mexico.* San Diego: Center for U.S.-Mexican Studies, University of California, San Diego.

Middlebrook, Kevin. 1995. *The Paradox of the Revolution: Labor, State, and Authoritarianism in Mexico.* Baltimore: Johns Hopkins University Press.

Migdal, Joel. 1988. *Strong Societies and Weak States.* Princeton: Princeton University Press.

Migdal, Joel, Atul Kohli, and Vivienne Shue, eds. 1994. *State Power and Social Forces.* New York: Cambridge University Press.

Mihyo, Paschal. 1995. "Against Overwhelming Odds: The Zambian Trade Union Movement." In *Globalization and Third World Trade Unions,* edited by Henk Thomas. London: Zed.

Miliband, Ralph. 1969. *The State in Capitalist Society.* New York: Basic Books.

Mills, C. Wright. 1956. *The Power Elite.* New York: Oxford University Press.

Mitchell, Timothy. 1991. "The Limits of the State: Beyond Statist Approaches and Their Critics." *American Political Science Review* 85, no. 1 (March): 77–96.

Moghadam, Valentine. 1996. "Making History but Not of Their Own Choosing: Workers and the Labor Movement in Iran." In *The Social History of Labor in the Middle East,* edited by Ellis Goldberg. Boulder, Colo.: Westview.

Moore, Barrington. 1966. *Social Origins of Dictatorship and Democracy.* Boston: Beacon Press.

Moore, Clement Henry. 1965. *Tunisia since Independence: Dynamics of a One-Party State.* Berkeley: University of California Press.

Moore, Clement Henry. 1970. *Politics in North Africa.* Boston: Little, Brown.

Morazé, Charles. 1968. *The Triumph of the Middle Classes.* Garden City, N.Y.: Anchor Books.

Morris, Stephen E. 1995. *Political Reformism in Mexico.* Boulder, Colo.: Lynne Rienner.

Murillo, Victoria. 1996. "A Strained Alliance: Continuity and Change in Mexico." Working Paper. Cambridge, Mass.: David Rockefeller Center for Latin American Studies, Harvard University.

Murphy, Caryle. 1995. "The Business of Political Change in Egypt." *Current History* 94, no. 588 (January): 18–22.

Muwaida, Mohamed. "Ittiḥād al-shughl fī al-dhikrā 41 lita'sīsihi" (The labor union on the forty-first remembrance of its founding). *Al-Mustaqbal*, 16 January 1987.

Mzid, Nouri. 1986. "Du pluralisme syndical." *Travail et développement* 8: 93–105.

Nerfin, Marc, ed. 1971. *Entretiens avec Ahmed Ben Salah*. Paris: François Maspero.

Niblock, Tim, and Emma Murphy. 1993. *Political and Economic Liberalization in the Middle East*. London: British Academic Press.

Norton, Augustus Richard, ed. 1995. *Civil Society in the Middle East*. Vol. 1. New York: E. J. Leiden.

O'Donnell, Guillermo. 1992. "Substantive or Procedural Consensus? Notes on the Latin American Bourgeoisie." In *The Right and Democracy in Latin America*, edited by Douglas Chalmers. New York: Praeger.

Offe, Claus, and Volker Ronge. 1975. "Theses on the Theory of the State." *New German Critique* 6 (Fall).

Offe, Claus, and Helmut Wiesenthal. 1980. "Two Logics of Collective Action: Theoretical Notes on Social Class and Organizational Form." *Political Power and Social Theory*, 1: 67–115.

Ogle, George. 1990. *South Korea: Dissent within the Economic Miracle*. London: Zed.

Owen, Roger. 1990. "State and Society in the Middle East." *Items* 44, no. 1 (March): 10–14.

Panitch, Leo. 1981. "Trade Unions and the Capitalist State." *New Left Review* 125 (January–February): 21–32.

Park, Young-Bum. 1993. *Labor in Korea*. Seoul: Korea Labor Institute.

Park, Young-Ki. 1979. *Labor and Industrial Relations in Korea*. Seoul: Sogang University Press.

Patton, Marcie. 1992. "Constraints to Privatization in Turkey." In *Privatization and Liberalization in the Middle East*, edited by Iliya Harik and Denis Sullivan. Bloomington: Indiana University Press.

Payne, Leigh. 1994. *Brazilian Industrialists and Democratic Change*. Baltimore: Johns Hopkins University Press.

Payne, Leigh, and Ernest Bartell, eds. 1995. *Business and Democracy in Latin America*. Pittsburgh: University of Pittsburgh Press.

Pennec, Pierre. 1964. *Les transformations des corps de métier de Tunis*. Tunis, ISEA-AN.

Perthes, Volker. 1994. "The Private Sector, Economic Liberalization, and the Prospects of Democracy: The Case of Syria and Some Other Arab Countries." In *Democracy without Democrats? The Renewal of Politics in the Muslim World*, edited by Ghassan Salame. New York: St. Martin's.

Perthes, Volker. 1995. *The Political Economy of Syria under Assad*. London: I.B. Taurus.

Petras, James, and Dennis Engbarth. 1988. "Third World Industrialization and Trade Union Struggles." In *Trade Unions and the New Industrialization of the Third World*, edited by Roger Southall. Pittsburgh: University of Pittsburgh Press.

Pfeifer, Karen. 1992. "Algeria's Implicit Stabilization Program." In *The Politics of Economic Reform in the Middle East*, edited by Henri Barkey. New York: St. Martin's.

Philipeaux, Jean. 1973. "Évolution de la politique économique en Tunisie." *Études* (Paris) (October).

Piore, Michael. 1979. *Birds of Passage: Migrant Labor and Industrial Societies*. New York: Cambridge University Press.

Pirson, Ronald. 1978. "Déstructuration et restructuration de la société tunisienne: du groupe à la classe sociale." *Cahiers internationaux de sociologie* 64 (January–June): 147–78.

Polling, Syliva. 1994. "Investment Law No. 10: Which Future for the Private Sector?" In *Contemporary Syria: Liberalization between Cold War and Cold Peace*, edited by Eberhard Kienle. London: British Academic Press.

Poncet, Jean. 1969. "L'économie tunisienne depuis l'indépendance." *Annuaire de l'Afrique du Nord*.

Ponte, Victor Manuel Durand. 1991. "The Confederation of Mexican Workers, the Labor Congress, and the Crisis of Mexico's Social Pact." In *Unions, Workers, and the State*, edited by Kevin Middlebrook. San Diego: University of California, San Diego.

Posusney, Marsha Pripstein. 1997. *Labor and the State in Egypt: Workers, Unions, and Economic Restructuring*. New York: Columbia University Press.

Poulantzas, Nicos. 1972. "The Problem of the Capitalist State." In *Ideology in Social Sciences*, edited by Robin Blackburn. London: William Callum and Sons.

Purcell, John, and Susan Purcell. 1977. "Mexican Business and Public Policy." In *Authoritarianism and Corporatism in Latin America*, edited by James N. Malloy. Pittsburgh: University of Pittsburgh Press.

Purcell, Susan Kaufman. 1981. "Business-Government Relations in Mexico—The Case of the Sugar Industries." *Comparative Politics* 13, no. 2 (January): 211–34.

Rakner, L. 1992. *Trade Unions in Processes of Democratization: A Study of Party Labour Relations in Zambia*. Bergen: Michelsen Institute.

Raulier, Anne. 1985. "Moins d'état, moins de syndicalisme: La Tunisie emportée dans la tourmente néolibérale." *Le monde diplomatique* 1 (December): 6–7.

Redjeb, M. S., and A. Dhifallah. 1987. "Étude comparative de la productivité des secteurs public et privé en Tunisie." Tunis. Unpublished manuscript.

Renan, E. 1883. *L'islamisme et la science*. Paris: Calmann-Lévy.

Richards, Alan. 1984. "Ten Years of Infitah: Class, Rent, and Policy Stasis in Egypt." *Journal of Development Studies* 21 (July): 322–38.

Richards, Alan, and John Waterbury. 1990. *A Political Economy of the Middle East*. Boulder, Colo.: Westview.

Robison, Richard. 1986. *Indonesia: The Rise of Capital*. Sydney: Allen and Unwin.

Robison, Richard. 1990. *Power and Economy in Suharto's Indonesia*. Manila: Journal of Contemporary Asia.

Roddick, Jackie. 1980. "Labor Relations and the 'New Authoritarianism' in the Southern Cone." In *Industrialization and the State in Latin America*, edited by Jean Carrière. Incidental Publications 14. Amsterdam: Center for Latin American Research and Documentation.

Rodinson, Maxime. 1978. *Islam and Capitalism*. Austin: University of Texas Press.

Romdhane, Mahmoud Ben. 1981. "L'accumulation du capital et les classes sociales en Tunisie depuis l'indépendance." Ph.D. dissertation, University of Tunis.

Romdhane, Mahmoud Ben. 1982. "Mutations économiques et sociales et mouvement ouvrier en Tunisie de 1956–1980." *Annuaire de l'Afrique du Nord* 21: 259–84.

Romdhane, Mahmoud Ben. 1984. "Les salaires et la distribution des revenues en Tunisie depuis 1970." *Le mensuel* 1 (May): 6–20.

Romdhane, Mahmoud Ben, and Azzam Mahjoub. N.d. *Transformations économiques et changements sociaux en Tunisie*. Cairo: Forum du tiers monde.

Romdhane, Mahmoud Ben, and Pierre Signoles. 1982. "Les formes récentes de l'industrialisation tunisienne, 1970–1980." *Géographie et développement* 5 (January 1982).

Rothchild, Donald, and Naomi Chazan, eds. 1988. *The Precarious Balance: State and Society in Africa*. Boulder, Colo.: Westview.

Rubio, Luis F. 1988. "The Changing Role of the Private Sector." In *Mexico in Transition: Implications for U.S. Policy*, edited by Susan Kaufman Purcell. New York: Council on Foreign Relations.

Rueschemeyer, Dietrich, Evelyne Huber Stephens, and John D. Stephens. 1992. *Capitalist Development and Democracy*. Chicago: University of Chicago Press.

Sadowski, Yahya. 1991. *Political Vegetables? Businessman and Bureaucrat in the Development of Egyptian Agriculture*. Washington, D.C.: Brookings Institution.

Salame, Ghassan, ed. 1994. *Democracy without Democrats: Renewal of Politics in the Muslim World*. New York: St. Martin's.

Sandbrook, Richard, and Robin Cohen, eds. 1972. *The Development of an African Working Class*. Toronto: University of Toronto Press.

Sassois, Jean Michel. 1971. "Problèmes du travail et la direction des entreprises dans l'industrialisation de la Tunisie." Master's thesis, University of Paris.

Satloff, Robert. 1992. "Jordan's Great Gamble: Economic Crisis and Political Reform." In *The Politics of Economic Reform in the Middle East*, edited by Henri Barkey. New York: St. Martin's.

Savada, Andrea, and William Shaw, eds. 1992. *South Korea: A Country Study*. Washington, D.C.: Library of Congress.

Scalapino, Robert, and Chong-Sik Lee. 1972. *Communism in Korea*. Vol. 1. Berkeley: University of California Press.

Schwartz, Adam, and Jonathan Paris, eds. 1999. *The Politics of Post-Suharto Indonesia*. New York: Council on Foreign Relations.

Schwartz, Frank. 2003. "What *Is* Civil Society?" In *The State of Civil Society in Japan*, edited by Frank Schwartz and Susan Pharr. New York: Cambridge University Press.

Sebag, Paul. 1951. *La Tunisie: Essai de monographie*. Paris: Éditions Sociales.

Seidman, Gay. 1994. *Manufacturing Militance: Workers' Movements in Brazil and South Africa*. Berkeley: University of California Press.

Sellami, Jaouida. 1975. "Le rôle du credit dans l'industrialisation du pays." Actes du séminaire sur l'industrie tunisienne. Mimeograph. Tunis: CERES.

Sfar, Chaabane Kamel. 1985. "Le conflit collectif du travail en Tunisie: Contexte et modes de résolution." Master's thesis, Institut du Travail, Tunis.

Signoles, Pierre. 1985. "Régime d'accumulation et modes de dépendance: Le cas de la Tunisie." Ph.D. dissertation, University of Paris I.

Sklar, Richard. 1979. "The Nature of Class Domination in Africa." *Journal of Modern African Studies*. 17, no. 4.

Skocpol, Theda. 1984. "Emerging Agendas and Recurrent Strategies in Historical Sociology." In *Vision and Method in Historical Sociology*, edited by Theda Skocpol. New York: Cambridge University Press.

Sofer, Eugene. 1980. "Recent Trends in Latin American Labor Historiography." *Latin American Research Review* 15, no. 1: 167–77.

Sohn, Hak-Kyu. 1989. *Authoritarianism and Opposition in South Korea*. London: Routledge.

Song, Byong-Nak. 1994. *The Rise of the Korean Economy*. New York: Oxford University Press.

Southall, Roger. 1984. "Third World Trade Unionism: Equity and Democratization in the Changing International Division of Labour." *Canadian Journal of Development Studies* 5, no. 1: 147–56.

Southall, Roger, ed. 1988. *Trade Unions and the New Industrialization of the Third World*. Pittsburgh: University of Pittsburgh Press.

Springborg, Robert. 1989. *Mubarak's Egypt: Fragmentation of the Political Order*. Boulder, Colo.: Westview.

Springborg, Robert. 1998. "Egypt: Repression's Toll." *Current History* 97, no. 1 (January): 32–37.

Starr, Paul. 1977. "Lebanon." In *Commoners, Climbers, and Notables*, edited by C.A.O. Van Nieuwenhuijze. Leiden: E. J. Brill.

Stepan, Alfred. 1985. "State Power and the Strength of Civil Society in the Southern Cone of Latin America." In *Bringing the State Back In*, edited by Peter Evans et al. Cambridge: Cambridge University Press.

Stone, Russell A. 1974. "Religious Ethic and the Spirit of Capitalism in Tunisia." *International Journal of Middle East Studies* 5: 260–73.

Stork, Joe. 1995. "Egypt's Factory Privatization Campaign Turns Deadly." *Middle East Report* 25, no. 1 (January–February): 29.

Suleiman, Ezra. 1975. "Industrial Policy Formulation in France." In *Industrial Policies in Western Europe*, edited by Steven Warnecke and Ezra Suleiman. New York: Praeger.

Suleiman, Ezra. 1978. *Elites in French Society: The Politics of Survival*. Princeton: Princeton University Press.

Sullivan, Denis. 1992. "Extra-State Actors and Privatization in Egypt." In *Privatization and Liberalization in the Middle East*, edited by Iliya Harik and Denis Sullivan. Bloomington: Indiana University Press.

Tangeaoui, Said. 1993. *Les Entrepreneurs marocains: Pouvoir, société, modernité*. Paris: Karthala.

Tarchouna, Mongi. 1984. "La liberté syndicale en droit du travail tunisien." *Travail et développement* 3–4: 29–66.

Therborn, Goran. 1977. "The Rule of Capital and the Rise of Democracy." *New Left Review* 103.

Therborn, Goran. 1983. "Why Some Classes Are More Successful Than Others." *New Left Review* 138 (March–April): 37–55.

Therborn, Goran. 1986. "Class Analysis: History and Defence." In *Sociology: From Crisis to Science*, edited by Ulf Himmelstrand. Beverly Hills, Calif.: Sage Publications.

Thompson, E. P. 1963. *The Making of the English Working Class*. New York: Pantheon.

Toumi, Mohsen. 1978a. "Le courant ouvriériste et populaire en Tunisie face au pouvoir d'état." *Revue française d'études politiques africaines* 149 (May): 95–102.

Toumi, Mohsen. 1978b. *Tunisie pouvoirs et luttes*. Paris: Sycamore.

Toumi, Mohsen. 1982. "Le discours 'ouvrier' en Tunisie: Usages syndicaux et usages politiques." *Annuaire de l'Afrique du Nord* 21: 305–18.

Tunisia. Ministry of Industry and Commerce (Direction des études et de la planification). 1987. "Atelier régional africain relatif aux entreprises publiques et leur environnement: Le cas de Tunisie." Internal Document.

Tunisia. Ministry of Industry and Commerce. Permanent Technical Committee of Manufacturing Industries Sector. 1986. *Préparation du VIIIe plan de développement économique et social, 1987–1991, rapport de synthèse*.

Tunisia. Ministry of Plan (Direction générale du plan). N.d. "Importance, évolution, et orientation des entreprises publiques." Internal document.

Tunisia. Ministry of Plan. 1984. "Liste des entreprises publiques." Internal document.

Tunisia. Ministry of Plan. Commission de synthèse du VIème plan. 1982. "Réforme des entreprises publiques." Internal document.

Tunisia. Ministry of Plan. *Plan triennal, 1962–64.*

Tunisia. Ministry of Plan. *Plan quadriennal, 1965–68.*

Tunisia. Ministry of Plan. *Troisième plan de développement, 1969–72.*

Tunisia. Ministry of Plan. *Quatrième plan de développement, 1973–76.*

Tunisia. Ministry of Plan. *Cinquième plan de développement, 1977–81.*

Tunisia. Ministry of Plan. *Sixième plan de développement, 1982–86.*

Tunisia. Ministry of Plan. *Septième plan de développement, 1987–91.*

Tunisia. Ministry of Plan. *Huitième plan de développement, 1992–96.*

Tunisia. Ministry of Plan. 1985. *Séries retrospectives, principaux agrégats, 1961–81.*

Tunisia. National Institute of Statistics (Institut national de statistiques). 1979. *Recensement des établissements: Tunisie entière, 1976–78.*

Tunisia. National Institute of Statistics. 1984. "Liste des entreprises publiques." Internal document.

Tunisia. National Institute of Statistics. 1987. "Recensement des entreprises industrielles." Internal document.

Tunisia. National Institute of Statistics. 1989. *Enquête nationale population emploi.*

Tunisia. Office of the Prime Minister. Commission nationale de la réforme administrative. 1986. "Rapport de la sous-commission des entreprises publiques." Internal document.

Turner, Bryan. 1978. *Marx, Weber, and the End of Orientalism.* Boston: Allen and Unwin.

Valensi, Lucette. 1969. "Islam et capitalisme: Production et commerce des Chechias en Tunisie et en France au XVIIIe et XIXe siècles." *Revue d'histoire moderne et contemporaine* 16 (July–September).

Vandewalle, Dirk. 1992. "Breaking with Socialism: Economic Liberalization and Privatization in Algeria." In *Privatization and Liberalization in the Middle East,* edited by Iliya Harik and Denis Sullivan. Bloomington: Indiana University Press.

Van Ginneken, Wounter. 1980. *Socio-Economic Groups and Income Distribution in Mexico.* London: Croom Helm.

Vellinga, Menno. 1980. "Working Class, Bourgeoisie, and State in Mexico." In *Industrialisation and the State in Latin America,* edited by Jean Carrière. Incidental Publications 14. Amsterdam: Center for Latin American Research and Documentation.

Vitalis, Robert. 1989. "Building Capitalism in Egypt: The Abbud Pasha Group and the Politics of Construction." Ph.D. dissertation, Massachusetts Institute of Technology.

Wallerstein, Immanuel. 1988. "The Bourgeois(ie) as Concept and Reality." *New Left Review* 167 (January–February): 91–107.

Warnecke, Steven, and Ezra Suleiman, eds. 1975. *Industrial Policies in Western Europe.* New York: Praeger.

Waterbury, John. 1970. *The Commander of the Faithful.* New York: Columbia University Press.

Waterbury, John. 1976. "Corruption, Political Stability, and Development: Comparative Evidence from Egypt and Morocco." *Government and Opposition* 11, no. 4.

Waterbury, John. 1991. "Twilight of the State Bourgeoisie." *International Journal of Middle Eastern Studies* 23, no. 1 (Winter).

Waterbury, John. 1994. "Democracy without Democrats: The Potential for Political Liberalization in the Middle East." In *Democracy without Democrats: Renewal of Politics in the Muslim World,* edited by Ghassan Salame. New York: St. Martin's.

Waterbury, John. 1997. "From Social Contracts to Extraction Contracts: The Political Economy of Authoritarianism and Democracy." In *Islam, Democratization, and the State in North Africa,* edited by John Entelis. Bloomington: Indiana University Press.

Whitehead, Lawrence. 1991. "Mexico's Economic Prospects: Implications for State Labor Relations." In *Unions, Workers, and the State*, edited by Kevin Middlebrook. San Diego: University of California, San Diego.

Whitt, J. Allen. 1980. "Can Capitalists Organize Themselves?" In *Power Structure Research*, edited by G. W. Komhhoff. London: Sage.

World Bank. 1994. *Republic of Tunisia: Private Sector Assessment*. Washington, D.C.: World Bank.

World Bank. 1995a. *Claiming the Future: Choosing Prosperity in the Middle East and North Africa*. Washington, D.C.: World Bank.

World Bank. 1995b. *Republic of Tunisia: Growth, Policies, and Poverty Alleviation*. 2 vols. Washington, D.C.: World Bank.

World Bank. 1996. *Tunisia's Global Integration and Sustainable Development: Strategic Choices for the Twenty-First Century*. Washington, D.C.: World Bank.

Zakarya, Khalid. 1977. "Syria." In *Commoners, Climbers, and Notables*, edited by C.A.O. Van Nieuwenhuijze. Leiden: E. J. Brill.

Zeghidi, Salah. 1990. *Tunisian Trade Unionism: A Central Pole of Social and Democratic Challenge*. Dakar: Council for the Development of Economic and Social Research in Africa.

Zghal, Abdelkader. 1980. "Classes moyennes et développement au Maghreb. In *Les classes moyennes au Maghreb*. Paris: CRESM.

Index

Abbud Pasha, 50
accountability of state, 149–50
accumulation versus distribution, 86–87
Achour, Habib, 92, 94–96, 106–8, 110–11, 113
Affes, Abdessalem, 78
Ahmed Bey, 13
Algeria, 147, 150
Ali, Mohamed, 90
alliance, power of, 136–37
Al-Sha'b, 106, 112, 117, 148
Arab nationalism/socialism, 20, 177, 180
"aristocratic" labor position, 151–52, 169, 171–72, 174
authoritarian states: alliance of capital and labor with, 144–57; autonomy of, 6–7, 80–84; "developmental paradox" of, 4, 7, 46, 79–80, 122–23; eroding power of, 6–7, 10, 174–85; LDCs and, 174–76; MENA countries, 176–85; society and, 7
automatic check-off policy, 96, 112, 119
autonomy, 6–7, 46–85; of authoritarian regimes, 6–7, 80–84; of capitalists, 6, 10, 46–47, 49–53, 72–80, 149; defined, 49–52; of labor, 6, 10, 88, 99–108, 121–23, 126–28, 137–43; power, distinguishing from, 47, 52–53, 128
Ayari, C., 24

Baccouche, Taieb, 110
Bahrain, 39
Bellagha, Bechir, 92, 96
Ben Abdallah, Mohsen, 74
Ben Achour, Ezzedine, 63
Ben Ali, Zine Abdine, 1–2, 56, 57, 60, 66, 79, 83, 115–20, 145, 156
Ben Ayed, Abdelwahab, 78

Ben Salah, Ahmed, 17, 22, 23, 25, 35, 62, 92–95, 99, 129
Bourguiba, Habib, 1, 17, 20–21, 56, 61, 62, 79, 82, 93–96, 100, 105–6, 108, 110, 112, 115, 118
Brazil, 3, 125, 130, 158–60, 165–67, 187
bureaucracy, 74–76

capitalist/private sector industrialization, 10, 46–85; access to capital, 16; authoritarian state and, 144–57; autonomy of, 6, 10, 46–47, 49–53, 72–80; colonialism and, 13–17, 89–90; contributions of, 1970s–1980s, 32–34; democratization, diffidence about, 145–47, 149–51, 160–67; democratization, liberal/Marxist interpretations of relationship to, 2–6, 152–53; Destour/Neo-Destour Party and, 55–57, 59–60, 145–46; and first liberalist experiment in Tunisia, 1956–1961, 17–19; growth of, 26–29, 40–42, 72; parasitic, 50, 72; power of, 46–71, 177–79; public-private cooperative ventures, 22; public-private division of labor, 34; public sector, private entrepreneurs moving from, 26; reform of 1986, effect of, 39–45; state-sponsored (*see* state-sponsored industrialization); Tunisia, genesis in, 11–45; and Tunisian Human Rights League (LTDH), 146; weaknesses in, 28–32, 42–43
Cárdenas, Cuauhtémoc, 169
case studies, value of, 9, 159–60, 167–68
Chamber of Commerce, Tunisian, 66–67, 68
chechia industry, 16
Chun Doo Hwan, 164, 170

233

Index 237

Pakistan, 188
pantouflage, 58
Park Chung Hee, 163, 170
patrimonialism, 15–16, 163
pay. *See* wages
personalization of problem-solving, 50, 58,
  65–66, 70, 73–80, 163
petroleum industry, 33, 35, 36, 100, 105
phosphates, 33, 36–37, 41, 100
planning and development policy, 20, 21,
  22
pluralization of power, 6–7
politics: cronyism, non-politicization of,
  77–79; direct participation of
  industrialists in, 57–60, 71, 177–78;
  economic decisions, non-political nature
  of, 77–79, 83–84; financing political
  parties and candidates, 56–57, 71;
  independent party, move to form, 106;
  Islamist movements, 1, 117–19, 121,
  136, 138, 150, 181, 185; labor
  movement and political discontent, 102;
  labor relations and political confidence
  of state, 87, 92–93, 99–100, 105–6;
  labor, repression/restoration of (*see*
  repression/restoration of labor and
  UGTT, cycle of); lobbying, 60–70, 179;
  measuring private sector influence over
  policy, 80–84; multiparty political
  competition, lack of, 56, 71, 85, 179;
  national origins, effect of, 90; public
  sector, political forces behind expansion
  of, 36; subversion of market, state-
  supported/politically motivated, 50,
  72–73
populist image, state concern with
  preserving, 60, 71, 96, 107–8, 117–19,
  123, 136, 180
Portugal, 35, 187
poverty, effects of, 150–52, 153, 154–55,
  176, 180
power, 7, 46–85; of alliance, 136–37;
  autonomy, distinguishing from, 47,
  52–53, 128; capitalist/private sector
  industrialism, 46–71, 80–84, 177–79;
  defined, 47–49; through financing,
  56–57, 71; ideological, 47, 48, 52,
  55–56, 71; instrumental, 47, 49, 52,
  56–70, 71, 177–78; of labor, 122–26,
  128–37, 140–43, 179–81; multiple
  means to, 52; pluralization of, 177–81;
  and statist variables and, 126, 131–35;

structural, 47–48, 52–55, 71, 84, 87,
  97, 99, 178; and structural variables,
  124–25, 128–31; Tunisia, evolution of
  power of labor in, 128–37
price controls, 26, 38
private sector. *See* capitalist/private sector
  industrialization
privatization, 38–39, 142, 181
public confrontation of policies,
  government unwillingness to tolerate,
  62, 63–65, 67, 69, 71
public nature of labor's route to power,
  effect of, 122, 127
public sector industrialism: dominance of,
  1970–1986, 34–36; political forces
  behind expansion of, 36; private
  entrepreneurs entering, 26; private-
  public cooperative ventures, 22; private-
  public division of labor, 34;
  privatization, 38–39, 142, 181; and
  socialist period in Tunisia, 1962–1969,
  19–22; union dues, automatic check-off
  policy, 96, 112, 119

Qaddafi, Muammar, 106
quotas and domestic market protections,
  25–26, 38, 39, 44–45, 82, 83

RCD. *See* Destour/Neo-Destour Party
real property, state ownership of, 20, 21
reform of Tunisian economy, 36–39, 72,
  84–85, 99
repression/restoration of labor and UGTT,
  cycle of: 1956–1970, 87–88, 92–98;
  1970–1978, 88, 98–104; 1978–1987,
  88, 105–15; 1988–present, 88, 115–20;
  during colonial period in Tunisia,
  89–92; labor power, effect on, 132–34,
  138–40; state sponsorship of labor and
  repression, relationship between, 86–87
Rhee, Syngman, 163, 170
rights. *See* civil liberties
rioting, labor-related, 106–7

Sadat, Anwar, 173
salaries. *See* wages
Saudi Arabia, 50, 72, 176
scarcity of labor, 124–25
Senegal, 79
Shurafā, 113–14
size of enterprises and elites, 27, 29–30,
  42, 43, 60, 65, 124, 129–30, 179